BUT SHE SAID

ELISABETH SCHÜSSLER FIORENZA

BUT SHE SAID

FEMINIST PRACTICES OF BIBLICAL INTERPRETATION

BEACON PRESS · BOSTON

Beacon Press
25 Beacon Street
Boston, Massachusetts 02108-2892

Beacon Press books
are published under the auspices of
the Unitarian Universalist Association of Congregations.

99 98 97 96 95 94 93 92   8 7 6 5 4 3 2 1

Calligraphy by Richard Lipton

Text design by Christine Leonard Raquepaw

Library of Congress Cataloging-in-Publication Data

Fiorenza, Elisabeth Schüssler, 1938–
But she said: feminist practices of biblical interpretation /
Elisabeth Schüssler Fiorenza.
p. cm.
Includes bibliographical references and index.
ISBN 0-8070-1214-9
1. Bible and feminism. 2. Feminist theology. I. Title.
BS680.W7F56 1992
220.6'082—dc20 92-9

The copyright page continues on page 262.

To Katie Cannon, Mary Hunt, Chung Hyun Kyung,
Diann Neu, Judith Plaskow, and Christine Schaumberger

Justice-Seeking Friends in the Struggle to Transform
Theological Imagination

With Critical Affection

> And I dream of our coming together
> encircled   driven
> not only by love
> but by lust for a working tomorrow
> the flights of this journey
> mapless   uncertain
> and necessary as water.
>
> Audre Lorde, "*Our Dead Behind Us*"

CONTENTS

ACKNOWLEDGMENTS

This book continues my work in charting a critical feminist biblical interpretation. Distinguished lectureships, workshops, and visiting professorships in North America and Europe have provided the rich challenges and probing questions that enable critical creative work. Letters and conversations with women from around the world have given me the courage and strength to continue raising feminist questions in the academy and church during these repressive times. The students in my courses, especially in "Gospel Stories of Women," which I have regularly taught for the past seven years, first at the Episcopal Divinity School and then at Harvard Divinity School in Cambridge, have inspired me with their intelligence, creativity, and commitment to serious theological work. To all the justice-seeking friends whom I have had the privilege to meet in the context of this work I am deeply grateful.

The manuscript would have never been finished without the hard work and support of my co-workers. I owe special thanks to Dr. Margaret Studier, my secretary, who has tirelessly corrected several drafts and has worked overtime to meet the deadline. She, together with Katherine Messina, my research assistant, have resolutely tidied up my idiosyncratic punctuation, spellings, and citations. Reading, correcting, and revising several different drafts and proofs, Katherine Messina, Shelly Matthews, and Michelle Lelwica patiently have not only sought to improve my style, weed out neologisms, and smooth out "germanisms," but also have given me critical feedback. Since they were not always successful in persuading me to choose a different word or turn of phrase, I take full responsibility for any awkwardness that remains.

I am especially grateful to Chris Schüssler-Fiorenza for baking a cake to encourage me for the end spurt and particularly for her willingness to proofread a text which must have been "very boring." As always, I am indebted to Francis Schüssler Fiorenza for his everyday support and care but chiefly for his "mail service" during the past months, bringing drafts back and forth from our home to the office.

Finally, special thanks to my editors at Beacon Press: Deborah Johnson and Deborah Chasman, who suggested to me the idea of a sequel to *Bread Not Stone*, and Lauren Bryant, who has encouraged and edited this book with great care.

September 17, 1991
Feast of Hildegard von Bingen

INTRODUCTION

Contact Lenses

Lacking what they want to see
makes my eyes hungry
and eyes can feel
only pain.

Once I lived behind thick walls
of glass
and my eyes belonged
to a different ethic
timidly rubbing the edges
of whatever turned them on.
Seeing usually
was a matter of what was
in front of my eyes
matching what was
behind my brain.
Now my eyes have become
a part of me exposed
quick risky and open
to all the same dangers.

I see much
better now
and my eyes hurt.[1]

Political Construction of Feminist
Biblical Interpretation

The Canadian writer Margaret Atwood has given us a political novel in *The Handmaid's Tale* that projects into the future a totalitarian society whose patriarchal structures and language are modeled after the Bible. The speaking subject is a woman whose real name and identity are not known. She is a Handmaid called Offred who lives in the Republic of Gilead. Gilead has replaced the United States of America and is ruled by a group espousing an ideology similar to that of the Moral Majority in the pre-Gileadean period of the 1980s. After the President and Congress of the United States have been massacred, the regime of this modern biblical republic is established. Women lose their right to property and employment; the black population, called the children of Ham, are resettled in segregated National Homelands; and Jews are repatriated through the Jewish boat-plans. In this biblical Republic, reading and writing are outlawed; the news media is censored and controlled; and everyone is required to spy on everyone else.

The stratifications of Gileadean society are marked by a special dress code and color scheme developed by the secret Think Tank of the Sons of Jacob. White women are classified according to their gender functions: The Wives of the Commanders of the Faithful are blue-clad and their daughters white-veiled. The Wives supervise the household and knit for the Angels, who are a kind of military police force. Those who do household work are called Marthas and have to wear a dull green. The wives of poor men, the Econowives, wear red, blue, and green striped dresses, because they have to perform all the functions that are divided among different women in the elite households. Finally, "unwomen" are women who have been shipped to the Colonies because they are childless, infertile, or old, as well as nuns, lesbians, and other insurrectionary elements.

The Handmaids are chosen for their reproductive capability. Their names—Offred, Ofglen, Ofcharles—are a patronymic composed of the possessive preposition and the name of the head of the household. Similar to surrogate mothers today, the Handmaids substitute as breeders for infertile Wives, since infertility is not officially acknowledged in husbands. Both

Handmaids and Wives are supervised by Aunts. As female overseers, the Aunts are expected to control women in the most cost-effective way for reproductive and other purposes. They seek, moreover, to resocialize women into the traditional biblical values of the Republic of Gilead. The Aunts also oversee the Salvaging, the public execution of female offenders who are hanged in order to save their souls.

Atwood's narrative displays the interconnections between patriarchy structured by sexism, racism, class differences, homophobia, and anti-Semitism, on the one hand, and the availability of the Bible as language of and legitimation for totalitarian ends, on the other. Through Offred's reflections and recollections of her former life, as well as through a retrospective closure in the form of a historical paper given at a Symposium on Gileadean Studies in 2195, Atwood's narrative also indicates democratic practices and biblical-cultural values that could be used for a politics of resistance.

Among such subversive practices are writing and reading. Books and magazines are forbidden. Women are not allowed to write at all. Holding the Commander's pen, Offred realizes why the motto in the rehabilitation center for Handmaids was "Pen Is Envy." "The pen between my fingers is sensuous, alive almost. I can feel its power, the power of the words it contains. I envy the Commander his pen. It's one more thing I would like to steal."[2] This play on pen/penis signifies the phallocratic valence of the word, and of reading and writing. The most important book which women are not allowed to read is the Bible. As the foundational document of the Republic of Gilead it is only to be read by men in power:

> The Bible is kept locked up, the way people once kept tea locked up, so the servants wouldn't steal it. It is an incendiary device: who knows what we'd make of it, if we ever got our hands on it? We can be read to from it, by him, but we cannot read. Our heads turn towards him, we are expectant, here comes our bedtime story. He takes his time, as if unconscious of us . . . He has something, we don't have, he has the word. How we squandered it, once.[3]

I have chosen Atwood's narrative in order to underscore the political context of scholarly discourses on biblical interpretation in the United States. I have done so in the full awareness that such an expressed political location may mark my reflections as unscholarly and ideological in the eyes of some colleagues. Yet liberation theologians and critical theorists have made us aware that all discourses represent political interests. Meaning is always politically constructed insofar as interpretation is located in social networks of power/knowledge relations that shape society. Scholarly discourse that remains unconscious of its rhetorical functions and which is abstracted from its political contexts is in danger of "squandering" the word.

I first read Atwood's novel during the 1988 presidential campaign in which Pat Robinson's rhetoric often resembled the biblical discourses of Gilead. In the past couple of years, whenever I have encountered women like those on Robinson's campaign staff, or seen the women of Operation Rescue on the nightly news, or read drafts of articles arguing that feminist interpretation must respect conservative women's attempts to construct meaning when reading patriarchal biblical texts, I have asked myself whether we "squander" the word. The question of how feminist biblical interpretation can keep our biblical readings from reinforcing the dominant patriarchal system and phallocentric mind-set of Gilead has become one of the driving forces behind my work.

Atwood's narrator not only discloses the dehumanizing horrors of the totalitarian patriarchal state but also alludes to the potentially "incendiary" character of the Bible if given into the hands of "the subordinate others," the "unwomen" or "nonpersons"[4] of Gilead. Aware that reading can be subversive, elite men in our current world keep the keys to biblical interpretation in their own hands. It is mostly elite men who still read and interpret their New Revised Standard Versions to us in liturgical celebrations and academic lectures. Emancipatory movements, on the other hand, have been fired up by the hope that the "incendiary power" of the Word would be released if women and other nonpersons could obtain the intellectual key of scholarship and biblical interpretation and thereby reach the positions held by elite men. The Word which is read from pulpits, cathedras, and at presidential press conferences, these movements hope, will then no longer be a bedtime story legitimating situations of oppression. Replacing men with women and other "unpersons" in pulpits, universities, courts, and State Houses, however, does not guarantee that the Word read to us will change. One cannot assume that the reading of the Bible from a woman's point of view will necessarily amount to a *feminist* reading; it does not suffice to ask what it means to read the Bible as a woman.[5] Rather, one must ask: What does it mean to interpret Scripture as a feminist, and what constitutes a feminist reading?[6]

The more that feminist interpretations of the Bible seek to approximate academic science or to speak from dogmatic denominational points of view, the more important it becomes to ask how feminists in religion can prevent our readings from functioning like the Aunts in Atwood's Gileadean Republic for whom the only way to survive was to serve the patriarchal system by co-opting and adjusting women's intellectual and spiritual de-

4

sires. Indeed, feminist readings of androcentric texts and patriarchal traditions are always in danger of recuperating the "Commander's readings to
us," of using the "biblical bedtime story" to quiet the anger and rebellion
of women and other "unpersons." In the end, to "own" the Word could
mean to own a word that legitimates the totalitarian patriarchy of Gilead.
Again, the most pressing questions are: How can a feminist biblical hermeneutics situate its readings of the Bible in such a way that they do not
reinscribe the patriarchal discourse of subordination and obedience? How
can feminist biblical interpretation challenge the totalizing rhetoric of
right-wing Christian neo-fundamentalism or liberal theological androcentrism and simultaneously empower women and other marginalized persons in their struggles for freedom, justice, and well-being? By placing this
question at the center of attention, I seek in this volume to pursue similar
questions to those explored in my 1984 volume *Bread Not Stone*.[7] However, I approach them within a different context.

In *Bread Not Stone* I sought to articulate a critical rhetorical paradigm
of biblical interpretation in order to place a critical feminist interpretation
for liberation within the context of biblical criticism, epistemology, and
hermeneutics. Feminist biblical hermeneutics, I have argued, raises questions and challenges that must be attended to by dominant historical-
literary studies and theological hermeneutics if biblical criticism is to maintain its critical edge. Conversely, feminist biblical interpretation can utilize
biblical criticism and theological hermeneutics as intellectual tools in emancipatory struggles against patriarchal oppression. Such an attempt to position a critical feminist biblical interpretation in the epistemological and
practical center of biblical studies and theology requires a reconceptualization and transformation of biblical studies—a transformation of their objectivist scientific or ecclesial doctrinal ethos into a critical rhetoric of the
ekklēsia.

Feminist biblical studies, I have argued in *Bread Not Stone*, must deconstruct the dominant paradigms of biblical interpretation and reconstruct
them in terms of a critical rhetoric that understands biblical texts and
traditions as a living and changing heritage, one which does not legitimate
patriarchal oppression but can foster emancipatory practices of faith-
communities. The hermeneutical center of such a biblical theological interpretation, therefore, can not be the patriarchal church. The center must be
women-church; the *ekklēsia* of women as the practice and vision of the
discipleship of equals which inspires those women and men in biblical
religion who struggle for liberation from patriarchal oppression.

Feminist reviewers of *Bread Not Stone* have charged that I naively
construct a continuity between the early Christian discipleship of equals,
which is understood as a historical fact, and women-church, conceived as

5

a feminist movement of self-identified women and men identified with women's struggles.[8] Such readings of my text misapprehend, however, the tension between the "already" and "not yet" of the *ekklēsia* of women. Nor do these readings grasp the distinction between the democratic notion of *ekklēsia* as the counter-space to patriarchy (which is understood as a pyramid of interlocking dominations), on the one hand, and feminist movement and struggle against patriarchal relations of ruling, on the other. Such appraisals alternately indict the book for being too much invested in either a theological hermeneutics of remembrance or a theological hermeneutics of suspicion. Consequently, it is difficult for them to apprehend my pragmatic proposal[9] for a theological hermeneutics of critical evaluation and proclamation because they reduce it to a feminist norm.

Although one can never prevent such (mis)readings of one's text, they raise important questions that need to be clarified. In the first place, a reading in terms of simplistic continuity between women-church and the discipleship of equals not only overlooks the tension between the "already" and "not yet," between the reality and vision of the *ekklēsia* of women. It also neglects the contradiction and conflict between egalitarian democratic understandings of community and the dominant reality of patriarchy as an interlocking system of discriminations and subordinations. Furthermore, this tension and conflict did not begin with the emerging Christian movements but can be traced back to classical Greece, as well as to early Israel. It is this tension and contradiction that provides for a fragile continuity of struggle. Indeed, emancipatory movements such as the early Christian "discipleship of equals" have always positioned themselves within this history of conflict and struggle.

Moreover, my concern was and is not with the modern problem of the unbeliever asking whether G-d[10] exists. Rather I am interested in liberation theology's question of the "nonperson"—a question which asks instead *what kind of G-d* the Bible proclaims and Christians believe in. It does not search for an abstract norm but must be understood as a question asked from particular sociopolitical locations and subject-positions. When speaking of G-d, a critical theology of liberation does not assume that biblical language is directly referential and descriptive of divine reality. Rather, such theological discourse positions itself within the tradition of "negative theology," which recognizes that all language about the divine is incommensurate with divine reality. Theological articulations are our responsibility since they are permeated by androcentrism and shaped by sociopolitical patriarchal power relations.[11]

Finally, the political valence of the *ekklēsia* of women is missed when it is argued that women-church, as the interpretive center of feminist hermeneutics, "sets up a privileged group of believers over nonbelievers."[12] Similarly, such political valence is overlooked when it is maintained that I argue that if women acknowledge their heritage, then they must "remain within a particular tradition."[13] To the contrary, I believe that feminists must develop a critical interpretation for liberation not in order to keep women in biblical religions, but because biblical texts affect all women in Western society.[14] Although I am writing as a Christian theologian, I am neither attempting to persuade women to remain members of biblical religions nor am I arguing that they should read the Bible, or why. Rather, I seek to work out a process and method for a feminist political reading that can empower women who, for whatever reasons, are still affected by the Bible to read "against the grain" of its patriarchal rhetoric. Moreover, such a critical feminist interpretation is not limited to canonical texts but can be equally applied to extracanonical sources and traditions. In short, *Bread Not Stone* searched for a theoretical framework which would allow feminists in biblical religions to deconstruct the patriarchal center of biblical traditions and to elaborate the alternative political discourse of the *ekklēsia* within biblical religions.[15]

The present volume not only seeks to clarify and advance my previous arguments for a critical feminist interpretation for liberation but also to approach the problem from a different perspective. In this book, I engage in a theoretical exploration of the hermeneutical conditions and epistemological possibilities for a critical feminist practice of reading androcentric texts by elaborating on such readings within the context of interdisciplinary feminist critical theory. My goal is not—as it was in *Bread Not Stone*—to position a critical feminist biblical interpretation for liberation within the center of biblical studies, but rather to theorize such an interpretation within the hermeneutical-rhetorical space created by feminist theory. I do not intend, however, to relinquish the center in favor of the margins. Rather I seek simultaneously to destabilize the center *and* the margins of "malestream" biblical studies by constructing the *ekklēsia* as a feminist counter-public-sphere from which a feminist biblical rhetoric can speak. Thus my present reflections do not cancel those in *Bread Not Stone*. Rather both books complement each other.

By contextualizing feminist biblical interpretation within the variegated space of feminist interpretive practices, this book seeks to situate a critical feminist interpretation for liberation *differently*. By problematizing women's voice and agency, by making women the subjects of biblical readings, by asking how feminist biblical interpretations remain implicated in the discourses of the "fathers," and by inquiring into the hermeneutical possibilities of women's ability to interject their "but" into the hegemonic discourse, I seek to articulate a critical feminist interpretation on feminist political terms. Such an articulation requires a different understanding of patriarchy, one which does not limit it to the sex/gender system but conceptualizes it in terms of interlocking structures of domination [i.e., *kyriarchal*, elite male, relations of ruling (*Herr-schaft*)].[16]

Although as a white educated European woman teaching at Harvard I speak from an "infinitely privileged position"—to borrow Gayatri Chakravorty Spivak's words—I have decided to retain the qualifier "feminist" rather than to speak of a "white Euro-American women's biblical hermeneutics" in analogy to Asian, Latin American, and African women's, womanist, and mujerista biblical interpretation. I have done so, not in order to maintain a white supremacist definition of feminism in terms of the universal sex/gender system. Rather I continue to use the expression feminist interpretation because the term feminism, as distinct from gender or woman, signifies a political concept and movement. Even though Third World feminists continue to challenge mainline feminist movements with regard to their cultural imperialism, white supremacy, and understanding of gender in terms of middle-class white women's experience, many have refused to give up the term feminism.[17] Instead, they insist that women of color have always been engaged with feminism or "feminist movement"—to use bell hooks's expression. Feminists of color therefore are more concerned with the participation of Third World women in "defining feminism than with changing the terminology . . . the term *feminism* sets this essay in a political context to which women are integral. Since 'modern day' feminism is still in the process of incarnation, especially at the international level, I question whether the coining of a new term simply retreats from the debate, running the risk of losing sight of the fair amount of universality in women's oppression."[18]

In order to minimize the possibility of its co-optation in the interests of Western patriarchy, I argue here, as I did in *Bread Not Stone*, that feminist biblical interpretation must place at the center of its attention everywoman's struggles to transform patriarchal structures, both in biblical times and in our own, rather than focusing only on the androcentric biblical text and its authority. Since, throughout the centuries, patriarchal theology and church have silenced women and excluded us from religious institutions of authority, feminist theology must seek to empower women to become theological subjects, to participate in the critical construction of biblical-theological meanings, and to claim their authority to do so. In reclaiming women's authority to shape and determine biblical religions, feminist theology attempts to reconceptualize the act of biblical interpretation as a moment in the global praxis for liberation.

If one contextualizes biblical interpretation within feminist discourses and within the intellectual traditions and struggles of "women of wisdom and valor," rather than those of "fathers and sons" or "masters and disciples," a *different* biblical reading will emerge. The theoretical challenge for feminist biblical interpretation that I seek to explore in this book consists precisely in this: to find "the words" that make well, to articulate a feminist theory of interpretation as a critical practice of freedom, to trace out the logic of liberation that can transform patriarchal oppression.

Yet, words that "make well" and give meaning to our lives are not just unearthed through analytical thinking but also envisioned in poetry. "A poem can momentarily heal not only the alienation of thought and feeling . . . , but can fuse the different kinds of knowing and for at least some instants weld mind back into body seamlessly."[19] If feminist theorists attempt to articulate the meaning and significance of women's struggles against *kyriarchal* relations of ruling, making such struggles visible and central to our sociocultural self-understanding, feminist poets seek a new "optic" and a different "voice" that can see the world anew and break through androcentric marginalization and silence. Since today, as in antiquity, poets are the seers and prophets of their people proclaiming new visions, I use a poem that articulates the "optic" of the chapter to open the theoretical deliberations of each chapter. Readers are invited to use the introductory poem as a hermeneutical key to the chapter's theoretical reflections.

In a fascinating article on biblical authority, Claudia Camp explores a feminist biblical hermeneutics in terms of three biblical women: Hulda, who authorizes the biblical word; personified Wisdom, who embodies the authority of the text; and Esther, who personifies the tradition of her people, binding authority and life together in shared celebration.[20] Like Camp, in the beginning of each chapter I also call on a woman's name to "figure" and "embody" the hermeneutical steps and rhetorical moves of a feminist critical hermeneutic and rhetoric of liberation. However, these steps are not simply linear and sequential, like the steps of a staircase, rather, like steps in a dance, they move backward and forward, encircle, repeat, and move ahead once more. The metaphor of movement and dance suggests that feminism is not defined by a core essence and substance but is embodied as a movement engendering change and transformation.[21]

The following chapters are to be envisioned as a spiraling circle dance, and repetitions in the argument as back and forward movement. I have called on Miriam to lead the dance (chapter 1). She is followed by Arachne,[22] weaving the word (chapter 2); Mary of Magdala, reclaiming the past (chapter 3); Justa, the just one,[23] constructing common ground (chapter 4); Sophia,[24] discerning the Spirit (chapter 5); Prisca, teaching Wisdom (chapter 6); and, finally, Sheba, the black queen,[25] who in the Hebrew Bible seeks to exchange wisdom and knowledge with Solomon (1 Kings 10:1–13; 2 Chron. 9:1–12). She again appears in one of the oldest Christian traditions as a figure inaugurating the eschatological future (cf. Luke 11:31, Matt. [Q]).[26] Rather than beginning with the trickster god Hermes, who has given hermeneutics its name,[27] I open with Miriam, who, along with the other six, beckons readers to join in the dance of a feminist rhetoric, exploring a critical process and feminist practice of biblical interpretation for liberation.

This dance has three main movements. In the first movement of the argument I explore various interpretive strategies developed in feminist biblical studies in order to further explicate the model of interpretation proposed in *Bread Not Stone*. The first chapter sketches different approaches in feminist biblical interpretation. In doing so, I understand these approaches not as competing practices that cancel each other out until the "best" method and reading (which is of course always that of the present writer!) emerges. Instead, I conceive of these interpretive practices in rhetorical terms, as reasoned arguments that are nevertheless still caught up in the framing conditions of their institutional locations. To be able to accept critical feminist and liberation theological readings on equal terms, biblical interpretation must be reconceptualized in rhetorical terms. Chapter two enacts the key moments in a critical process of interpretation through a reading of the story of Martha and Mary (Luke 10:38–42). For this staging of a critical process of interpretation I have chosen a Lukan text because the work of Luke-Acts is generally held to be one of the biblical writings which is most affirming of women. My reading seeks not only to tease out the dynamics of the androcentric text but also to contextualize this text in its historical and contemporary rhetorical debates.

The second movement of my text seeks to explore the hermeneutical process of a feminist biblical rhetorics of interpretation. Key steps in this movement are a historical, a political, and a theological hermeneutics. The third chapter centers on the question of how to read the silences and gaps in historical records. It explores the silence of Luke's Gospel about the Syro-Phoenician in terms of an alternative model of historical imagination and reconstruction. Such a reconstructive model attempts to trace the struggles and tensions in the first century between radical democratic and patriarchal discourses inscribed in early Christian texts.

In chapter 4 I explore the problems involved in constructing a feminist political hermeneutics. I look for a feminist analytic framework that can contextualize a critical feminist interpretation for liberation. If texts are communicative practices which are contextually determined, then a feminist political hermeneutics must develop a complex analysis that can assess the meaning of biblical texts in relation to existing power structures. Any attempt to construct a site from which feminist biblical interpretation can speak, I argue, must take into account the various forms of oppression that women suffer, rather than construct a universal feminist position. A cursory review of the debate on essentialism and constructionism in feminist theory indicates that the discursive construction of woman, gender dualism, or the feminine can not constitute the site from which to read as a feminist liberation theologian. Instead, I argue, feminist identity must be conceived not in terms of the Western logic of identity but in terms of the logic of democracy. The conceptualization of the *ekklēsia* of women as a radical democratic praxis, I propose, provides a symbolic space in which a feminist critical reading of the Bible is possible. Chapter 5 turns from a historical and political to a theological rhetoric. In this chapter I review the attempts to situate a feminist theological rhetoric within debates on the canonical authority of biblical texts. Rather than position itself within the space of the theological "canon within the canon debate," I argue, a feminist theological hermeneutics must speak from within the emancipatory struggles of the *ekklēsia* of women. Particularly, the prophetic traditions and struggles of the "sisters of the Spirit" provide such a different contextualization for a feminist theological rhetoric.

The third major movement of this book introduces two very different examples of a critical feminist practice of biblical interpretation for liberation: one addressing the question of biblical theological education, the other engaging in the reading of a second Lukan text within the rhetorical space of the *ekklēsia*. The sixth chapter concerns the social location of biblical studies and the problems women face when entering a professional domain that for centuries was restricted to elite males. In light of this, I argue that a feminist self-understanding as *resident alien* in theological education allows women faculty and students to speak "in a different voice."[28] The seventh and final chapter returns to the practice of reading a particular biblical text in a different way. It concentrates on a reading of the Lukan story about the woman bent double who was healed (Luke 13:10–21), contextualizing it within different frames of reading or registers of interpretation. In sum, throughout these chapters I attempt to trace the different rhetorical moves, spaces, silences, and crevices between the logic of patriarchy and the logic of democracy that may engender emancipatory practices of feminist biblical interpretation.

The title of this book refers to the Gospel story of the foreign woman from Syro-Phoenicia who interrupts Jesus' retreat and enters into a theological argument for the sake of her daughter. She represents the biblical-theological voice of women, which has been excluded, repressed, or marginalized in Christian discourse. Whether one situates the story's rhetorical practice in the life of Jesus, or in that of the early church, or limits its present narrative context to Mark's or Matthew's Gospel, Jesus is seen as engaging in an argument that discloses religious prejudice and exclusivist

11

identity. In challenging his ethnocentrism the Canaanite woman becomes a paradigm for feminists who transgress intellectual and religious boundaries in their movements toward liberation. The woman, characterized ethnically and culturally as a religious outsider, enters theological argument, turns it against itself, overcomes Jesus' prejudice, and achieves the well-being of her little daughter. As distinct from all other controversy stories, Jesus does not have the last word. Rather, the woman's argument prevails and her daughter is freed from the destructive spirit.

I have chosen the intervention of this woman for the sake of her daughter to explore the discursive problems encountered by a critical feminist interpretation for liberation. The text does not recognize the woman either by her own name or by that of her father or husband. Rather she is characterized by her cultural, religious, and ethnic identity as an outsider who enters the house into which Jesus has withdrawn. Her disruptive entrance into (male) theological argument is fueled by her interest in the well-being of her daughter.

This story is found in the Gospels of Mark and Matthew but not in the Gospel of Luke, even though Luke is believed to favor women's stories. It is told in two different versions which have different rhetorical aims. Yet both versions speak about a foreign woman arguing with Jesus about the boundaries of liberative practice. She engages in this debate, however, neither to become a part of male discourse nor to be discipled as one of its reproducers. Rather she argues for the sake of the well-being of her daughter, who is possessed by an evil power that destroys her life.

Read in a *kyriocentric*, i.e., master-centered, frame the story functions as one more variation of woman's story as outsider in the symbolic worlds and social constructions of male discourse. A substantial part of the manuscript tradition seeks to portray the woman as an example of humble submissiveness by inserting "yes" into the text,[29] and thereby downplaying the "but" of the woman: "But the woman answered and said, yes Lord . . ." Moreover, both gospels contrast the woman outsider with the *master* figure of Jesus who, according to Mark, has withdrawn inside the house, while in Matthew he is surrounded by his disciples. Whereas Matthew calls her by the antiquated scriptural name Canaanite, Mark elaborately characterizes the woman as a Greek who was a Syro-Phoenician by birth. Not only by virtue of her gender, but also because of her ethnicity and cultural-religious affiliation, the woman enters the site of canonical male discourse as a "triple" outsider.

The story concludes in Matthew with Jesus praising the woman's "great faith," and in Mark with the announcement that her daughter is freed from the demon because of her word or because of her teaching. Although this is one of the few gospel stories in which a woman character is accorded "voice," when read in an androcentric register the concluding promise gives Jesus the last word and underlines that the authority of the text rests with the "master" voice of Jesus. The woman's argument serves to enhance its resonance. Standard scholarly commentaries also tend to engage in an apologetic defense of the master Jesus if they comment at all on the woman and her significance.[30] Thus they amplify the marginalizing tendencies not only of the biblical text but also of critical scholarship.[31]

Like the woman in this gospel story, feminist biblical interpretation meets resistance when it seeks to enter scholarly discourses on equal terms. In recent years, feminist biblical interpretation has continually sought to enter the "house" of biblical criticism as an "insider" to interrupt biblical criticism's androcentric isolation and to challenge its prevailing discourses. Yet, like the woman in Matthew's gospel, such attempts to enter the discourses of the discipline on equal terms often receive no response at all— "but he did not respond to her word"—or they are met with the reaction of Jesus' male disciples, who wish to send the woman away because her voice is too loud and noisy.

Finally, when read in a feminist rather than androcentric contextualization, the story displays yet another level of meaning that refers readers back to the title of *Bread Not Stone*. The saying about "the children's bread" and the woman's "teaching" gestures toward another female figure and voice: Divine Sophia-Wisdom who has been sent particularly to Israel (Sir. 24:8, 10–12) and who offers the bread of understanding (Sir. 15:3). The saying about the children's bread recalls the stories about the "bread" of the miraculous feedings (Mark 6:34–44 and 8:1–10).[32] The signifier "bread/loaves" which occurs fifteen times in this section 6:30–8:21 (out of eighteen occurrences in Mark) is used here as a metaphor for what Jesus offers to the people of Israel as their teacher. Sophia-Jesus feeds them with the bread of life and abundantly satisfies their hunger. Jesus-Sophia insists that the "bread" belongs to the children of Israel.

A reader familiar with the Jewish and early Christian Sophia traditions would have understood these allusions to Divine Wisdom inscribed in the text. Divine Wisdom speaks with pride among her people. She offers life, rest, knowledge, and the abundance of creation to all who accept her. She is all-powerful, intelligent, unique, people-loving, an initiate of God's knowledge, a collaborator in God's work. She is the leader on the way out of the bondage of Egypt, the preacher and teacher in Israel, and the architect of God's creation. She shares the throne of God and lives in symbiosis with the Divine. One can sense how much the language of the biblical texts speak of her struggles to characterize Chokma-Sophia as divine in the theological framework of monotheism.

This theological tradition of Divine Wisdom has been cut off in both

Jewish and Christian theology. Yet traces of her theology, of sophialogy, have survived to be rediscovered and amplified by biblical scholarship. Although earliest Christian theology understood Jesus first as Divine Wisdom's messenger and prophet and later as Sophia-Teacher-Incarnate, most Christians have never heard of her. The Sophia-God of Jesus could not make her home among her people.

> Wisdom built herself a house and
> set a table
> dispatched her maidservants and
> proclaimed in public
> "Come and eat of my bread
> drink the wine, I have prepared"
>
> Wisdom, worker of justice
> knowledge and life are Her signature
> prophets and poets Her messengers
>
> Calling forth the *ekklēsia*
> Gathered Around Her Table.[33]

Sophia's offer of "bread," of well-being, beauty, and knowledge presents rich possibilities for the future of biblical interpretation in a different key.

Mark 7:24–30 (RSV)	Matthew 15:21–28 (RSV)

Mark 7:24–30 (RSV)

24 From there he set out and went away to the region of Tyre.

He entered a house and did not want anyone to know he was there. Yet he could not stay hidden,

25 But a woman whose little daughter had an unclean spirit immediately heard about him, and she came and bowed down at his feet.

26 Now the woman was a Greek, a Syro-Phoenician by origin.

And she asked him to cast the demon out of her daughter.

27 And he said to her. "Let the children be fed first, for it is not fair to take the children's food and throw it to the dogs."

28 But she said to him in response: "Yes, Lord, but even the dogs under the table eat the children's crumbs."

29 And he said to her, "Because of this word, you may go—the demon has left your daughter."

30 And she went to her house, found the child lying on the bed, and the demon gone.

Matthew 15:21–28 (RSV)

21 Jesus left that place and went away to the district of Tyre and Sidon.

22 And behold a Canaanite woman from that region

came out and shouted, saying, "Have mercy on me, Lord, Son of David; my daughter is severely tormented by a demon."

23 But he did not answer her at all.

And his disciples came and urged him, saying, "Send her away, for she keeps shouting after us."

24 He answered, "I was sent only to the lost sheep of the house of Israel."

25 But she came and knelt before him, saying, "Lord, help me."

26 He answered, "It is not fair to take the children's food and throw it to the dogs."

27 She said, "Yes, Lord, yet even the dogs eat the crumbs that fall from their masters' table."

28 Then Jesus answered her, "Woman, great is your faith! Let it be done for you as you desire."

And her daughter was healed instantly.

STRATEGIES OF FEMINIST
BIBLICAL INTERPRETATION

P A R T

1
MIRIAM –
LEADING THE DANCE

Learning to Read

And I longed to read my Bible,
    For precious words it said;
But when I begun to learn it,
    Folks just shook their heads.

And said there is no use trying,
    Oh! Chloe, you're too late;
But I was rising sixty,
    I had no time to wait.

So I got a pair of glasses,
    And straight to work I went,
And never stopped till I could read
    The hymns and Testament.

Then I got a little cabin,
    A place to call my own—
And I felt as independent
    As the queen upon her throne.[1]

Charting the Field of Feminist

Biblical Interpretation

When one remembers Miriam, Hulda, Hanna, Mary of Magdala, Prisca, Beruriah, Proba, Macrina, Hildegard of Bingen, Teresa of Avila, Margaret Fell,[2] Sojourner Truth, Antoinette Brown,[3] Christine de Pizan,[4] Elizabeth Cady Stanton, Jarena Lee, or Katherine C. Bushnell,[5] it becomes apparent that women have always interpreted the Bible. Moreover, books about women in the Bible, as well as studies of prescriptive biblical male texts on women's role and place, have been numerous throughout the centuries.

However, women often have interpreted the Bible within theological or spiritual frameworks articulated by elite men. Therefore, women's biblical readings are not necessarily identical with feminist biblical interpretation. While women always have read and interpreted the Scriptures, feminist hermeneutics—the theoretical exploration of the exegetical and sociocultural presuppositions of biblical interpretation in the interest of women—is of very recent vintage. Only in the context of the women's movement in the last century, and especially in the past twenty years or so, have women scholars begun to explore the implications and possibilities of a biblical interpretation that takes the institutional ecclesial silencing of women into account.[6] Books and articles on biblical women's studies have not only enlisted a wide readership in the churches and synagogues, but they are also very slowly making substantive inroads into the academy.

Women's studies in religion seek to articulate women's religious questions and to argue for women's presence in biblical religions. Biblical women's studies in turn attempt to alter the questions and approaches of malestream[7] biblical scholarship in such a way that women's and other marginalized persons' active participation in biblical religions can be attended to. Re-claiming the theological subjectivity of women in shaping and determining biblical religions, biblical women's studies have asked new questions in order to recover women's biblical heritage as religious empowerment for the present and the future.

In conjunction with feminist biblical literary criticism, critical postmodern theories, and feminist historiography, feminist biblical studies have developed several interpretive approaches and strategies for reading the Bible. All of these strategies acknowledge two seemingly contradictory facts. On the one hand, the Bible is written in androcentric language, has its origin in the patriarchal cultures of antiquity, and throughout its history has inculcated androcentric and patriarchal values. On the other hand, the Bible has also served to inspire and authorize women and other non-persons in their struggles against patriarchal oppression. Whereas scholars who still identify with biblical religion tend to downplay the first insight, postbiblical feminists tend to regard the second contention as an instance of "false consciousness." Biblical women's studies in one way or the other presupposes and seeks to address this dual problematic. What Adrienne Rich has said about the research of Marie Curie, that "her wounds came from the same source as her power," can equally be said of women's biblical heritage as one and the same source for women's religious power and suffering.[8]

I.
STRATEGIES OF INTERPRETATION

As is true with all taxonomies, the following attempt to classify different approaches in feminist biblical interpretation is rhetorical in character. Insofar as it typifies and thereby simplifies complex interpretive approaches, its classifications must be scrutinized and debated.[9] Yet, by charting multiple approaches I seek not only to overcome the reformist/radical and the biblical/postbiblical splits in feminist studies in religion, which have obscured the pluriform strategies and critical accomplishments of feminist biblical interpretation;[10] I also seek to show that biblical women's studies has developed as a distinct field of inquiry and rich area of research within biblical criticism. Although established biblical scholarship often does not explicitly recognize this development, a growing number of serious critical studies have charted biblical women's or gender studies as a new terrain of inquiry.

REVISIONIST INTERPRETATION

A *first* approach in feminist biblical interpretation has both a remedial and a revisionist aim. When I ask my students to list at least a dozen biblical women only a very few can do so. Many of them can recall Eve and Mary, the mother of Jesus; some might have heard about Jezebel or the woman at the well; and some might remember Mary Magdalene as the sinner and prostitute. Rarely, though, do they know anything about Prisca or Hulda. By contrast, however, even those who have no religious training have no trouble naming the leading male figures in the Bible. And yet, Miriam Therese Winter discovered, to her great surprise, that she could identify sixty-four women individually in the New Testament, not counting references to groups of women. She asks: "Why is it that male apostles from the time of Jesus figure prominently in the accounts of the early church, while women of the Gospels are replaced with a whole new cast of female characters after Pentecost?"[11] This lack of general knowledge about the women of Scripture is partially due to the androcentrism of religious instruction and liturgical anamnesis that has decisively shaped Christian imagination. Marjorie Procter-Smith has pointed out that contemporary lectionaries tend to include women associated with male heroes, while they omit texts about women such as Rachel, Leah, Deborah, Judith, Tabitha, Lydia, Prisca, or the daughters of Phillip.[12] It is necessary, therefore, to develop a remedial approach that attempts to rediscover all the information about women that still can be found in biblical writings. Since most religious people know the Bible through liturgical readings and the celebration of biblical feast days, the selection of liturgical readings about women and ritual celebrations of biblical women becomes an important remedial strategy for reshaping biblical interpretation and imagination.

Such a remedial approach does not, however, restrict itself to the canonical writings; rather, it fosters extracanonical and crosscultural research about women in antiquity. Its inquiries have rediscovered leading women in the Apocryphal Acts, in Gnostic writings, in the texts of the so-called Church Fathers, as well as in Jewish apocryphal, Rabbinic, and Greco-Roman writings. Moreover, such remedial research is not restricted to textual analysis, for it also searches extratextual remnants for new information about women.

After gathering information about women, scholars often then catalogue and systematize these texts and traditions about women in a dualistic fashion. For instance, they isolate positive and negative statements in order to point to the positive traditions and biblical teachings about women. Such positive texts about women and the feminine are considered separate from "texts of terror," which are stories of women's victimization.[13] Other scholars catalogue biblical statements about woman and feminine imagery about God as positive, ambivalent, or negative. Whereas negative elements are said to permeate the Hebrew Bible and the intertestamental and post-biblical writings of Judaism, such images are seen to be limited to the writings of the Church Fathers in the Christian tradition.[14] Such a dualistic classification favoring Christian over and against Jewish traditions, however, perpetuates anti-Jewish attitudes and interpretations,[15] although its apologetic intent is to reclaim the Bible as support for Christian women's emancipation.

Other revisionist attempts posit as an interpretive contrast not the negative role of women in Judaism but the depravity of women in Greco-Roman culture. For instance, in 1849 Antoinette Brown published an article on 1 Cor. 14 and 1 Tim. 2, texts that forbid women to speak. This article investigated whether the injunctions of these New Testament texts apply to women's public speaking. Her approach was clearly revisionist, in that she tried to show that these two passages cannot be used as "proof-texts" against women. They do not prohibit women's public teaching in general but only forbid a certain kind of faulty teaching. To make her point Antoinette Brown resorted to two interlocking historical arguments: the depravity and low status of women in the surrounding cultures of Judaism and Greco-Roman antiquity and the misbehavior of church women. To quote her: "Now because the women of that and of any other age of the church, who have been kept in an ignorant, degraded, and unchristian subjection, when placed suddenly upon the gospel platform of equality, should be led into the snare of the adversary, and attempt to *teach over man* and to usurp authority over him, . . ."[16]

This first approach in feminist biblical interpretation, however, not only seeks to recover forgotten traditions about women, but also to remove the layers of centuries of androcentric interpretation that cover up the supposed original meaning of the biblical text. Feminist scholars have for instance shown that biblical commentaries have either neglected women's presence in the text or distorted the original meaning of female characters in biblical stories. A feminist revisionist strategy asserts that biblical texts themselves are not misogynist. To the contrary, biblical texts have been patriarchalized by interpreters who have projected their androcentric cultural bias onto biblical texts. Consequently, the Bible must be "de-patriarchalized" because, correctly understood, it actually fosters the liberation of women.[17]

This revisionist strategy was already articulated and adopted in the last century and has strongly influenced subsequent interpretations. Sarah Moore Grimké, for instance, protested not only the false translation of some passages but also "against the perverted interpretations of the MEN who undertook to write commentaries."[18] She expresses her conviction that when admitted "to the honor of studying Greek and Hebrew," women will produce readings of the Bible quite different from those of men. In a similar vein, Lucretia Mott argued that women ought to examine and compare biblical texts with other biblical passages so that a different reading would become possible.[19] Finally, Frances Willard stated categorically: "I think that men have read their own selfish theories into the book."[20]

23

This revisionist strategy has its roots in women's and other subordinates' struggles for emancipation in which the Bible has played a significant ideological political role. In response to those who quote the Bible to support the sociosymbolic patriarchal order, a feminist apologetic approach asserts that the Bible does not prohibit but rather authorizes the equal rights and liberation of women. In the last century, feminists therefore have learned Greek and Hebrew in order to correct false translations and commentaries. Today evangelical feminists often engage in a very fine-tuned exegesis and careful reading in order to show that the literal sense of the text is liberating. In response to this approach, a feminist theological hermeneutics which explicitly addresses the belief that Scripture speaks with divine authority has taken center stage in feminist biblical interpretation. Since several feminist hermeneutical positions have crystallized in confrontation with the doctrinal claim that the Bible is authored and authorized by God Himself, I will focus on a feminist theological hermeneutics in the following chapter.

TEXT AND TRANSLATION

A *second* approach in feminist biblical interpretation is concerned with the androcentric character of biblical texts and discusses their proper translation.[21] Biblical criticism began with textual criticism documenting that we no longer can know the "pristine original" of the verbally inspired text, but only its subsequent diverging manuscript forms. Scholars select a version from among diverse manuscript readings in order to establish the "original" text, translate the selected text into English, and then comment on the biblical writings from the vantage point of their own androcentric-patriarchal knowledge of the world. However, androcentric tendencies that marginalize women can be detected not only in subsequent translations and redactions; such tendencies are already evident in the biblical writers' selection and redaction of traditional materials, as well as in the selective canonization of early Christian texts.

From studies of the transmission of biblical texts and their variant readings, it appears that texts about women's leadership actually were actively eliminated. The example of Col. 4:15 is well known.[22] Here the author extends greetings to the community of Laodicea (4:13) and then to a person by the name of *Nympha(s)* and the church in her/his/their house. The accusative form *Nymphan* can refer to a man named Nymphas or to a woman whose name was Nympha. If one accepts the variant reading of Codex Vaticanus, some Minuscles, and the Syriac translation—"and the church in her [*autēs*] house"—then the greeting refers to a woman as the leader of a house church. If one reads with the Egyptian text "their"

24

[*autōn*], then the author greets either Nympha(s) and her/his family or Nympha(s) and her/his friends. The Western and Byzantine textual variants leave no doubt that the person in question is a man. The church met in his (*autou*) house. According to general methodological rules the most difficult reading (*lectio difficilior*)—"in her house"—probably represents the original text, since in later times women were not admitted as leaders of local churches. Nevertheless, until very recently most Bible editions have chosen "his house" as the most original reading.

Although feminist theory has problematized the power of discourse and language, surprisingly little critical analysis has been devoted to the actual functioning of androcentric language that purports to be generic.[23] Greek, like German, possesses what is called grammatical gender. *Grammatical gender* is a three-way classification into masculine/feminine/neuter which does not divide word meanings into male/female/inanimate. Rather, it conveys the "fact that nouns can behave in three different ways when it comes to the agreement of adjective, the choice of article, replacement by a pronoun and inflectional patterns (word endings)."[24] For instance in Romans 16:1–2 a woman by the name of Phoebe is given the title *diakonos*, a title which has a grammatically masculine form.[25]

English in distinction to Greek has what is called *natural gender*, in which only words referring to biological sex can be masculine or feminine. The majority of words are neither masculine nor feminine, or, if they refer to persons (e.g., friend, professor, or driver), they have *common gender*. Some languages have more than three types of gender, whereas others have no noun classification that could be labeled as gender at all.

Since grammatical gender in a language can function either simply as a classificatory device or to refer to natural gender, the translation of such language depends very much on its textual as well as cultural context. Moreover, the intellectual framework and sociopolitical location of the translator and interpreter have a decisive influence on how the "contextual markers" of such "generic" language are read. Grammatically masculine language generally subsumes women under "generic man" and mentions them explicitly only as a special case—either as the exception to the rule or as a problem. Whereas grammatically masculine language is presumed to include both women and men, this is not the case for language and images referring to women, because common gender exhibits a sexual asymmetry. For instance, although most schoolteachers are actually women, we do not say the "teacher and her class" but "the teacher and his class" when referring in a general way to teaching.

In short, androcentric, grammatically masculine texts are not simply descriptive reflections of reality. Rather, they produce women's marginality and absence from public consciousness by subsuming them under mas-

25

culine terms. How we read the "silences" of such unmarked grammatically masculine generic texts and how we fill in their blank spaces depends on the contextualization of our readings in historical and present experience, which must be assessed in terms of a systemic critique of patriarchy.

Feminist interpretation has paid much attention to the implications of grammatical gender in the translation of biblical texts, especially with regard to its function in the liturgy.[26] Recognizing the alienating effect of androcentric scriptural texts that are proclaimed as the "word of God" in the liturgy, feminist scholars have argued and worked for an inclusive translation of the lectionary. This focus on gender-inclusive translations of liturgical readings has not only caused much emotional debate[27] but has also led to the construction of emancipatory language for liturgical celebrations.[28] However, an inclusive translation is not necessarily identical with a feminist translation. Insofar as an "inclusive translation" masks the patriarchal meanings of biblical texts, it must be accompanied by a critical assessment of biblical texts and their patriarchal contextualizations to arrive at an historically and theologically *adequate* translation—namely, a translation which makes those who have been absent in historical and theological records present. Such a translation can not rely on linguistic determinism or structuralist theories of language. Rather, it must be informed by a critical theory of rhetorics which acknowledges that issues of power permeate linguistic theory, grammatical rules, and cultural translations.

IMAGINATIVE IDENTIFICATION

A *third* approach in feminist biblical interpretation is not so much concerned with biblical language and translation. Instead it is interested in personal identification and biblical imagination. This strategy not only focuses on the women characters of biblical stories, but also imagines women characters in so-called "generic" stories that do not explicitly mention women but allow for their presence. For instance, it might make explicit in storytelling and bibliodrama that not only the "sons of Israel" but also the daughters gathered at Sinai, or that the audience of Jesus' preaching included not only men, but also women.

From its inception, feminist/womanist/mujerista[29] interpretation has sought to actualize biblical stories in role-play, storytelling, bibliodrama, dance, and song.[30] In order to break the marginalizing and obliterating tendencies of the androcentric text, feminists tell biblical stories in which women are silenced or not present at all *differently*.[31] Whereas such a retelling of biblical stories in midrash or legend is quite familiar to Jewish[32] and Catholic women, it is often a new avenue of interpretation for white Protestant women. Since the ancestors of African-Americans, who are predominantly Protestant, were forbidden to learn to read and write, their biblical interpretations imaginatively elaborated in story, sermon, and songs certain key figures (Moses) and paradigmatic events of the Bible in terms of their hopes and struggles for liberation from slavery. It was especially the story of the liberation of Israel from the slavery of Egypt that fired the imagination of the spirituals: "Faith became identification with the heroes and heroines of the Hebrew Bible and with the long-suffering but ultimately victorious Jesus."[33]

Feminist imaginative reinterpretation of biblical texts sometimes argues openly for a gender-specific biblical hermeneutics in terms of Jungian archetypal psychology and cultural glorification of femininity, motherhood, and true womanhood.[34] Most of the time, however, such imaginative biblical recreations unconsciously reproduce the Western romanticist and individualist ideal of the "White Lady."[35] If imaginative biblical reinterpretation does not go hand in hand with a *hermeneutics of suspicion* but instead uncritically embellishes the women characters in the androcentric text, it invites readers to identify positively with the feminine role models that the androcentric text constructs. In so doing, such a reinterpretation actualizes and reproduces the very images and myths of true womanhood from which it seeks to be free.

Since popular books on "the women of the Bible" often utilize biblical stories about women to inculcate the values of conservative womanhood, a feminist interpretation must approach not only the biblical stories but also its own redramatizations of them with a hermeneutics of suspicion. Not only the history of the stories' interpretation but also their function in the overall rhetoric of the biblical text and its contemporary contexts needs to be critically analyzed. For instance, within the African-American tradition of storytelling, Renita Weems creatively reconstructs the "possible emotions and issues that motivated biblical women in their relation with each other" in order to draw "attention to the parallels between the plight of biblical women and women today." Weems, however, is aware that the only way she can "let the women speak for themselves" is by wresting their stories from the presumably male narrators.[36]

Since women's stories are embedded in and structured by patriarchal culture and religion, they must be subjected, I argue, to a process of critical evaluation and displacement. Such a critical interpretation for liberation must question the emotions which androcentric stories evoke and the values and roles they project before it can reimagine and recreate them in a feminist key.

A cultural biblical approach also stresses the importance of visual expression and pictorial elaborations of biblical women's stories. Realizing that in the past and still today many women have not been able to read and

27

write,[37] this approach appreciates the power of images, especially for illiterate, barely literate, or postliterate contemporary audiences. Artistic or popular depictions of biblical women are not only a source of instruction but also shape the imagination of religious and secular communities. Just as medieval art—the "Bible of the poor"—depicts biblical figures and stories in the colors and customs of its own time, so the biblical paintings by Nicaraguan peasants[38] and the slide sequences of *Parables Today* told in the Basic Christian Communities in São Paulo, Brazil are set within the socioeconomic and political realities of the poor in Latin America.

Such sociocultural biblical criticism has explored the countless variations in the depictions of Eve and Mary, the Mother of Jesus, or it has rediscovered Martha, the wise virgin and dragon-slayer in medieval art.[39] It has uncovered artists' fascination throughout the centuries with the figure of Judith, while it has problematized the figuration of female nakedness in the religious and cultural depictions of the Christian West.[40] Such a strategy of cultural criticism is rediscovering a rich but implicated cultural heritage by tracing the figure of Divine Sophia[41] or the image of Mary Magdalene[42] in literature and art.

Some feminist artists seeking to create new visual interpretations of biblical figures and events have depicted the crucified Jesus as a woman, or created images of God the Mother;[43] others focus on women of the Bible.[44] The South African painter Dina Cormick writes of her own work:

> The paintings were "in celebration of women" so I colored them all very brightly and decoratively, and each heroine is always dressed in gold with bright psychedelic green daisies. My intention was also to deliberately expose situations in which these biblical women were abused and misused. I was quite unprepared for the overwhelming enthusiastic response to these paintings.[45]

WOMEN AS AUTHORS AND BIBLICAL INTERPRETERS

A *fourth* strategy in feminist intepretation seeks to recover works written by women in order to restore critical attention to female voices and intellectual traditions.[46] This work has restored many forgotten or obscured women writers. In early Christian studies, scholars have argued for instance that the Gospels of Mark (e.g., Paul Achtemeier) and John (e.g., Sandra Schneiders) were written by a woman evangelist. Others have pointed out that at least half of the Lukan material on women must be ascribed to a special pre-Lukan source (e.g., Leonard Swidler) that may have owed its existence to a woman evangelist. Other scholars argue that women's traditions still surface in the gospels (e.g., Elaine Wainwright).

Adolf von Harnack's argument—published over ninety years ago—that the Epistle to the Hebrews was authored by Prisca is famous to this day.[47] Such suggestions of female authorship[48] not only expand our historical-theological imagination, but they also communicate that women have participated in articulating and shaping biblical traditions and texts.

One can not assume, however, that texts are liberating just because they are articulated by a woman. While the Pastoral Epistles, for instance, forbid leading women to teach and have authority over men (1 Tim. 2:11), they also instruct women elders as "good teachers" to encourage younger women to practice their patriarchal household duties, "so that the word of G-d may not be discredited." (Titus 2:3–5) Elizabeth A. Clark has pointed out that in the fourth century, Proba, in her Virgilian poem *Cento*, "elaborates upon the biblical materials in ways that render woman's status worse than it actually is in the Bible."[49] In distinction to the so-called Church Fathers, Proba does not extol asceticism but rather recommends as ostensibly Christian values those traditional patriarchal Roman values" of respect for parents and kin, sanctity of home, and marital chastity."[50] Instead of assuming there is an essential feminine style of thinking and writing that enhances the well-being of women, one needs to critically explore whether, or to what degree, the androcentric text communicates patriarchal values and visions through women. Women, too, have internalized cultural feminine values and consequently tend to reproduce the patriarchal politics of otherness in their speaking and writing.[51]

Until now only scant attention has been paid to the intellectual history of biblical interpretation by women. Introductions to biblical interpretation still recount only the history of interpretation of elite white men rather than that of "the others." William Myers has detailed how Eurocentric biblical-theological education focuses on the interpretive history and questions of white Euro-American men while neglecting the traditions and questions of the African-American hermeneutical tradition.[52] We lack sustained research into the history of biblical interpretation not only by African, Asian, and Hispanic Christians but also by women of all cultures. In addition, writers of women's religious history have not paid sufficient attention to the different ways that nineteenth-century black and white women, for instance, read the Bible.[53] Here, a rich store of knowledge awaits the feminist intellectual and social historian and interpreter. A history of biblical interpretation by women would not only give us much insight into the ways women have read and used the Bible throughout the centuries but would also make us conscious of a rich feminist history now almost completely lost to us. Such a reconstruction of a feminist intellectual history of biblical interpretation could not only reclaim women's theological work, but it would also "make clear that for centuries women have

been saying many of the things that we are saying today and which we
have often sought as new . . . There are industries built upon the discussion
of men's ideas, and for women it would be a productive change to build
upon, elaborate and modify the ideas of our foremothers."[54]

HISTORICAL INTERPRETATION

A *fifth* strategy of feminist interpretation focuses on biblical history, which
will be elaborated from a methodological perspective in chapter 3. Historical studies of women in the Bible or of Jewish, Greek, or Roman women
are generally *topical* studies, which understand androcentric texts and archeological artifacts *about women* as descriptive source texts. These sources
are taken as comprehensive and reliable data about women in the biblical
worlds. They are understood as "windows" to and "mirrors" of women's
reality in antiquity. Sourcebooks on women in the Greco-Roman and Jewish biblical worlds assemble literary documents, inscriptions, and papyri
in English translation about women's religious activities in Greco-Roman
antiquity.[55] Since textual and archeological source materials about women's
historical agency are very limited, scholarly and popular historical accounts
tend to conclude that women did not play a significant role in ancient
history. Thus, although collections and translations of source materials
about women provide helpful information, they are nevertheless in a certain sense pre-critical insofar as they obscure the nature of androcentric
texts as ideological constructions. Consequently, they must be utilized with
a hermeneutics of suspicion and placed within a feminist model of analysis
and reconstruction.

In distinction to women's or gender studies, a feminist historical interpretation conceptualizes women's history not simply as the history of
women's oppression by men but as the story of women's historical agency,
resistance, and struggle against patriarchal subordination and oppression.
Recognizing the absence and marginalization of women in androcentric
texts, feminist historians address the problem of how to write women
back into history, of how to recapture women's historical experience and
contributions. The historian Joan Kelly[56] has succinctly stated the dual goal
of women's history as both to restore women to history and to restore
history to women. Women have made sociocultural contributions and challenged dominant institutions and values, and they have wielded destructive
power and collaborated in patriarchal structures of exploitation.

Feminist scholars in religion have begun to open up many new areas of
research by asking *different* historical questions that seek to understand
the socioreligious life-worlds of women in antiquity. Some of these ques-

tions are: What do we know about the everyday life of women in Israel, Syria, Greece, Egypt, Asia Minor, or Rome? How did freeborn women, slave women, wealthy women, or businesswomen live? Could women read and write? Do we know of any women philosophers, poets, or religious thinkers?[57] What rights did they have? How did they dress? Which powers and influence did they gain through patronage? What did it mean for a woman of Corinth to join the Isis cult, the synagogue, or the Christian group? What did imprisonment mean for Junia? How did women in Philippi receive Luke-Acts?[58]

Although many of these questions still need to be researched and might never be answered, asking them has engendered several important insights. For example, asking such questions has made it possible to rediscover Junia, the apostle; to document the history and leadership of women in ancient Israel[59] and Judaism[60] as well as in early Christianity;[61] to locate the household-code texts in Aristotelian political philosophy; and to subject gnostic writings to gender analysis.[62] Sociohistorical studies have illuminated the daily life of women in the ancient worlds and underlined the class divisions between women.[63] However, insofar as historical studies do not sufficiently challenge the assumption that androcentric source-texts are descriptive and reliable evidence for sociohistorical reality, their focus on women's history remains caught up in the marginalizing tendencies of the androcentric text which subsumes women under male terms.

SOCIOCULTURAL RECONSTRUCTION

In *In Memory of Her* I have sought to develop a *sixth* strategy of feminist biblical interpretation, which reconceptualizes the task of early Christian historiography. Such a reconstructive approach is not only indebted to epistemological explorations in feminist historiography, but it can also be further theorized in light of discussions of the "New Historicism." Such discussions do not understand history in a positivist sense but as a consciously constructive narrative, as the story of power relations and struggles.[64] Recognizing the rhetorical character of biblical texts, Susan Ackermann, for instance, argues that historians of ancient Israelite religions

> must examine the biblical presentations of the orthodox with an eye to the heterodox, seeking, for example to look without prejudice at those cultic practices that the biblical writers so harshly condemn. Only when we acknowledge the polemical nature of many biblical texts can we see underlying their words evidence of the multifaceted nature of ancient Israelite religion . . . , [especially of] an often overlooked aspect of ancient Israelite religion: women's religion.[65]

31

A feminist sociorhetorical construction of early Christian history attempts to move away from the method of isolating and focusing on texts *about women* toward a theoretical elaboration of sociopolitical and cultural-religious models which allow one to place women,—freeborn and slave, Jewish and Greco-Roman, African and Asian, privileged and poor— in the center of early Christian struggles and history. Texts about women do not directly describe women's actual historical reality and agency, they are only indicators of it. Such texts mention women and marginalize them at the same time. Androcentric biblical texts tell stories and construct social worlds and symbolic universes that mythologize, reverse, absolutize, and idealize patriarchal differences and, in doing so, obliterate or marginalize the historical presence of the devalued "others."[66] Biblical texts about women therefore are like the tip of an iceberg, intimating what is submerged and obliterated in historical silence. They have to be read as touchstones of the historical reality that they both repress and construct.

As rhetorical texts, canonical texts and their interpretations construct a world in which those whose arguments they oppose either become the "deviant others" or are no longer present at all. To displace the marginalizing dynamics of the androcentric biblical source-text or artifact, a critical feminist interpretation must take the texts about women out of their contextual frameworks and reassemble them like mosaic stones in a feminist design which, rather than recuperating the marginalizing or oppressive tendencies of the text, is able to counteract it. To that end, one has to elaborate models of historical and sociocultural reconstruction that can subvert the androcentric dynamics of the biblical text and place the struggles of those whom the androcentric text marginalizes and silences in the center of the historical narrative.

Readers of the Bible are generally not aware that biblical histories are neither reports of events nor transcripts of facts but rather rhetorical constructions that have shaped the information available to them in light of their religious or political interests. The earliest attempt to chart early Christian beginnings already utilizes a geopolitical model of reconstruction. Luke-Acts tell the story of early Christian beginnings in such a way that the gospel moves from Galilee to Jerusalem. After Jesus' and the early Christian mission's rejection in Jerusalem, the gospel moves to the Greco-Roman world. Acts ends with the gospel's arrival in Rome, which was then the geopolitical center of the inhabited world. This early Christian model has not only anti-Jewish but also imperialist and Eurocentric implications.

Some other examples of reconstructive early Christian models are the doctrinal models of orthodoxy-heresy[67] and of Jesus-apostolic succession. The model of orthodoxy-heresy postulates, instead of theological diversity, a pristine orthodox unity of early Christianity from which heretics, often under the leadership of women, deviated. The model Jesus-apostolic succession on the other hand assumes that Jesus called and ordained only male apostles to the priesthood, who in turn ordained their male successors, who ordained their successors, guaranteeing male succession throughout the centuries. Although both models are not tenable in historical terms, they nevertheless are still very influential theologically. Confessional theological variations include both the Protestant model of rapid deterioration from Jesus and his first followers to early Catholicism, and the Roman Catholic model which assumes that early Christian beginnings contained the seeds for the development that climaxed in the Roman papacy. Such theological models are genderized insofar as they assume that women's leadership in early Christian communities signals heresy or that Jesus chose only male apostles as his successors.

The reconstructive model of "background" and "center" is equally flawed. For instance, reconstructions of early Christian women's history that construe Jewish or Greco-Roman women's history as "background" in order to assert the liberated status of Christian women over and against that of Jewish or pagan women employ a Christian supremacist model. Equally gendered are sociological models that oppose charismatic equality and patriarchal institution, male ascetic itinerant radicalism and familial love-patriarchalism, or masculine honor and feminine shame, since such models perpetuate the dualistic framework of the Western cultural gender system. Feminist scholars must insist that the sociological or anthropological reconstructive models that they use be tested for their androcentric theoretical implications and patriarchal limitations. Social-scientific frameworks that are not open to a feminist critique of ideology but are utilized by biblical scholars in a positivistic way do not displace the marginalizing dynamics of the androcentric source-text. On the contrary, they reify it.

Finally, a critical feminist historical reconstructive approach challenges dominant scholarship by insisting that history must be written not from the perspective of the "historical winners" but from that of the silenced or marginalized. In order to achieve an historically adequate description of the sociocultural and religious worlds of the Bible, scholars no longer can limit their investigations to the history of Western elite men. Rather, they must reconceptualize early Christian history in such a way that the voices of the "vanquished of history" can be heard again.

Although a critical feminist reconstructive approach recognizes the provisionality and multiplicity of knowledges as particular, situated, and "embodied," it does not abandon the claim to relative objectivity and historical validity of its reconstructions. The objectivity and adequacy of such critical feminist historical reconstructions must be assessed in terms of whether and how much they can make present the historical losers and their arguments—that is, how much they can make visible the symbolic world-constructions of those who have been made "invisible" in androcentric texts. One is still able to disclose and unravel "the politics of otherness" constructed by the androcentric text because it is produced by a historical reality in which "the absent others" are present and active. In order to reconstruct the past, feminist scholars therefore utilize a feminist theoretical analysis of women's experience as scientific resource and significant indicator of the reality against which our interpretations and reconstructive models are to be tested.

IDEOLOGICAL INSCRIPTION

A *seventh* approach in feminist biblical interpretation concentrates on the ideological inscriptions of androcentric texts.[68] Whereas historical interpretations of the Bible tend to be caught up in the factual, objectivist, and antiquarian paradigm of historical studies, structuralist and formalist rhetorical studies reject the "referential fallacy" by insisting that we are not able to move beyond the androcentric text to the historical reality of women.[69] They rightly reject the idealist understanding of the biblical text as a transparent reflection of the past in favor of an understanding of it as a construction of patriarchal ideology.

Whether they are formalist, reader-response oriented,[70] structuralist, or narratological,[71] feminist literary studies carefully show how androcentric texts construct the politics of gender and feminine representation. Such diverse analyses rightly argue that the relationship between androcentric text and historical reality cannot be construed as a mirror-image but that it must be decoded as a complex ideological construction.[72] The silences, contradictions, arguments, prescriptions, and projections of biblical texts, as well as the Bible's discourses on gender, race, class, or culture, must be unraveled to show their ideological inscription of the patriarchal politics of otherness.

Feminist literary studies, for instance, attend to the "woman's point of view" inscribed in biblical texts,[73] as well as to the ideological inscriptions of androcentric dualism and the politics of gender in cultural and religious texts. Yet, by tracing out the feminine/masculine binary structures of the biblical text,[74] or by focusing on the "feminine" character constructs (e.g., mother, daughter, bride)[75] of biblical narratives, structuralist and deconstructionist readings run the risk of re-inscribing rather than dislodging the dualistic gender politics of the text. Although feminist literary criticism seeks to foster a hermeneutics of resistance that deconstructs, debunks, and rejects the androcentric politics of the canonical text, by adopting linguistic determinism it cannot but reinscribe the totalizing dynamics of the androcentric text—a text which either marginalizes women and other non-persons or which eliminates them altogether from the literary record.[76] For instance, feminist literary analyses have shown that the androcentric narrative of Mark's and Matthew's Gospel assumes male gender as a requirement for becoming a disciple. According to this reading these gospels restrict discipleship to male characters while they accord followership to the disciples, the crowds, and to the women characters. Such a reading that accepts the narrative construction of the androcentric text as a "given" is neither able to problematize the rhetorical function of androcentric language nor to question its own framework that inscribes the distinction between discipleship and followership which the text leaves fluid. A purely deconstructive reading also can not but relinquish the heritage of women, be it cultural or religious, since not only the Bible but all cultural classics are determined by the patriarchal politics of the androcentric text.

In contrast, a critical feminist rhetorical interpretation, I have argued, seeks to break the hold of the sacred androcentric text and its unquestioned authority by resisting its ideological patriarchal directives and hierarchically arranged binary oppositions. It seeks to undo the patriarchal politics of biblical texts and interpretations by rejecting textual absolutism and tracing the intimate interaction between text and sociopolitical reality. By elucidating not only the sexual but also the patriarchal politics of biblical texts, it seeks to enable women readers to resist the prescriptive rhetorics and identity formation that these texts espouse. Such a critical feminist strategy for dislodging texts from their patriarchal frame by reading them against their kyriocentric, or master-centered, grain would be misapprehended if it were construed as one more sophisticated form of theological apologetic that recuperates the powers of the androcentric sacred text and thus co-opts women's religious energies for patriarchal biblical religions.[77]

WOMEN AS SUBJECTS OF INTERPRETATION

An *eighth* strategy of feminist interpretation shifts attention from the androcentric text to women as reading subjects.[78] Feminist reader-response criticism makes us conscious of the complex process of reading. By showing both how patriarchal discourse constructs the reader, and how gender, race, and class affect the way we read, such an approach underlines the importance of the reader's textual and sociocultural location. Reading and thinking in an androcentric symbol-system entices biblical readers to align themselves and to identify with what is culturally normative, that is, culturally "male." Thus reading the Bible can intensify—rather than challenge—women's embeddedness in the cultural patriarchal discourses which alienate us from ourselves.

Carol Newsom, for instance, has interpreted Proverbs 1–9 in terms of discourse theory. Communication always takes place between a speaker and an audience, an "I" and a "you." The author of Proverbs 1–9 does not conceal the text's speaking subject but openly constructs the text as a communication between father and son. The speaking voice of the text lays claim to the authority of the father, who sanctions notions of righteousness, justice, and equity but vilifies rival discourses, namely, the symbolic practices that are embodied by women, lady wisdom, and the strange woman. In the process of reading, readers are continually invited or summoned (interpellated) to take the patriarchal subject-position of the son who submits himself to the authority of the father. In taking this subject-position offered to them by the text, women readers identify themselves at one and the same time as subordinated male subjects and as female objects of speech. The subjectivity of women readers, i.e., the ability to construct oneself as a subject in and through language, becomes fractured. Yet women readers can resist the summons of the text by refusing to take on the subject-position it offers and identifying themselves instead with the dissident voices in the text.

To read the text against its patriarchal grain is a way of becoming a resisting reader. The androcentric biblical text derives its seductive as well as critical "power" from its generic aspirations. For instance, women may read stories about Jesus without giving any significance to the maleness of Jesus.[79] Yet, reading such stories in the theological contextualization of recent Vatican statements, for instance, that emphasize the maleness of Jesus not only reinforces women's cultural patriarchal self-identity, but also founds Christian identity as masculine identity.[80] Focusing on the figure of Jesus, the Son of the Father, when reading the Bible, "doubles" women's oppression. Women in the act of reading not only suffer from the alienating division of self against self but also from the realization that to be female is to be neither "divine" nor "a son of God."

Women's reading of generic androcentric biblical texts however, does not necessarily have to lead to the reader's patriarchal self-identity. Women readers can deactivate an essentialist cultural-theological framework of masculine/feminine gender in favor of an abstract degenderized reading. Empirical studies have documented that men and women read so-called generic masculine language ("man," "he") differently. Whereas men associate male images with such language, women do not associate any images at all with the androcentric text but read it in a generic, abstract sense. This is possible because of the ambiguity of generic grammatically masculine language. In each instance, women have to decide whether or not they are addressed by a statement. In the absence of any clear contextual markers, a statement such as "all men are created in the image of

36

G-d" can be understood either as generic-inclusive of women or as masculine-exclusive. How readers decide on the meaning of a generic text greatly depends on their experience. Fifty years ago readers would have concluded a sentence such as "all professors in divinity schools are . . ." with "white educated men." The presence of white women and African, Hispanic, or Asian faculty at theological schools—however small and tenuous their presence—no longer allows for such a "common-sense" conclusion.

However, patriarchal biblical language is not only androcentric; it is also kyriocentric. It does not just lead to the woman reader's "immasculation" but also to her colonization. For instance, Chung Hyun Kyung notes that the biblical story of Jesus' suffering and death is held up as a model for Asian women, whose lives are filled with suffering and obedience. She relates a story about a Korean Sunday school teacher whose life was threatened by domestic violence. The woman testified that she had experienced G-d's love through her husband's judgment. When she accepted that she had to obey her husband as G-d's representative, her old self was dead and her new self was born. She concluded her testimony, receiving applause from the congregation: "There have been no arguments and only peace in my family after I nailed myself on the cross and followed God's will."[81] Such a reading of the key Christian biblical story about the suffering, death, and resurrection of Jesus that focuses on Jesus' obedience and suffering cancels the text's cultural masculinizing tendencies in favor of the inculcation of patriarchal submission.

When women recognize their contradictory ideological position in a kyriocentric language system, they can become readers resisting the *master-identification* of the androcentric, racist, classist, and colonialist text. If this contradiction is not brought into consciousness, however, it leads to further self-alienation. For change to take place, women and other unpersons must concretely and explicitly claim as their very own the human values and visions that the androcentric text ascribes to "generic" elite, white man.

SOCIOPOLITICAL LOCATION

A *ninth* strategy of feminist biblical interpretation insists on articulating the sociopolitical, global-cultural, and pluralistic religious locations and contexts of biblical readings. This strategy is advocated by those who in various ways seek to fashion new models and approaches for a biblical reading that can support people's struggle for justice, self-determination, and freedom.[82] Advocates of this strategy often speak from the social location of double or triple marginalization. As African-American, Hispanic, or Asian-American women scholars they are a tiny minority in the white male European-American academy not only because of their race or culture but also because of their gender. They are the quintessential Other in the hegemonic discourses of Euro-American elite men. Neither Jerome nor Thomas, Bultmann nor Albright, Troeltsch nor Geertz, Derrida nor Foucault are their exegetical or theoretical "Godfathers." Rather, they share the theoretical interests which have emerged across academic disciplines in discourses of resistance. Thus they speak from social contexts, hermeneutical points of view, and theological interests quite different from those of European and American biblical scholarship. Those who are marginalized in the academy and in society but who in fact constitute the majority of the world's people—women of all colors and men exploited by racism, classism, and colonialism—insist over and against modern scientific claims to value-neutrality and disinterestedness in biblical scholarship on the validity of their own presuppositions and interests.

For instance, when womanist scholars name racial slavery as the sociopolitical context of biblical interpretation,[83] they ask about the kind of socioethical values and symbolic constructs which have enabled the dominant white Christian church and academy to justify, both biblically and theologically, chattel slavery. They highlight the degree to which dominant hermeneutical frameworks of biblical interpretation are determined by economic, institutional, cultural, and racial interests. Just as the legitimization of slavery has determined the biblical readings of white churches, so the experience of slavery has shaped African-American biblical interpretation.

The contributions of Asian women theologians[84] in turn are not situated in a Euro-American but in a global cultural and religious context. Asian women's theoretical explorations focus on the colonialist implications of biblical interpretation. They explicitly articulate biblical hermeneutics in a religiously pluralistic context, especially in dialogue with Asian religions. For instance, Sister Vandana, an Indian exegete, interprets John's Gospel with reference to Indian Sacred Scriptures and the help of Dhvani, a method that stresses the evocative power, the inner beauty, and the emotive grip of a text.[85]

Latin American feminist theologians claim the "hermeneutical privilege of the oppressed," when reading the Bible from a "woman's perspective."[86] Elsa Tamez stresses that every Latin American reading of the Bible must have the poor as its point of departure. To read the Bible with "women's eyes" and "from women's perspective" means to become conscious of the existence of individuals who are exploited and oppressed because of their sex. This approach distinguishes Latin American women's reading of the Bible from all other liberation theological approaches. It requires both "gaining distance" from "macho" culture, religion, and texts and "coming closer" to the everyday experience of Latin American women. Although this approach is not restricted to women, "women as victims of sexist oppression will obviously perceive with less difficulty those aspects that affect them. Their experience, their bodies, their social upbringing, their suffering and specific struggles give them keys (insights) to this reading."[87]

Utilizing quite different historical-literary critical methods and theoretical models of interpretation, these "minority discourses" nevertheless articulate common insights and critical challenges that white Euro-American biblical scholarship can no longer disregard. Committed to the liberation struggle and rooted in the Christian community, such discourses on the social location of biblical interpretation establish the principle that an "interested" reading of biblical texts is not less scholarly or less historically adequate. To the contrary, such a reading is more capable of doing justice to the rich dimensions of biblical texts and their sociohistorical contexts. Rather than advocating value-free scholarship, they require a public articulation of scholarly values and commitments. They draw their critical intellectual force neither from scientific rationalism nor from academic antidogmatism but rather from their commitment to the liberation struggle of their people. What the African-American writer June Jordan says about poetry also expresses the self-understanding of liberation theologians who seek to fashion a critical biblical interpretation for liberation:

> Our art does not arise from the academy, and neither publication nor critical praise may define the motivating substance of our ambition. Our terms for creation, our artistic goals exist indissoluble from the living conditions and the political objectives of those whom we hope to serve well. We are the poets of our people. . . . A distinctively Black Poem will consciously seek to qualify as an instrument of survival for the poet, for her people.[88]

II.
A CRITICAL MODEL OF FEMINIST INTERPRETATION

Positioning my work within the context of feminist studies and liberation movements, as well as within academic-theological studies, I have sought to develop a distinct *tenth* approach in biblical women's studies. In developing this approach I have learned much from the rich variety of reading strategies developed in biblical women's studies. I do not seek to replace them but to utilize and integrate them in a rhetorical model of a critical feminist interpretive process for transformation. I do not subscribe to one

39

single reading strategy or method, but rather employ a variety of theoretical insights and methods to articulate my own analytical frameworks and interpretive practices in order to recast biblical studies in rhetorical terms.[89]

A CRITICAL FEMINIST RHETORICAL MODEL

A critical model for reading the Bible seeks to articulate feminist interpretation both as a complex process of reading and reconstruction and as a cultural-theological practice of resistance and transformation. To that end it utilizes not only historical and literary critical methods, which focus on the rhetoric of the biblical text in its historical contexts, but also storytelling, role-play, bibliodrama, pictorial arts, dance, and ritual to create a "different" historical imagination.

Such an interactive and multistrategic model of interpretation seeks to overcome the methodological split between feminist historical studies, on the one hand, which understands its sources in positivist terms as windows on and descriptions of historical reality, and feminist literary studies, on the other hand, which tend to understand texts in positivist terms as completely turning on themselves and thus as reinscribing the binary structures and dualistic representations of the androcentric text as universal laws. A rhetorical approach also seeks to exploit the contradictions and silences inscribed in the text for reconstructing not only the symbolic "world of the biblical text," but also the sociohistorical worlds which have made possible the particular world construction of the text. It does so by analyzing the sociorhetorical functions of the text, as well as by articulating models for historical reconstruction that can displace the dualistic inscriptions of the androcentric text. It does not deny but recognizes that androcentric texts are rhetorical texts, produced in and by particular historical debates and struggles. In short, a critical model of feminist interpretation for liberation seeks to articulate a rhetorical practice that can *displace* objectivist and depoliticized academic practices of biblical interpretation— practices which at present seem to be gaining ground in biblical women's studies.

Peggy L. Day, for instance, locates feminist gender studies within the academic paradigm. She distinguishes feminist theological interpretations, on the one hand, which according to her seek out the significance of biblical texts for today, and gender studies, on the other hand, "adopting and applying feminist critical approaches developed in the secular humanities and social sciences to the field of biblical studies."[90] Yet, if feminist theory and biblical interpretation no longer position themselves within the women's movement but orient themselves toward a "scientific" male audience and primarily seek to win its respect, the "critical energies of feminism" are in danger of being recuperated into the dominant ideology of biblical studies. The integration of biblical women studies into the academy will bring "increased pressure" to accommodate itself and to make compromises, "abandoning in the process the political priorities and the concerns for the personal that have made it so effective in the past."[91]

Insofar as feminist studies in religion seek to transform academic as well as ecclesial biblical interpretation, they must always have both a theoretical *and* a practical goal. This praxis-orientation locates a feminist biblical interpretation for liberation in the context of emancipatory movements in society and religion, as well as at the intersection of feminist critical theories and liberation theologies. Since feminist studies, in distinction to gender studies, are explicitly committed to the struggle to change patriarchal structures of oppression in religious and cultural institutions, they must disentangle the ideological (religious-theological) functions of biblical texts for inculcating and legitimating the patriarchal order.

Feminist biblical interpretation must remain a practice of rhetorical inquiry engaged in the formation of a critical historical and religious consciousness. Whereas hermeneutical theory seeks to explore and to appreciate the meaning of texts, rhetorical interpretation and its theoethical interrogation of texts and symbolic worlds pays attention to the kinds of effects biblical discourses produce and how they produce them. A focus on the theory and the practice of struggle for transforming patriarchal relations of domination and subordination is a descriptive as well as normative principle for a critical feminist interpretation for liberation. To that end a rhetorical process of a biblical interpretation for liberation must rely on a critical rather than a deterministic conception of language.

Feminist linguistic theory has developed two reading strategies based on different understandings of the nature of language; one assumes linguistic-symbolic determinism, the other understands androcentric language in rhetorical terms as a conventional tool for creating and negotiating meaning in specific contexts.[92] These different understandings of language continue the debate on whether grammatical gender is natural, or is a classificatory system that does not reflect any common-sense division of word meanings into masculine/feminine/inanimate-neuter. This debate was not introduced by feminism but has been carried on by grammarians and linguists since antiquity. Whereas grammarians and linguists tend to obfuscate the sociopolitical significance of this debate, feminist analysis stresses the significance of language and symbolism in women's struggle against androcentric self-alienation and patriarchal oppression. The debate around the Inclusive Language Lectionary has amply documented the import of this discussion.

The first deterministic understanding of language takes the androcentric

41

cultural sex/gender language system as a self-contained closed system which signifies reality. It works with the assumption that androcentricity (male as central, female as peripheral), exclusivity (male as focal point, female as marginal), isolation (male as self, female as other), and subjectification (male as agent and subject, female as passive object) are universal structures of language and representation. Insofar as feminist scholars accept this self-contained naturalized sex/gender system at face value, their reading strategy consists either in tracing its inscription in biblical texts, that is, in uncovering the text's underlying universal deep structures, or in revalorizing female/feminine over and against male/masculine representation. Such a feminist analysis, for instance, traces and highlights a biblical text's grammatically masculine language that makes women invisible or marginal in the text. Pointing to androcentric biblical representations in language, it maintains not only that the inscribed and the intended author and audience of biblical texts are male, but also that the symbolic universe and world of the Bible is masculine.

Focussing on the androcentric linguistic medium, such a reading strategy, for instance, critiques biblical symbolic constructions of evil as "gendered." Women are symbolized in male terms either as "the whore" or as "the good woman." Reading the Bible through the "eyeglasses" or grid of the sex-gender system makes one conscious of the all-pervasive androcentric ideology of Western culture in the interpretation of biblical texts and traditions. Such a purely hermeneutic reading in terms of the sex-gender system does not allow one however to challenge the text's cultural androcentric perspective of reality. Rather by elaborating a text's sex/gender inscriptions such a reading re-inscribes this system as a self-contained totality that does not depend on its sociohistorical rhetorical contexts. Thus a feminist biblical interpretation that understands language in positivist terms can make readers conscious of internalized male identifications, but it can not read cultural texts and traditions "against the androcentric grain" in order to reclaim them for women.

The second theory of language understands language as a tool which enables readers to negotiate and create meanings in specific contexts and situations. Consequently, it consciously asserts the interpreter's agency, subjecthood, contextuality, particularity, stance, and perspective. It does not focus, therefore, on the androcentric linguistic medium but on the practice of reading.

If language is not a straitjacket into which our thoughts must be forced, that is, if it is not a naturalized closed system but rather a medium that is affected by social conditions and that changes in response to social changes, then writing, translation, and interpretation become acts of struggle for change.[93] In distinction to linguistic determinism, such a rhetorical understanding of language does not identify grammatical gender with "natural" sex. It understands that grammatically masculine language can function both as gender-specific and as generic language. In their interaction with a text, readers decide how to read such language in specific linguistic and social contexts. If they borrow critical methods and theories that valorize the sex/gender system and grid of reading, they risk magnifying women's marginalization, objectification, alienation, and negation in the text. To break the power of the cultural "reading glasses," "grid" or "register" of the totalizing sex/gender system, feminist interpreters must adopt approaches that undermine the androcentric reality-construction of the text. Throughout the centuries women have read and identified with great literature not because they were totally self-alienated, but because they read it as "common literature" with whose "humanist" values and visions they could identify.

A critical feminist interpretation for liberation seeks to engage a rhetorical reading strategy in three ways: Firstly, it translates and reads the grammatically masculine language of the Bible as conventional generic language unless its interrogation indicates that in a particular context such language functions as gender-specific language and seeks to instill patriarchal meanings. Secondly, it translates and reads the explicitly gendered language and images of the Bible as "conventional" language that must be understood in its traditional and present-day meaning contexts. For instance, both whoring and fornication as metaphor for idolatry, as well as the symbolic understanding of Israel as the bride and wife of Yahweh, are part and parcel of the prophetic-apocalyptic tradition.[94] They must be subjected to a feminist critique. Their "gendered" meaning cannot be assumed as the primary meaning within the narrative contextualization of biblical writings, since such language is part and parcel of a naturalized "common-sense" gender framework.

Finally, a critical feminist interpretation reads biblical texts not just in terms of the sex/gender system but with reference to the Western patriarchal system with its interlocking structures of racism, classism, colonialism, and sexism. Such a reading, for instance, does not only pay attention to the sexual characterization of biblical figures but also to their characterization in terms of high status, ruling power, egregious wealth, and divine aspirations. Such a complex analysis is important because multicultural studies have shown that so-called "First World" writers and readers place sexual-psychological problems in the foreground, whereas those from the so-called "Third World" focus on sociopolitical experience.[95]

To engage in such a differentiated critical reading of androcentric biblical language and text in interaction with alternative interpretations, a feminist liberationist strategy of rhetorical reading must employ not only literary-cultural, but also historical-theological modes of analysis. Moreover, it must seek to transform individualistic and scientistic modes of biblical interpretation into rhetorical, public-political models of reading.

The dominant understanding of religion and the Bible that has developed in modernity is not political but individualistic and belongs to the private sphere. This modern understanding of religion works with four basic assumptions:

1. Privatization. The biblical message addresses the individual; it has no validity for the ordering of social and political life.

2. Historical limitation. The biblical message can only claim relevance for the situation of its origin; it belongs to a totally different world and can not claim significance for today.

3. Interiorization. The biblical message pertains to the life of the soul, redemption from personal sin, and eternal life. The *basileia*—the domination-free world of God—is "not of this world."

4. Individualist ethics. The biblical message proclaims universal moral values and attitudes which appeal to the conscience of the individual. Therefore it is the task of religion and not that of science to ascertain the moral sense of Scripture.[96]

In contrast to this religious/theological understanding of the Bible, modern biblical scholarship claims to be scientific, objective, and disinterested. Nevertheless, it is also practiced from within a community of interpretation. The sociopolitical location of modern biblical scholarship is the university, with its preconceived notions of language and reality. Biblical scholars no longer read the Bible as a code with which to decipher moral directives for individual spiritual edification. Rather, they either use the Bible as a historical source whose information can be objectively transcribed, or they understand it as religious literature whose indeterminate meaning can never be fixed. Both "scientific" strategies of interpretation share the social location of the Enlightenment university, an interpretive community dedicated to rational, scientific, and value-detached inquiry that prides itself on being apolitical.

The scientific ethos of biblical reading insists that readers must silence their own interests and abstract themselves from their own sociopolitical situation in order to respect the "alien" character and historical chasm between us and the biblical text. This rhetoric of disinterestedness and bias-free exegesis silences reflection on the political interests and functions of biblical scholarship. Its claim to public scientific status suppresses the rhetorical character of biblical texts and readings and obscures the power relations through which it was constituted. It does so by asserting that a given interpretation of the text represents an objective scientific reading that is able to comprehend the definitive meaning intended by the author. True, exegetical commentary is not free from rhetorical argument, but such argument must be restricted to showing how competing interpretations have misread the text. This scientific model of interpretation shares in the pathology of modernity, which, according to J. Habermas,[97] consists in the splitting-off of expert cultures from everyday cultural practices and life. By understanding the "first" meaning of the biblical text as a deposit of the definitive meaning of the author, historical biblical interpretation runs the risk of "shutting up" the "meaning" of the text in the past and turning it into an artifact of antiquity accessible only to the expert of biblical history or philology.

Theologians and ministers in turn are interested in the religious "spiritualized" meaning of biblical texts for today. Through "application" they seek to liberate the text from its "historical captivity" in order to rescue the message of the Bible for Christians today.[98] One form of this "liberation" of the text is accomplished by "updating and actualizing" aspects of it: by "translating" and rendering its mythic images contemporary, by selecting passages which still speak to us and illumine our own questions, by reducing its world of vision to theological or ethical principles and themes. Another form of theological "application" of biblical texts is achieved by correlating the text's discursive situation with present-day religious problems. Whereas theological liberals frustrated by the mythological content or outdated injunctions of the Bible look for commentaries which enable them to "squeeze" the living water of revelation and theological truth out of the hard stone of ancient biblical facts, biblical fundamentalists insist on the inerrant literal sense of the text as a fact.

Insofar as scientific exegesis seeks not only to facilitate understanding but also to close off the text's multivalent meanings by interpreting the text from a particular sociotheological location, it engages not just in a hermeneutical but also in a rhetorical practice. Yet the practice of interpretation does not simply understand and comprehend texts and symbols (hermeneutic); it also produces new meanings, speaking from different sociopolitical locations and for changed rhetorical situations (rhetoric).[99] Since the sociohistorical location of ancient rhetoric is the public of the Greek city-state (the *ekklēsia*), a rhetorical conceptualization of text and interpretation situates biblical scholarship in such a way that its public character and political responsibility become an integral part of our literary readings and historical reconstructions of the biblical world.

Biblical scholarship as a rhetorical or communicative practice seeks to display how biblical texts and their contemporary interpretations are both political and religious. Authorial aims, point of view, narrative strategies, persuasive means, and authorial closure, as well as the audience's perceptions and constructions, are rhetorical practices which have determined not only the Bible's production but also its subsequent interpretations.

This understanding of rhetoric as a communicative practice that involves interests, values, and visions must be carefully distinguished from the popular use of the expression. Popular parlance often labels statements "rhetoric" or "rhetorical" which it believes to be "mere talk," stylistic figure, deceptive propaganda, in short, any clever form of speech that is not honest, or lacks substance. Rhetoric is often misunderstood as "mere" rhetoric, as stylistic ornament, technical device, or linguistic manipulation, as discourse utilizing irrational, emotional devices contrary to critical thinking and reasoning. When I reclaim the term "rhetoric" for a critical feminist interpretation of liberation, I do not use it in this colloquial sense. Indeed, I seek to utilize rhetorical analysis not as one more method of literary or structural analysis, but rather to analyze how biblical texts and interpretations create or sustain oppressive or liberating theoethical values, sociopolitical practices, and worlds of vision.

In distinction to formalist or structuralist literary criticism, a critical feminist rhetoric insists that context is as important as text. What we see depends on where we stand. One's social location or rhetorical context is decisive for how one sees the world, constructs reality, or interprets biblical texts. Biblical scholarship that continues to subscribe to a value-neutral epistemology covertly advocates an apolitical reading of canonical texts and does not take responsibility for its political assumptions and interests. Once biblical scholarship begins to acknowledge its own social locations and interests, whether of race, gender, nation, or class, it can become accountable to its wider audience and responsibly explain why it privileges one particular interpretation over other possible readings.

A critical construction of feminist biblical interpretation seeks to replace the depoliticizing practice of modern scientific interpretation with a practice of rhetorical inquiry engaged in the formation of a critical historical and religious consciousness. Whereas hermeneutics seeks to explore and to appreciate the meaning of texts, rhetorical interpretation pays attention both to the kind of sociosymbolic worlds and moral universes biblical discourses produce, and to the way these discourses produce them. If the Bible has become a classic of Western culture because of its normativity, then the biblical scholar's responsibility cannot be restricted to giving contemporary readers clear access to the biblical writers' original intentions. It must also include the elucidation of the ethical consequences and political functions of biblical texts and scholarly discourses in their historical as well as contemporary sociopolitical contexts. Just as literary critics have called for an interpretive evaluation of classic works of art in terms of justice, so theologians, preachers, and all readers of the Bible must learn how to examine not only the rhetorical aims of biblical texts but also the rhetorical interests emerging in the history of interpretation or in contemporary scholarship.

A religious-ethical rhetorics and feminist pragmatics of biblical interpretation does not simply seek to evaluate the ideas or propositions of biblical texts; it also attempts to determine whether the Bible's very language and composition promote stereotypical images and linguistic violence. What does a reading of the Bible "do" to someone who submits to its world of vision? Not detached value-neutrality, but an explicit articulation of one's rhetorical strategies, interested perspectives, ethical criteria, theoretical frameworks, religious presuppositions, and sociopolitical locations for critical public discussion are appropriate in such a rhetorical paradigm of biblical scholarship.

Consequently, therefore, the shift from a hermeneutical paradigm[100] to a rhetorical one has far-reaching consequences for the theoethical practice of proclamation.[101] By proclamation I do not mean just preaching but all theoethical inquiry that is concerned with the uses and effects of biblical texts in contemporary society. Such a broad understanding of theological biblical interpretation is necessary, because biblical texts affect the perceptions, values, and imagination not only of Christians, but of Western cultures and societies. Most importantly, the transformation of the scientific-positivist ethos of biblical studies into a rhetorical-ethical one creates a theoretical space in which feminist and other liberation theologies can participate in the center rather than on the margins of biblical interpretation. In such a paradigm of reading, all interpretations are understood to be rhetorical-perspectival interventions.

In sum, a critical feminist rhetorical interpretation for liberation does not assume that the biblical text is an unclouded window to the historical reality of women. Nor does it consider biblical injunctions and prescriptions as once and for all given divine revelations and norms. It does not understand the Bible simply as a historical source of evidence documenting women's reality, but it sees the Bible as a perspectival rhetorical discourse constructing theological worlds and symbolic universes in particular historical-political situations. Such a feminist rhetorical model of reading is not an individualistic accomplishment. Rather, it must be situated in its own rhetorical situation of origin. Such a model owes its articulation to the feminist liberation movements within biblical religions and society at large, as well as to its critical engagement with feminist critical theory in general, and alternative strategies of feminist biblical interpretations in particular.

The practice of biblical interpretation in terms of a feminist rhetorics seeks to make present the different voices inscribed both in the text and in its ancient and contemporary contexts. The following historical re-imagination[102] of the story of Herodias, which precedes that of the Syro-Phoenician in Mark's Gospel (Mark 6:14–29), is an example of such a feminist interpretation in rhetorical terms. This creative re-presentation combines the methods of critical historical exegesis with creative imagination in order to recover the voice of Herodias, suppressed in the rhetorics of Mark's narrative:

"Let me warn you, my Sisters, before I begin, that in this story from Mark there is but a kernel of actual historical evidence. According to the historian Josephus, John the Baptist was put to death by my husband, Herod Antipas, but the rest of what you read and hear in this biblical account is merely legendary embellishment. According to Josephus even the motive differs—Herod wanted to be rid of John—fearing an uprising due to his growing popularity."

With this as a backdrop, let me respond to Mark 6:17–29 as it is written.

"For Herod had sent and seized John and bound him in prison for the sake of Herodias, his brother Philip's wife; because he had married her."

Herod does the deed, but immediately Mark focuses the blame on me. I become responsible. Is this man, Herod, not responsible for his own choices—for his own actions? Does Mark really see me as strong and powerful and Herod as weak and powerless? Or is it that Mark needs a focus for condemnation, and affords me power (like my foresister, Eve) only in the doing of an evil act. I feel exploited—pulled into this story from outside as the Woman to blame—the sinner—the temptress.

"For John said to Herod, 'it is not lawful for you to have your brother's wife.' And Herodias had a grudge against him and wanted to kill him."

Did you hear that? "John told Herod." A man to man encounter—the androcentric framework is clear. I am an intelligent, educated woman in my Greco-Roman world—aware of the male domination in this patriarchal system. I admit that I struggle to be visible, involved, and active in a world that tries to break my spirit—to make me conform to its submissive, passive image of woman. And so, were this story true, I would have had a grudge against John. I'd be angry and there would have been moments when I'd have wanted to kill him for ignoring my personhood. It takes two to tango and I see our marriage (right or wrong) as a partnership. Yet John, in this account, sees and speaks to one person—Herod. He doesn't speak to me but about me, and not even by my name. I am not even marginal in this discussion; I'm not even there. Obviously John, Mark, or both accepted the patriarchal view of marriage as a property relationship. It is not lawful for Herod to *have* me. I *belong* to another man. I want to scream out from my voiceless place in this text, "I, too am a fully human person; I, too, have a mind, a heart and emotions." There is another person in this relationship—another half to this world—voices not heard. *Voices crying in the wilderness.*

"*But she could not kill John, for Herod feared him, knowing he was a righteous and holy man, and kept him safe, when he heard him, he was perplexed; and yet he heard him gladly.*"

Again here I am at the mercy of a writer who tells you I am the Woman behind the scenes with the evil scheme, but powerless to play it out because of one man's ability to recognize goodness in another man. I am presented as evil to the core, while in both men there is evidence of goodness. John is holy; and even in my Herod Mark shows a "glimmer of hope," depicting Herod as recognizing goodness and as keeping John safe from my destructive desires. Though perplexed, my dear Herod hears John gladly.

"*But an opportunity came when Herod on his birthday gave a banquet for his courtiers and officers and the leading men of Galilee. For when Herodias' daughter came in and danced, she pleased Herod and his guests and the king said to the girl, 'Ask me for whatever you wish and I will grant it.' And he vowed to her, 'Whatever you ask me, I will give you, even one-half of my kingdom.'*"

Josephus, the historian, does not include this banquet event, but in this rendering attributed to Mark, notice that even the world of celebration excludes women. I am not included among my own husband's birthday guests. At this point Mark's legendary sources, or his own imagination, run wild. He brings in my daughter, Salome—but only to delight the men and to serve as a vehicle for me to accomplish my wicked deed. Believe me, my daughter would never have danced before such an audience. It was not becoming of her social status. As I read this story by a man about women, I, myself, feel a desire to dance—not a dance to delight, but a dance of *anger*.

"*And she went out and said to her mother, 'What shall I ask?' and she said, 'The head of John the Baptizer.' And she came in immediately with haste to the king, and asked saying, 'I want you to give me at once the head of John the Baptist on a platter.'*"

Though Mark is careless with his historical facts, he is careful and consistent in keeping women in their place. We, women, are always outside—entering only to delight men or to take the blame. Salome now goes outside this world of men and celebration to consult with "Mommie

Dearest." Without hesitation, my evil mind and heart spew out the wicked request. Mark has me asking for a *head* when I could have had half a kingdom (another historical error, by the way; Herod was not a king and in no position to give away half a kingdom).

"And the king was exceedingly sorry; but because of his oaths and his guests he did not want to break his word to her. And immediately the king sent a soldier of the guard and gave orders to bring his head. He went and beheaded him in prison; and brought his head on a platter, and gave it to the girl; and the girl gave it to her mother."

In this gory story by Mark, my poor, remorseful Herod emerges slightly tarnished—the victim of my manipulation and influence—and John becomes the innocent victim of my violence and revenge. Yet, in truth, am I not the *victim?* Yes, I did historically exist, and I was the wife of Herod; but, though the name is the same, the facts have been changed to protect the *guilty.* I am the victim of a patriarchal world that has refused me voice and showered me with accusations, and, for centuries, I have been condemned by Bible readers for a crime I never committed. Like women before and after me, my story has never been told.

"When his disciples heard of it, they came and took his body, and laid it in the tomb."

And so—along with the entombment of John—we had the burial of my true self. The truth of who I am was gagged, bound, and entombed these many centuries, while a legendary figure by the same name has stalked your biblical world in the guise of truth—accepted, protected, and proclaimed by a patriarchal church as the "Word of God."

My Sisters, I reach across the centuries to speak to you today: In your search for truth about women of the past—even women of biblical times—*beware*—because often what you find are stories by men about women.

To know me may not have been to love me, BUT
To know me only from this biblical text is NOT to know me.
My hope now lies in YOU, My Sisters—
Have courage to question
to be suspicious of biblical texts about women like me found on pages dubbed
GOOD NEWS and proclaimed as WORD OF GOD.
Be tenacious in your struggle to know the truth
to name the oppression where you find it
and to set free and proclaim a
LIBERATING WORD . . .

2
ARACHNE –
WEAVING THE WORD

In Colcha embroidery, I learn,
women use ravelled yarn from old wool blankets
to trace out scenes on homespun woollen sacks—
our ancient art of making out of nothing—
or is it making the old life serve the new?
The impact of Christian culture, it is written,
and other influences, have changed the patterns.
(*Once they were birds perhaps*, I think, *or serpents.*)
Example: here we have a scene of flagellants,
each whip is accurately self-directed.
To understand colonization is taking me
years. I stuck my loaded needle
into the coarse squares of the sack, I smoothed
the stylized pattern on my knee with pride.
I also heard them say my own designs
were childlike, primitive, obscene.
What rivets me to history is seeing
arts of survival turned
to rituals of self-hatred. This
is colonization. Unborn sisters,
look back on us in mercy where we failed ourselves,
see us not one-dimensional but with
the past as your steadying and corrective lens.[1]

The Practice of Interpretation:

Luke 10:38–42

The feminist literary critic Nancy K. Miller[2] has argued that postmodern literary theory has replaced the notion of text as a "veil," behind which is to be found a more or less hidden truth or reality, with the notion of the text as texture, tissue, lace, or weaving. This language of textiles privileges the spider's web over the spider, the threads of lace over the lace-maker, the trophology of the loom over the weaver. Such a recasting of the text as texture not only spells the "death of the author," but it also forecloses the discussion of the writing, reading, and interpreting subject insofar as it assumes that "lost in this tissue—this texture—the subject unmakes himself [sic] like a spider dissolving in the constructive secretions of [her] web."[3] Miller suggests that a feminist poetics must replace the neologism of the text as "hyphology" with the notion of "arachnology," that is, with the study of the woman weaver of texts. Such a study is a "critical positioning which reads *against* the weave of indifferentiation to discover the embodiment in writing of a gendered subjectivity; to recover within representation the emblems of its constructions."[4]

Since such a critical positioning is not a fixed standpoint but a shifting and moving position, I suggest that we add to the image of spider and text that of the dance. Insofar as the feminist biblical critic repeats strategic moves of interpretation, she is best imaged as a dancer who engages in a circle-dance that spells not only movement but also embodiment.[5] The biblical figures of Miriam, Judith, and Sophia come to mind as leaders in the ongoing, never closing, shifting movement of a feminist biblical interpretation for liberation.

In *Bread Not Stone* I have proposed *four reading strategies* which I seek to further theorize here. The crucial moments in a critical feminist hermeneutical process are: ideological suspicion, historical reconstruction, theoethical assessment, and creative imagination. However, these strategies of interpretation are not undertaken in a linear fashion. Rather, they must be understood as critical movements that are repeated again and again in the "dance" of biblical interpretation.

These four rhetorical movements can only be sustained when contextualized in a feminist critical process of *"conscientization,"* or learning to recognize sociopolitical, economic, cultural, and religious contradictions.[6] This process of conscientization strives to create critical consciousness and has as its goal both a praxis of solidarity and a commitment to feminist struggles that seek to transform patriarchal relations of subordination and oppression.[7] Such a process of conscientization is engendered by experiences of cognitive dissonance. These "breakthrough" and "disclosure" experiences bring into question the "common-sense" character of patriarchal reality. Such "breakthrough" experiences and the systemic critique of oppressive patriarchal reality are made possible through emancipatory movements. The critical feminist paradigm of reading as a "transformative dance of interpretation" must thus begin with the critical moments of *consciousness raising* and *systemic analysis.*[8] For these two moments are the ingredients of a *hermeneutics of suspicion.*

Although these four interpretive strategies can be distinguished theoretically, they interact with each other in the process of interpretation. A hermeneutics of suspicion, for instance, must be applied not only to biblical texts and interpretations, but also to an imaginative feminist retelling. The *hermeneutics of imagination,* on the other hand, is a crucial ingredient in historical reconstruction and critical evaluation. Moreover, before engaging historical, literary, and theological reading strategies and methods within a critical feminist paradigm of reading, a feminist practice of interpretation must interrupt the perspectives and relations between text, reader, and context which have been construed by dominant doctrinal, literary, or historical reading formations.

A hermeneutics of suspicion is misunderstood if it is labeled "paranoid" and construed as assuming a "conspiracy" of biblical writers and contemporary interpreters.[9] Rather, such an interpretive method turns its searchlight first on the reader's own reading practices and assumptions. It seeks to detect and analyze not only the androcentric presuppositions and patriarchal interests of the text's contemporary interpretations and historical reception but also those of biblical texts themselves. Rather than presuppose the feminist character and liberating truth of biblical texts, a hermeneutics of suspicion rests on the insight that *all* biblical texts are articulated in grammatically masculine language—a language which is embedded in a patriarchal culture, religion, and society, and which is canonized, interpreted, and proclaimed by a long line of men. Without doubt the Bible is a *male-centered* book!

A *hermeneutics of remembrance,* therefore, can not take grammatically masculine, allegedly generic language and texts "about women" at face value. Instead, it must read them as intimations that much of what remains

53

is submerged in androcentric historical consciousness. If the reading strategies of a hermeneutics of suspicion can be likened to the practices of a detective or a sleuth, those of a hermeneutics of remembrance resemble the activity of a quilt-maker who stitches all surviving historical patches together into a new overall design. To that end, a hermeneutics of remembrance must develop designs or models for historical reconstruction which can dislodge the eradicating frame of the androcentric biblical text. In positive terms, such reconstructive models must allow one to reintegrate women and other marginalized people into history as agents and at the same time to write biblical history as the history of women and men. A hermeneutics of historical remembrance reconstructs early Christian history not as reified artifact, but as memory and heritage for the *ekklēsia* of women.

While a hermeneutics of remembrance seeks to recover all possible remnants of textual and material information in order to rearrange them in a different and more plausible historical picture, a *hermeneutics of proclamation* insists that texts which reinscribe patriarchal relations of domination and exploitation must not be affirmed and appropriated. In theological terms, they should not be proclaimed as the word of G-d but must be exposed as the words of men. Otherwise, Christian discourses about G-d continue ultimately to legitimize patriarchal oppression. If the first two hermeneutical strategies can be likened to the practices of a detective and of a quiltmaker, this third strategy resembles the activity of a health inspector who tests all food and medicine for possible harmful ingredients.

Like a health inspector, a heremeneutics of proclamation, for the sake of life and well-being, ethically evaluates and theologically assesses all canonical texts to determine how much they engender patriarchal oppression and/or empower us in the struggle for liberation. Such an ethics of interpretation transforms our understanding of Scripture as "the foundation stone of truth" to that of "nourishing bread and food." Like a public health investigator, it not only attempts to test which foods are poisoned and which are not, but it also seeks to judge to whom and under what circumstances such "food" can be given. For instance, one might agree that a biblical injunction such as "love your neighbor" does not promote oppressive relations. Yet when it is quoted by a minister who is counseling a battered woman to remain in a destructive marriage, such an injunction serves patriarchal purposes.

Finally, a *hermeneutics of liberative vision and imagination* seeks to actualize and dramatize biblical texts differently. The social function of imagination and fantasy "is to introduce possibilities . . . [for] we can work toward actualizing only that which we have first imagined."[10] Creative re-imagination employs all our creative powers to celebrate and make present the suffering, struggles, and victories of our biblical foresisters and foremothers. It utilizes all kinds of artistic media to elaborate and enhance the textual remnants of liberating visions. It retells biblical stories from a different perspective and amplifies the emancipatory voices suppressed in biblical texts. It elaborates on the role of marginal figures and makes their silences speak. Lynn Gottlieb captures the goals of such a creative re-imagination:

> . . . some of us remain at the beginning, the word still to be formed, waiting patiently to be revealed, to rise out of the white spaces between the letters in the Torah and be received. I am speaking of the tradition of our mothers, our sister-wives, the secret women of the past. How would they have spoken of their own religious experiences, if they had been given a space to record their stories? . . . In order for Jewish women truly to be present in Jewish history and everyday life we must find the female voices of the past and receive them into our present.[11]

Whereas in the first chapter I have situated a critical feminist process of interpretation for liberation within a rhetorical paradigm of reading, in this chapter I seek to engage such a feminist model of interpretation in the reading of a Lukan text. Luke 10:38–42, the story about Martha, Mary, and Jesus, is only found in Luke's Gospel, where it is part of the so-called Lukan travel narrative. It reads in the RSV translation as follows:

> Now as they went on their way, he entered a village; and a woman named Martha received him into her house. And she had a sister called Mary who sat at the Lord's (*tou kyriou*) feet and listened (*ēkousen*) to his teaching (*ton logon autou*). But Martha was distracted with much serving (*diakonian*); and she went to him and said: "Lord (*kyrie*) do you not care that my sister has left me to serve (*diakonein*) alone? Tell her then to help me." But the Lord (*ho kyrios*) answered her: "Martha, Martha, you are anxious (*merimnas*) and troubled about many things; one thing is needful. Mary has chosen the good portion, which shall not be taken away from her.

The great emotional attraction which this story has for many biblical readers is eloquently expressed in the following introductory statement to an essay on this text:

> And there is something else about this story. It simply will not let us go. I mean at the personal level. It is many years now since the Martha and Mary story first took hold of my attention. Since then I have spent

many hours of study on it and many more pondering and reflecting on what it might mean. Each time when I put it down or let it go, it clings to me and refuses to let me go. I know that I have not yet gotten to the heart of its mystery. . . . We may be able to say some things which point toward the story's greatness, and we may enable others and ourselves to see various aspects of the story which we had not noticed before. But to define and possess it? Can we possess the greatness of the flowers of the field? Greatness is recognized, not defined.[12]

How does a feminist critical interpretation approach this text, which is so highly valued by biblical scholars and theologians? Feminist biblical interpretation begins with experience. Many women greatly identify with Martha's plight. Traditionally women have been told that their feminine vocation is to take care of men and their children. They do all the work in the house and in the kitchen, clean and shop, give dinner parties for the advancement of their husbands, and at the same time are supposed to be relaxed, entertaining, and well-groomed. In the church they wash the altar linen, run the bingo games, and hold bake sales. They do all of this, often without ever receiving a "thank you." They secretly identify with Martha who openly complains, and they resent Jesus who seems ungrateful and unfair in taking Mary's side. Yet because Jesus is not supposed to be faulted, women repress their resentment of Jesus' action. Instead they vent their resentment against other women who, like Mary, have abandoned traditional feminine roles. The right-wing backlash in society and church feeds on this resentment of women who feel that their work and contributions are not valued but that it would be unfeminine to express their resentment.

Other women feel guilty because they are not able to fulfill Martha's role of perfect housekeeper and entertaining hostess. Pondering this story, one student writes of her mother:

> I watched my own mother neglect the housekeeping in order to talk to someone or listen or read and I joined my father in feeling embarrassed about the untidy house. I was ashamed about the mess and always surprised when my friends wanted to come home with me. Some have later explained that my mother made them feel welcome and important and they liked that housekeeping wasn't the first priority . . . Yet within her own family and within herself this was a conflicted issue. I am sure my mother shared this conflict with Martha.

Such an exploration of women's experience with the Martha and Mary story calls for a hermeneutics of suspicion even though this passage is usually hailed as one of the most positive biblical texts about women.

I.
A HERMENEUTICS OF SUSPICION

A *hermeneutics of suspicion* seeks to explore the liberating or oppressive values and visions inscribed in the text by identifying the androcentric-patriarchal character and dynamics of the text and its interpretations. Since biblical texts are written in androcentric language within patriarchal cultures, a hermeneutics of suspicion does not start with the assumption that the Martha and Mary story is a feminist liberating text just because its central characters are women. Rather it seeks to investigate *how and why* the text constructs the story of these two women as it does. [13]

The meaning of this passage is most difficult to establish because of the textual critical problems in verses 41 and 42. [14] Jesus' pronouncement is the climax of the story and therefore key to the meaning of the story. The six textual variations indicate that the story was controverted very early on. The variations represent, basically, two different readings. The longer reading, on the one hand, assumes a meal setting: "Martha you are anxious and troubled about many things; few things are needful or one," could mean, as one commentator puts it, that a couple of olives, or even one, will suffice at present. Mary has the main course already. The shorter reading, on the other hand, which is preferred by most contemporary interpreters, reads: "Martha you are anxious and troubled about many things, one thing is needful." The "one thing" probably refers to the activities of the two protagonists. The climactic word of Jesus then asserts that Mary has chosen the one thing, the good part.

Since the text does not directly refer to a meal or explicitly to "serving at table" but uses the more general expressions *diakonian, diakonein* the longer reading's assumption that a meal is being served cannot be justified. Moreover, the climactic word of Jesus does not mention *diakonia* or *diakonein* but reproaches Martha because she is anxious and troubled about many things. The Greek expression for being anxious—*merimnan*—reminds one of Luke 12:22.26, where the disciples are told not to worry about eating, drinking, and clothing, and not to be anxious about their lives. Instead they should seek God's *basileia*.

No consensus can be found among interpreters as to the story's basic meaning. A critical review of divergent interpretations can distinguish two basic approaches, which highlight in different ways the text's dualistic character.[15]

An *abstractionist* interpretation reduces the two sisters to theological principles and types. It is supported by the form-critical classification of the text as a biographical apophthegm, that is, an ideal scene or construct for the climactic saying of Jesus in which the many worries of Martha are contrasted with the one thing needful chosen by Mary. Such abstractionist interpretations, for example, have understood Martha and Mary as ciphers for the theological principles of justification by works and justification by faith, alms-giving and prayer, Judaism and Christianity, synagogue and church, people who are preoccupied with worldly cares and those who listen to God's word and seek spiritual things.

According to traditional interpretations of the story, Martha and Mary symbolize either the labors of this world and the bliss of the world to come (Augustine) or the active and the contemplative life in this world, or life according to the flesh and according to the Spirit (Origen). The contemporary version of this traditional interpretation emphasizes the importance of love of God over and against the social activism that stresses the importance of love of neighbor. Such interpretations not only dehistoricize the narrative, but they also make women historically invisible. They obscure the androcentric dynamics of the text which uses *women* to make its point.

Those interpretations which acknowledge that Martha and Mary are two female characters, that is, that actual women are the protagonists of the story, work with a "good woman/bad woman" polarization. The traditional Catholic interpretation gives women the choice of two lifestyles in the church: active (Martha) and contemplative (Mary). There are those women who serve God and those women who serve men. Active women do the housework, rear the children or take care of the sick, and concern themselves with mundane business. Contemplative women do not allow worldly things to interfere with their quiet study, prayer, contemplation, and service to the Lord. Women are either laywomen or nunwomen, secular or religious, serving their husbands or serving the Lord, their heavenly bridegroom.

Protestant interpreters have a more difficult time with this story since the Reformation replaced the role of nuns with that of the "pastor's wife," and the ascetic lifestyle with the cult of domesticity. Therefore they insist that women must fulfill their duties as housekeepers. Nevertheless, they must not overdo it. In other words, they should be accomplished hostesses of dinner parties and church suppers, but they should take some time out to "listen, to pray and to learn." Martha is told that only "a few things" are needed. She must still be the hostess, yet she has to keep it simple so that she can also fulfill her religious obligations. To quote a widely read work, *Women in the Ministry of Jesus*, Jesus' "remarks, however, are neither an attempt to devalue Martha's efforts at hospitality, nor an attempt to attack a woman's traditional role; rather Jesus defends Mary's right to learn from Him [sic] and says this is the crucial thing for those who wish to serve Him [sic]. Jesus makes clear that for women as well as men one's primary task is to be a disciple; only in that context can one be a proper hostess."[16]

Apologetic feminist interpretations in turn continue this dualistic interpretation. They focus on Mary's rejection of the traditional housewife role and stress her option for theology. They celebrate her vindication by Jesus without carefully analyzing the androcentric implications of Luke's story. Mary is compared to a student or disciple of a rabbi since she is seated at Jesus' feet. Just as Paul was the Pharisaic student of Gamaliel (Acts 22:3), so Mary is a disciple of Jesus, dedicated to listening to his word. Mary's role is characterized as very unusual in view of the place of women in Jewish culture whose work was to serve but not to study with a rabbi. Unlike any Jewish rabbi, it is then asserted, Jesus accepts women as disciples studying the Torah, while he rejects the role of housewife as women's proper role.

However, this interpretation highlights Christian women's role as disciples at the expense of Jewish women and their tradition. It assumes that Jewish women were relegated to the kitchen and excluded from the study of the Torah. Apologetic feminist interpretations have not invented such an anti-Jewish explanation; rather, they have uncritically taken it over from malestream exegesis. They do so in order to show that Christianity, far from being anti-women, has actually liberated women. Nevertheless, a feminist critical hermeneutics of liberation must reject such an anti-Jewish interpretation, because it seeks to eliminate the oppression and marginality of Christian women by historically perpetuating that of Jewish women. It overlooks that both Mary and Martha are Jewish women.

Another way to "save the story" from its critics emerges in the interpretive attempt to psychologize and eroticize its protagonists. One psychological reading, for instance, stresses that Mary showed sympathetic understanding toward the anguish of Jesus, who was on his way to Jerusalem where he was to face death, whereas Martha could not meet his needs. Jesus expected such a sympathetic understanding, though it was almost unheard of that a woman would be sought out as a confidante or that a man would discuss matters of life and death with a woman.[17] Other psychological readings understand the competition between Martha and Mary as either sibling rivalry or sexual jealousy. Martha, the older of the two sisters, expects Mary, the younger, to take over her share of work. Since John 11:5 states that Jesus "loved Mary and her sister," it is asked what sort of love this was: "Could there indeed have been sexual jealousy between the sisters for the attention of Jesus? Or was it platonic, a friendly relationship? As lively, physical human beings we cannot discount the possibility that there was more than friendly interaction between the three, a factor which could have entered into the resentment Martha expresses."[18]

Such psychologizing readings of the story overlook the insight of historical-critical exegesis that biblical texts are not interested in the psychological attitudes and emotions of their protagonists. They also perpetuate the patriarchal cultural stereotype of women as rivals, as merely the emotional support or love object of a man, or as both. Finally, such an interpretation also relies on the negative contrast of Jewish society.

In short, a hermeneutics of suspicion indicates that in one way or another most interpretations of Luke 10:38–42 underline the dualistic antagonism either between the two women or between the timeless principles or lifestyles which they symbolize. One must therefore ask whether such an androcentric dualism is a projection of traditional and contemporary interpretations, or whether it is generated by the text itself.

The same two women are also mentioned in John 11:1–44 and 12:1–11.[19] In distinction to the Fourth Gospel, the writer of Luke-Acts mentions neither the name of the town, Bethany, nor the brother of the two sisters, Lazarus. We can no longer know with certainty whether this silence is due to redactional considerations, or whether Luke did not have the same information about the two sisters as the Fourth Evangelist had. Nevertheless, a comparison between the gospels of John and of Luke indicates that the dualistic opposition characterizing Luke's text is absent from that of the Fourth Gospel.

A form-critical analysis shows that Luke's story itself constructs this opposition between Martha and Mary. Bultmann therefore classifies this story form critically as a biographical apophthegm, rather than as a controversy dialogue that was composed as an ideal scene to illustrate the final word of Jesus.[20] Apophthegms or pronouncement stories generally utilize antagonistic characterization to make a point and to espouse behavioral norms. The narration tends to stylize and typify certain persons or situations so that readers can identify with them and imitate their behavior. What seems to be clear is that the Lukan account is not concerned with the two women as individuals; rather, it is interested in them as representatives of two competing types or roles of discipleship: *diakonia-service* and *listening to the word.*

A linguistic-structural analysis further underlines the text's dualistic-oppositional structure.[21] In such an analysis, Mary functions as the positive figure to which the figure of Martha serves as a negative foil. The text itself inscribes the oppositions: rest/movement; lowliness/upright posture;

listen/speak. Martha's intervention as a speaking subject reinforces this contrasting opposition:

Mary	Martha
student	householder
listening	speaking
rest	movement
receptiveness	argument
openness	purposefulness
passivity	agency
better choice	rejection

In addition, a narrative analysis that charts the interventions of the characters can highlight the dualistic dynamics of the text. The three characters of the story are Martha, her sister Mary, and the *Kyrios*, the Lord. The relationship of Martha and the Lord in the beginning of the story is that of "equals": Martha welcomes Jesus into her house. Mary's relationship to the Lord is that of a "subordinate": she seats herself at his feet. Martha is absorbed in the preoccupations of *diakonia*; Mary gives her whole attention to the "word of the Lord." This opposition already hints at a conflict in which Martha becomes the protagonist. Martha's speech has two parts, one referring to the present and one pointing to the future, insofar as she aims to change the situation. Whereas the first part consists of a question which contains two accusations, the second is an imperative sentence which contains two demands. Martha's strong reference to her own person and needs contrasts with Mary's silence and passivity as she is focused on the *Kyrios* (v.39bc). Both parts of Martha's speech are directed explicitly to the *Kyrios* and only indirectly to Mary.

Martha does not speak to Mary directly but she appeals to Jesus[22] as a little girl might run to her father to tell on a sibling who misbehaved. She complains to the Lord about her sister[23] and asks him to use his authority to tell Mary to share in the work. In doing so she relinquishes the more egalitarian relationship between hostess and guest in favor of the dependency relationship between child and parent. The Lord rejects Martha's appeal and sides with Mary. He approves of Mary's choice to listen to him but discredits Martha's choice of *diakonia*, which is not the "one thing necessary."

In the beginning, the emotional dynamics of the scene lead us to expect an intervention of the *Kyrios* in favor of Martha. Readers understand her impatience with Mary's self-absorption and sympathize with her. Yet, Martha's active intervention shifts the reader's sympathy against her. Whereas in the beginning the story opposes Martha's welcoming of Jesus

61

and attention to service to Mary's position at his feet and attention to his word, the end of the narrative stresses Martha's exaggerated service, anxiety, and worry in contrast with Mary's choice of the better part which will not be taken away from her. Martha's desire to change the situation is rejected as too much worrying and busybodiness. In the course of the narrative, Martha, the independent and outspoken woman, is rebuffed in favor of the dependent Mary, who chooses the posture of a subordinate student.

In short, the story places the *Kyrios* in the center of the action. Insofar as he is characterized in masculine terms, the story is clearly kyriocentric, i.e., master-centered. Moreover, Mary, who receives positive approval, is the *silent* woman, whereas Martha, who argues in her own interest, is *silenced*.[24] Those who praise Mary's extraordinary role as a disciple generally overlook the fact that Mary's discipleship only includes listening but not proclamation. Finally, the text is not descriptive of an actual situation. Rather the narrative is *prescriptive*, pitting sister against sister in order to make a point. But what is the point that Luke wanted to make in his own social-ecclesial situation?

II.
A HERMENEUTICS OF REMEMBRANCE

A *hermeneutics of remembrance*[25] seeks to move against the grain of the androcentric text to the life and struggles of women in the early churches. It seeks to reconstruct early Christian history as the history of men and women, as memory and heritage for women-church. Rather than taking the androcentric text or historical model of Luke-Acts at face value, a hermeneutics of remembrance seeks to uncover both the values inscribed in the text and the patriarchal or emancipatory interests of its historical contextualization. When discussing the role of women in early Christianity, exegetes usually affirm that women have a prominent place in the Lukan double-work. However, they generally situate Luke's stories about women in the life of the historical Jesus rather than in the situation of the early Christian communities to whom Luke writes. Such an interpretive move allows them to psychologize and historicize the characters in the text and to stress, for example, Mary's personal relationship to Jesus.

That Luke 10:38–42 was generated by and addressed to a situation in the life of the early church—rather than an episode in the life of Jesus—is linguistically signaled by the title *Kyrios*. The text appeals not to the authority of the historical Jesus but to that of the resurrected Lord. Thus it is important to explore the story's inscribed historical situation and rhetorical function in order to identify the theological-pastoral interests of the author. Exegetes have pointed out that the inscribed historical situation is that of the early Christian missionary movement which gathered in house-churches.[26] Therefore, the householder Martha welcomes the Lord into her house. One reading of the story contextualizes it in terms of Gerhard Theissen's claim that the Jesus movement consisted of itinerant (male) missionaries and local households who supported the apostolic mission with material means.[27]

The text supports such an interpretation insofar as the *diakonein* of Martha refers back to that of the women in Jesus' and the apostles' company (Luke 8:1–3). As such a local householder, Martha makes too much fuss about hosting Christian itinerant preachers. Just as the twelve apostles (Luke 9:1–6) and the seventy (Luke 10:1–24) are admonished to stay as officially authorized delegates at the same house, to eat and drink whatever is put before them (10:7–8, cf. 9:4), and not to worry about their sustenance (12:22–26), so Martha's worries about hosting such traveling missionaries are rejected in favor of listening to their words. Such a construction of the historical subtext not only presupposes Theissen's historical reconstructive model of the Jesus movement, but in so doing it relegates women householders to providing hospitality for male preachers. Ultimately, such an interpretive model colludes with and reinscribes Luke's editorial interests, which relegate the *diakonein* of the women disciples to wealthy women's patronage and support for the apostolic male leaders.

Luke 8:1–3 is best understood as a Lukan editorial summary account (see 4:14f; 6:17; 9:51) which changes the Markan tradition by distinguishing clearly between the circle of the twelve and that of their female supporters. By adding Joanna, the wife of Herod's steward, he underlines that they are wealthy women who support Jesus and his male followers. They are not characterized as disciples *akolouthein* as in Mark, but they are motivated by gratitude because Jesus heals them.[28] That Luke intends to downplay women's equal discipleship comes to the fore not only in his attempt to subordinate women to the circle of the male disciples, but also in his characterization of them as wealthy benefactors. Studies of the social world of Luke have pointed out that he uses the Greco-Roman patron-client relationship as a model for his construction of the social world of Jesus, but that he insists on its modification.[29] Such patron-client relationships are characterized by inequality in status and power, as well as by exchange and reciprocity. "A patron has social and economic resources; in return a client can give expression of solidarity and loyalty. Generosity from the patron can be translated into honor and power."[30]

The Greco-Roman patron-client exchange system was a significant opportunity for marginalized wealthy but low-status people, such as freeborn women or freed persons, to achieve status and power. Are we then to understand that in exchange for their economic service the women who supported Jesus and the male apostles were to gain honor, status, and power equal to that of the male apostles? In fact, this is not the case, because the Lukan Jesus insists again and again that the expected behavior is the opposite of that produced by the patron-client relationship. The text insists that wealthy persons and leaders cannot expect to receive repayment in the form of honor and influence. Their only reward is from G-d, who is the only patron.

By undercutting the reciprocity of the patron-client system, the Lukan narrative produces the power-inequality between rich and poor men, male leaders and their subordinates. In doing so, it forecloses a significant social avenue to status and influence in the church for wealthy freeborn women and freedpersons. Thus the Lukan rhetoric of 8:1–3 undercuts women's equal discipleship on several levels: The women followers of Jesus are portrayed not only as serving Jesus and the male apostles with their possessions but also as owing gratitude to Jesus for having been healed. At the same time the text introduces "class" differences between women by turning the women disciples into elite married women and wealthy patrons. Ultimately, a historical reading that contextualizes the Martha and Mary story in terms of Luke's historical model as it has been theorized by G. Theissen is not able to break the hold of the androcentric texts but reinscribes it. Consequently, one must ask whether another reading is plausible.

It is important to note that the text itself does not directly place Martha in the kitchen preparing and serving a meal. In fact, the text merely states that she is preoccupied with too much "serving." *Diakonia* and *diakonein* had already become technical terms for ecclesial leadership in Luke's time. Traveling missionaries and house-churches were central to the early Christian mission, which depended on special mobility and hospitality. According to the Pauline literature, women as well as men were traveling missionaries and leaders of house-churches. The house-church provided space both for the preaching of the word and for eucharistic meal celebrations. Scholars project patriarchal bias onto the early Christian missionary movement, however, when they conclude that the *diakonia* of women consisted either in serving traveling male missionaries and doing housework for communal gatherings or that it was restricted to the house.

In early Christian usage, *diakonia* refers to eucharistic table service in the house-church. It was not, however, restricted to such service, since it also included the proclamation of the word. That this was the case comes to the fore in Acts 6–8 despite Luke's redactional interests to the contrary. Although the "seven" Hellenists are said to have been appointed to devote themselves to the *diakonia* of the tables so that the twelve could dedicate themselves to the preaching of the word, they nevertheless become the initiators of the Christian missionary movement and are depicted as powerful preachers and founders of communities. They are characterized similarly to the rival missionaries, preachers, and apostles of Paul in Corinth.

The structural affinity of Acts 6:1–6 and Luke 10:38–42 has long been recognized.[31] Just as Martha complains that Mary leaves (*katalipein*) the *diakonein* to her in order to listen to the word (*ton logon*) of the *kyrios*, so the twelve apostles maintain that they cannot leave (*katalipein*) the word (*ton logon*) of G-d in order to serve (*diakonein*) at tables. Luke's text not only distinguishes the *diakonia* of the word from that at table and restricts both to different groups, but, in so doing, Acts 6:1–6 subordinates one to the other. Lukan redactional interests seem remarkably similar to those of the Pastoral Epistles, which also distinguish between ministers who labor "in preaching and teaching" (1 Tim. 5:17) and those who "serve" (1 Tim. 3:8ff).

Luke 10:38–42 stresses that the *diakonein* of Martha is not the "one thing needful" and hence must be subordinated to "listening to the word." However, it must not be overlooked that the "good portion" chosen by Mary is not the *diakonia* of the word: it is not the preaching but rather the listening to the word. The characterization of Mary as a listening disciple corresponds to the narrative's interests in playing down the leadership role of women.

It has often been pointed out that it is a major Lukan literary strategy to parallel a story about a woman with one about a man and vice versa.[32] One of the earliest feminist articles has therefore argued that this male-female dualism reflects the "important constituency of women and men who shaped the missionary and catechetical movement."[33] Such an observation is correct in that it describes the audience of Luke's "catechetical" instruction as consisting of women and men. Yet the Lukan text represses the knowledge that women and men have *shaped* the missionary movement, insofar as the gospel does not parallel a single story about a leading male disciple, such as Peter, with that of a leading female disciple, such as Martha. By paralleling stories about male and female characters who are the objects of healing and instruction, the Lukan work genderizes membership in Jesus' community of disciples while simultaneously subordinating the women disciples to the male leaders.

This portrayal of women as *members* but not leaders of the Jesus movement corresponds to Luke's picture in Acts of the role of women. Acts tells us that women as well as men listen to the Christian message and become disciples.[34] However, the public speeches in Acts use the address "men, brothers" (*andres, adelphoi*) eleven times.[35] More importantly, Acts does not tell us a single story of a woman preaching the word, leading a congregation, or presiding over a house-church.

While the Pastoral Epistles explicitly prohibit women to teach men, the Lukan work fails to tell us stories about women preachers, missionaries, prophets, and founders of house-churches. Thus while the Pastorals silence our speech, Acts deforms our historical consciousness. In addition, Luke plays down the ministry of those women leaders of the early church whom he has to mention because they were known to his audience. Martha and Mary are a case in point.

Such a critical feminist interpretation of the Lukan text has met with strong disagreement.[36] These objections assert that the above interpretation does not sufficiently take into account the story's contextualization in the so-called travel-narrative and the overall tendencies of the Lukan redaction that are widely held to be positive with regard to women.[37] Such objections insist that the story characterizes Mary as a disciple of Jesus contrary to contemporary religious-cultural expectations. My point, however, is not that Mary is not to be understood as a follower or disciple of Jesus, but rather that she is not seen as a "minister of the word."

Even a cursory review of the placement of the story in the Lukan macrotext can substantiate my argument. Jesus is on his way to Jerusalem (9:51) and the reader knows he will die there. Chapter 10 begins with the official commissioning of the seventy-two disciples. They are told to expect food and shelter and to eat and drink what is set before them when they are received into a house (10:7). The vignette of the Martha and Mary story explicitly directs readers back to the sending out of the seventy-two disciples in that it refers to the journey and to the reception of Jesus in Martha's house. In doing so it clearly distinguishes between the disciples, who, like Jesus, are sent to proclaim the good news, and those in the community, who receive the disciples and listen to their preaching. The Lukan contextualization of the story thus marks Mary's discipleship as being like that of the members of the Christian community.

In addition, the placement of the Martha and Mary story in the immediate context of instructions for Christian practice is telling. The story is sandwiched between the example story of the Good Samaritan (10:25–37) and Jesus' teaching on how to pray (11:1–4).[38] While the story of the Good Samaritan addresses the question, "Who is my neighbor?", the section 11:1–4 answers the disciples' request for Jesus to teach them how to pray. The Martha and Mary story in turn climaxes in the assertion that Mary has chosen "the good portion."

Finally, the Lukan travel narrative in which the Martha and Mary story is situated has three journey sections. These are marked in 9:51, 13:22, and 17:11. The first narrative complex (9:52 to 10:42) in the first journey section (9:52 to 13:21) of the macrotext ends with the Mary/Martha story.[39] Whether the example story of the Good Samaritan and the pronouncement story of Martha and Mary are interrelated is debated. Yet both can be read as answering the question of the lawyer, "What am I to do to inherit eternal life?" Both are thus explications of the great commandment. They teach members of the Christian community what true discipleship is all about. They express the same message in narrative form as the blessing of Jesus in Luke 11:28, which praises those "who listen to the word of God and observe or do it (see 8:21)."[40] In short, the contextualization of the Martha/Mary story within Luke's macrotext of the travel narrative supports my argument that, although Luke's rhetorical strategy acknowledges women as members of the Christian movement,[41] it downplays their apostolic leadership.

That Martha and Mary were well-known apostolic figures in the early churches can be seen from the Fourth Gospel. Martha, Mary, and Lazarus are characterized as Jesus's friends whom he loved (11:5). They are his true disciples and he is their teacher. After expressing her faith in Jesus' word, Martha goes and calls Mary (11:20), just as Andrew and Philip called Peter and Nathanael. According to the Fourth Evangelist, Jesus' public ministry climaxes in the revelation that he is the resurrection and the life (11:1–54). While in the original miracle source the resurrection of Lazarus was the heart of the story, in the gospel the climax is the christological confession and dialogue of Martha and Jesus.

As a "beloved disciple," Martha becomes the spokeswoman for the messianic faith of the community. Her confession parallels that of Peter (6:66–71), but hers is a christological confession in the fuller Johannine sense: Jesus is the revealer who has come down from heaven. Indeed, Martha's confession has the full sense of the Petrine confession at Caesarea Philippi in the Synoptics, especially in Matthew 16:15–19. Thus Martha represents the full apostolic faith of the Johannine community, just as Peter does for the Matthean community.

While Martha of Bethany is responsible for articulating the community's christological faith, Mary of Bethany exemplifies the right praxis of discipleship. She is explicitly characterized as the "beloved disciple" whom the teacher has specifically called. She has many followers among her people who came to believe in Jesus (11:45). Though in the narrative of John 11 Mary plays a subordinate role to Martha, in 12:1–8 she is the center of the action. That Martha "served at table" could be an allusion to Luke 10:40, but in John 11 and 12 she is characterized as fulfilling both the ministry of the word and of the table.

Moreover, in John the two sisters are not seen in competition with each other or played out against each other as they are in Luke. Mary is not portrayed as Martha's opposite but as Judas' counterpart. The centrality of Judas both in the anointing and in the footwashing scene emphasizes the evangelistic intention to portray the true female disciple, Mary of Bethany, as the alternative to the unfaithful male disciple, Judas, who was one of the twelve. This opposition lends itself to an anti-Jewish reading if it is overlooked that Mary is portrayed as a leading Jewish woman. Whereas according to Mark 14:4, "some," and according to Matthew 26:8, "the disciples," protest the waste of precious oil, in John it is Judas who objects.[42] The male objection to Mary's ministry is discredited and rejected by Jesus' harsh rebuke: "Let her alone." Mary not only prepares Jesus for his hour of "glory," she also anticipates Jesus' command for each to wash the feet of the other as a sign of the agape praxis of true discipleship.

To sum up: A hermeneutics of remembrance can show that both Luke and the Fourth Gospel repress but nevertheless inscribe the struggle of early Christian women against the patriarchal restrictions of their leadership and ministry at the turn of the first century.[43] The Fourth Gospel indicates how women might have told stories which portrayed women as leaders in the Jesus movement to legitimate their own ministry and authority. By contrast, the rhetorical construction of Luke 10:38–40 pits the apostolic women of the Jesus movement against each other and appeals to a revelatory word of the resurrected Lord in order to restrict women's ministry and authority. The rhetorical interests of the Lukan text are to silence women leaders of house-churches who, like Martha, might have protested, and to simultaneously extol Mary's "silent" and subordinate behavior. Such a reconstruction of women's struggles in the early church also indicates why women have always identified more with Martha than with Mary. That is, it confirms women's "suspicion" that in the Lukan account Martha received a "raw deal." Yet it is not the *Kyrios* but the writer of Luke 10:38–40 who promotes such patriarchal restrictions.

III.
A HERMENEUTICS OF EVALUATION AND PROCLAMATION

The preceding critical feminist theological exploration of this Lukan text has important implications for contemporary feminist readings, for preaching, counseling, and individual Bible study. Such a hermeneutics has two significant interfaces: first, a critical assessment of the text, and, second, a critical assessment of the reading situation or context.[44]

First, instead of reinscribing the dualistic, oppositional, and kyriocentric dynamics of the biblical texts, a hermeneutics of proclamation must critically assess the values and visions the text promulgates in order to help women to name their alienation from and oppression within biblical religions. My critical exploration of the literary dynamics of Luke 10:38–42 has shown that the androcentric tendencies of traditional and contemporary interpretations are not completely read into the text; rather, they are generated by it. If this is the case, a feminist interpretation that defends the story as positive for women cannot but perpetuate the androcentric dualism and patriarchal prejudice inherent in the original story. This text is patriarchal because it reinforces the societal and ecclesiastical polarization of women. Its proclamation denigrates women's work while insisting at the same time that housework and hospitality are women's proper roles. It blames women for too much business and simultaneously advocates women's "double role" as "super women." Women ought to be not only good disciples but also good hostesses, not only good ministers but also good housewives, not only well-paid professionals but also glamorous lovers. A hermeneutics of proclamation therefore must insist that theologians not clothe such a patriarchal text with divine authority and proclaim it as the word of God. Instead it must be proclaimed as the word of Luke! We must evaluate all aspects of such a text to assess whether, how much, and in what kind of situations it continues to sustain patriarchal internalization in the name of G-d or Christ.

To say that we cannot simply proclaim Luke 10:38–42 as the liberating and salvific word of G-d does not, however, mean that we should not critically use this text in preaching and teaching. Since women and men have internalized its androcentric and patriarchal tendencies as the "word of G-d," Bible studies and sermons must critically explore its oppressive functions and implications. Not only the hermeneutics of suspicion, but also a hermeneutics of remembrance enables us to do so, since the androcentric character and patriarchal interest of Luke 10:38–42 can be elaborated with the help of historical reconstruction. A comparison with the Fourth Gospel's depiction of Martha and Mary, for example, helps one to understand that Luke's story functioned as prescriptive rhetoric in women's struggle against the gradual patriarchalization of the church at the turn of the first century. Such a comparison can also help readers to break the dualistic construction of the Lukan text and to celebrate the two female characters as historical and independent apostolic figures in their own right. In short, it allows us to reclaim the speech as well as the theological agency of these two women.

Second, a hermeneutics of proclamation must not only evaluate the androcentric dynamics inscribed in the structures of the text, it must also assess the sociopolitical contextualizations that determine how the Lukan text is read and heard today. Since such contextualizations are complex, I will outline four possibilities in order to emphasize the need for a critical evaluation for proclamation.

1. Ever since antiquity, Western culture has especially praised elite women's silence as proper feminine behavior. Mary, sitting at or lovingly washing the feet of Jesus and silently listening to his word, becomes the example par excellence for the proper feminine behavior of elite educated women in such a cultural context. Yet, when contextualized in the life of lower and working-class women, Mary's audacity in taking time out from work to sit idle and to relax in good company can have a liberating effect. As Janice Radway has pointed out, while the content of romance novels insists on the desirability and benefits of heterosexual feminine behavior, the act of *reading* itself for many women readers is oppositional. It allows women readers of romance fiction to take time out from work and family obligations and to "refuse momentarily their selfabnegating role." Such an act of reading is a "declaration of independence" and a way to say to others, "This is my time, my space. Now leave me alone." A homily stressing Mary's right to study and to read can therefore be liberating in a community where women's activity is restricted to caring and working for others in the family, on the job, or in the church. However, the example of Mary should not be used just to encourage the practice of biblical or religious reading; such a practice can also stifle the desire to struggle for satisfaction in real life insofar as women's emotional needs are successfully met in fantasy.[45]

2. The dualistic character of Luke's story is not discarded if the figure of Martha is held up to women as an exemplary figure fulfilling women's role of service. By taking the author's picture of Martha and the other women supporters of the Jesus movement at face value and interpreting such a picture in terms of sacrificing service, apologetic or literary feminist readings neither question nor subvert the androcentric tendencies of Luke's redaction. Therefore, they cannot but reinforce cultural stereotypes of femininity internalized by women and men. Such interpretations reinscribe cultural-religious gender, class, and race stereotypes when they stress, for instance, that the women "have given all for Jesus," or when they assert that the women "whom Luke so fondly speaks of" need not be remembered as "simply idle wealthy women."

A feminist interpretation which understands the Lukan texts about women in a historicizing way and which uncritically follows the patriarchalizing tendencies of the Lukan rhetoric cannot but recuperate these tendencies in its own reading. The women disciples are then seen as female workers who sacrificed everything to follow the "man" Jesus. Like women today, these women disciples are pictured as carrying a double burden.

They too traveled with Jesus, along with the male disciples, but they were not only teaching; they also did the cooking and the mending. They were not just donating their funds, but also their time. Just as faithful, sacrificing church women have always done! Ben Witherington III puts it succinctly: "Being Jesus' disciples did not lead these women to abandon their traditional roles in regard to preparing food, serving, etc. . . . The transformation of these women involved not only assuming new discipleship roles, but also resuming their traditional roles for a new purpose."[46]

3. Whereas feminist theology has challenged the restriction of women's roles to housework and service, it has not sufficiently questioned the notion of ministry as service. In spite of the feminist critique of the cultural and religious socialization of women and other subordinated peoples to self-sacrificing love and selfless service for others, the notion of ministry as service is still a powerful symbol for Christian feminists. They have argued that Christian theology cannot avoid the expression, despite its oppressive overtones, since *diakonia* is central to the understanding of the mission and ministry of Christ, as well as to that of the church.[47] Such a feminist retrieval of servanthood-ecclesiology basically divides along two strategies of interpretation: The first elaborates the early Christian distinction between *diakonein* and *douleuein* to stress that freely chosen service means liberation. *Diakonia*-service is to be differentiated from servility. Servanthood without choice is not *diakonia* but slavery (*douleia*). However, "servanthood through choice" is said to be an act of the total self. The powerlessness of servanthood can be redemptive only when it results from "free and conscious choice." Such "freely chosen" servanthood is not to be understood as self-denial, self-elimination, self-ignorance, or self-immolation. Rather it is said to be the "capacity to look beyond ourselves to see the needs of others." It is the "empathy" that wants to help and the skill that knows how to help.

Jesus models such "freely chosen" service, according to this interpretation, because he made the choices of self-giving and self-sacrifice rather than allowing society to dictate his behavior. Thus *diakonia* is realized in the life of Jesus, who came "not to be served but to serve and to give his life as ransom for many" (Mark 10:45). If "servanthood is being in love with the world as God is in love with it," then servanthood in the final analysis means liberation. "We find ourselves liberated into servanthood."[48] However, this feminist proposal for the theological recuperation of servanthood does not take into account that people who are powerless in a patriarchal culture and church; those singled out and socialized into subservience and a life of servanthood are not able to "choose servanthood freely."

By revalorizing service and servanthood theologically, this interpretive

71

strategy extends the theological "double-speak" about service to the theological concept of liberation. For those who are destined by patriarchal culture and sociopolitical structures to become "servants" to those who have power over them, the theological or ecclesiological retrieval of "service/servant/slave/waiter" cannot have a liberating function as long as patriarchal structures continue to divide people into those who serve and those who are served. Rather than elaborate the theological symbols of service/servitude/self-sacrifice, a critical feminist theology of liberation must seek biblical concepts such as *dynamis/exousia/soteria*, i.e., power/authority/well-being, that can critically challenge the cultural-religious production of a servant mentality.

4. Another feminist theological strategy for retrieving the theology of service for ministry concentrates on redefining ministry. By combining the theology of "freely chosen" service with an understanding of ministry not as "power over" but as "power for," it seeks to recover the early Christian understanding of ministry as serving G-d and building up the community. It also takes Jesus Christ and his incarnation as "suffering servant" as the model of Christian ministry:

> Such dismantling of clericalism is implied in the Gospel concept of ministry as *diaconia* or service. Diaconia is kenotic or self-emptying of power as domination. Ministry transforms power from power over others to empowerment of others. The abdication of power as domination has nothing to do with servility. . . . Rather ministry means exercising power in a new way, as a means of liberation of one another.[49]

Although this reconceptualization of ministry seeks to retrieve the New Testament model of *diakonia*—service for a feminist ecclesial self-understanding in and through a redefinition of power—it nevertheless valorizes the patriarchal concept and institution of service/servanthood theologically. The theological language of ministry as service, i.e., as "power for" rather than "power over" the church and the world, obfuscates the fact that the patriarchal church continues to exercise its ministry as "power over" its people as long as it is structured into a hierarchy of power-dualisms: ordained/nonordained, clergy/laity, religious/secular, church/world. Continuing to use the theological notion of service as a central feminist category for ministry, this approach reduplicates the cultural pattern of self-sacrificing service for women and other subordinate peoples, while at the same time it continues to serve as a moralistic appeal to those who have positions of power and control in church leadership. Dependence, obedience, second-class citizenship, and powerlessness remain intrinsic to the notion of "service/servanthood" as long as society and church structurally reproduce a "servant" class of people. Therefore, when seeking to define women's ministry, a feminist ecclesiology of liberation must reject the categories of service and servanthood as disempowering to women.

Luke and later theologians did not understand the radical paradox of the discipleship of equals when they called those in positions of wealth and power to "charitable service," which did not question but actually confirmed their patriarchal status and privileges. In the interest of "good citizenship," the post-Pauline writers advocate adapting the Christian community as "the household of God" to its patriarchal societal structures. The restriction of women's ministry and the separation of the *diakonia* of the word and that of the table, of proclamation and service, go hand in hand. Religious authority and power is no longer used for the service and well-being of people; it is no longer understood as enabling power but as controlling power, as patriarchal superordination and subordination.

Since this patriarchal adaptation of some segments of the early church has defined mainline Christian self-understanding and community and has institutionalized structures of "domination and authority," a feminist theology of ministry must deconstruct such a patriarchal Christian self-understanding and structure, refusing to perpetuate it by valorizing the notion of service and servanthood. The ministry of women is no longer to be construed as "service" or as "waiting on someone." Instead, ministry should be understood as "equality from below," as a democratic practice of solidarity with all those who struggle for survival, self-love, and justice. Since the *ekklēsia* of women as the discipleship of equals has been overshadowed by the reality of the patriarchal church, we need to re-envision women's ministry as such a practice of solidarity and justice.

IV.
A HERMENEUTICS OF IMAGINATION

Finally, a *hermeneutics of creative imagination and ritualization* seeks to articulate alternative liberating interpretations that do not build on the androcentric dualisms and patriarchal functions of the text. It allows women to enter the biblical text with the help of historical imagination, narrative amplifications, artistic recreations, and liturgical celebrations.[50] Such imaginative embellishments and retellings of the text, however, must also always be submitted to a hermeneutics of suspicion. For instance, a cursory survey of feminist retellings of the Martha and Mary story shows that many such feminist re-creations remain caught up in the cultural

73

feminine role expectations when they place Martha "in the kitchen" preparing a meal for Jesus.[51]

The following is an attempt at an imaginative feminist reinterpretation, made by a participant in one of my workshops:

> That Mary is invited to sit at Jesus' feet is only to coopt Mary, but not necessarily to set her free. Freedom would have come if Jesus and Mary would have shared the work so that everyone could have "the good portion." Jesus does invite Martha to put down her burdens and partake. He does lift up and validate Mary's choice to change roles. However, the pause still lingers on "one thing is needful." If the one thing that will help Martha with her anxieties and troubles is a shift in her view of herself and her role, the repercussions will be told around the world. She will no longer speak through a male authority figure, she will no longer put up with a group who expect to be waited on, she will take the good portion as she wants it and demand it as it is forthcoming. She will find a relationship to God Herself that fits for her which may well include both preaching and serving at table. She will reclaim her friendship with Jesus. She will raise hell.[52]

While this revisioning of the Mary and Martha story is articulated in terms of women's contemporary experience, the following account attempts a feminist retelling of the Mary and Martha story that allows us to discard the message that divides, subordinates, and alienates one sister from another. It allows us to understand the struggles of women in Luke's time and our own against patriarchal subordination, silencing, and oppression as one and the same struggle for liberation and wholeness. Out of the distorted web of history it lifts women of power and action and calls us to solidarity with them. One might want to quibble with its historicizing narrative, but I suggest that the following account is useful for illustrating a *hermeneutics of creative imagination:*

> I am Martha the founder of the church in Bethany and the sister of Mary, the evangelist. All kinds of men are writing down the stories about Jesus but they don't get it right. Some use even our very own name to argue against women's leadership in the movement. Our great-great granddaughters need to know our true stories if the discipleship of equals is to continue.
>
> They had been travelling for a long time when they finally came to our village. I invited them to join my sister Mary and me. Jesus and the disciples with him sat down and began talking. Mary sat at the teacher's feet and I joined her in asking him about his latest journeys. He told us the story of the Syrophoenician who came to him asking that her daughter who was possessed be healed. Preoccupied

with all the ministry to be done in Galilee Jesus refused: "I have come to serve only the lost and outcast of my own people."

But to his great surprise—Jesus continued—the woman persisted and started to argue with him: God's gracious goodness is so abundant that the crumbs falling from Israel's table are sufficient for nourishing those who do not belong to God's special people. Her argument and faith was like a flash of revelation in which Jesus realized that the good news of liberation and God's power of wholeness was for all people, gentile and Jew, male and female, slave and free, poor and rich. And her daughter was healed.

By the time the teacher finished this story, evening had approached and it was time for sharing the meal. I asked Jesus if he would stay to eat with us. He said yes, and added: "Martha don't go to a lot of trouble. Whatever you were going to have will be fine. Let me help you." We started toward the kitchen when one of the males hollered: "The women can go but you, Jesus, stay here. After all we have important things to talk about and they don't really understand theology."

But an Essene who had become one of the disciples travelling with Jesus said: "Isn't God's word for all people? Before I joined your movement I had always studied the Torah with other women. Are we women disciples to be excluded? After all, didn't your story about the woman from Syrophoenicia show that your message isn't just for some but for all, women and men, Gentile and Jew, slave and free, rich and poor?" And Jesus replied: "Susanna thank you for speaking out. You are much blessed by Holy Wisdom, for you are right." And he asked me to preside at the breaking of the bread and invited Susanna to say the blessing and to teach the Torah lesson for the day. There was grumbling among the men, but we women were excited by the new possibilities God had opened up to us.

My sister Mary helped me to write this down. May God Herself speak to us now and forever.[53]

In this chapter I have sought to exemplify the "dance of interpretation" as a critical rhetorical process. Such a critical practice of interpretation for liberation is not restricted to biblical texts but can be applied successfully to other religious or cultural classics. I am told that it has been used for instance in graduate education, in parish discussions, in college classes, in interreligious dialogue, or in work with illiterate Andean women.

The *ekklēsia* of women, I have argued in *Bread Not Stone*, constitutes the practical center and normative space for the hermeneutical circle-dance of a critical feminist rereading of the Bible for liberation. Since such a critical process of biblical interpretation seeks not just to understand biblical texts but also to change biblical religions and cultures in the interest of all women and other marginalized people, it requires a theological reconception of the Bible. Such a reconception construes the Bible as a formative root-model rather than as a foundational archetype. In this understanding the canon is neither the foundational constitution nor a set of norms defining Christian community and identity. Rather, as the formative prototype of biblical faith and community, the Scriptures offer paradigms of struggles and visions that are open to their own transformations through the power of the Spirit in ever new sociohistorical locations.

This model of the Bible as formative prototype conceives of biblical interpretation as a site of struggle and conscientization. It raises several sets of questions which not only require a reconceptualization of historical and theological hermeneutics in rhetorical terms, but also challenge biblical scholarship in general and feminist interpretation in particular to become more sophisticated by attending to its sociopolitical locations and religious contextualization, as well as its rhetorical interests and functions in the struggle for a more just church and world.

THE HERMENEUTICAL SPACE
OF A FEMINIST RHETORIC
OF LIBERATION

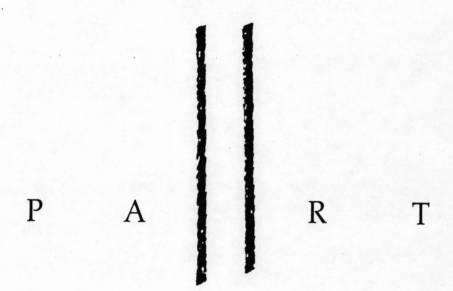

P A R T

3

MARY OF MAGDALA –
RE-MEMBERING THE PAST

Song of Praise

A wandering tribeswoman was my mother.
In Egypt she bore slaves.
Then she called to the G-d of our mothers
Sarah, Hagar, Rebecca, Rachel, Leah.
Praise G-d Who Hears, Forever.

A warrior, judge, and harlot was my mother
G-d called her from time to time
to save and liberate her people
Miriam, Jael, Deborah, Judith, Tamar
Praise G-d Who Saves, Forever.

A Galilean Jew was my mother.
She bore a wonderful child
to be persecuted, hated and executed.
Mary, mother of sorrows, mother of us all.
Praise G-d Who Gives Strength, Forever.

A witness to Christ's resurrection was my mother.
The apostle to the apostles
Rejected, forgotten, proclaimed a whore
Mary of Magdala, vanguard of women-church
Praise G-d Who Lives, Forever.

An apostle, prophet, founder, and teacher was my mother
called to the discipleship of equals
Empowered by the Sophia-G-d of Jesus
Martha, Phoebe, Junia, Priscilla, Myrta, Nympha, Thecla
Praise G-d Who Calls, Forever.

A faithful Christian woman was my mother.
A mystic, witch, martyr, heretic, saint, uppity woman
A native American, a black slave, a poor immigrant, an old
hag, a wise woman
May we, with her, in every generation
Praise G-d Who Images Us All.[1]

Because of Her Word:

Feminist Historical Reconstruction

Women have always transmitted history, told stories and kept memories alive. However, history has by and large been written by elite men as their own story and in their own interests. The apostle Peter, who according to some traditions was the first witness to the resurrection, has been hailed through the centuries as first among the apostles, whereas the apostle Mary of Magdala, who according to other traditions was the primary witness to the resurrection, has lived in Christian memory as repentant whore and sinner. The task of the feminist historian who seeks to recover history as heritage for women is aptly characterized by the Caribbean writer Michelle Cliff:

> To write as a complete Caribbean woman, or man for that matter, demands of us retracing the African past of ourselves, reclaiming as our own, and as our subject a history sunk under the sea, or scattered as potash in the canefields, or gone to bush, or trapped in a class system notable for its rigidity and dependence on class stratification. On a past bleached from our minds . . . It means realizing our knowledge will always be wanting. It means also, I think, mixing in the forms taught us by the oppressor, undermining his language and co-opting his style and turning it to our purpose.[2]

Like historians of other oppressed groups, feminist historians of early Christianity seek to break through the silences and biases of historical records to reappropriate the past of women who have participated as historical agents in social, cultural, and religious transformation. In order to reconstruct early Christian history *differently*, as the history of the *ekklēsia* of women or as that of the discipleship of equals, feminist historical studies in religion must not only question the prevailing accounts of the past. They must also situate their historical reconstructions within a critical rhetorical paradigm of historiography that can conceptualize the writing of history not as an antiquarian science but as a rhetorical practice. In other words, the point of a feminist historical reconstruction cannot be to distill, for instance, the factual "truth" of Mary of Magdala, one of Jesus' disciples, from its discursive representations. Nor can such a reconstruction attempt to recover the "real" Mary of Magdala. And neither should it try to establish the "actual event" of her first encounter with Jesus. Rather, a critical emancipatory historiography seeks to open up to historical memory what has been suppressed in traditional historiography in order to examine the exclusions and choices that constitute our historical knowledge of early Christian beginnings.

As we've seen, by positioning a feminist critical historiography in the rhetorical space of the *ekklēsia* of women, one is able to conceptualize early Christian history as a struggle between the dominant patriarchal discursive practices and those of the discipleship of equals. Such a positioning provides a theoretical vantage point from which the problems of text and history and past and present are brought into different focus. Moreover, from such a vantage point, the interests, political functions, responsibilities, and communicative practices of a critical feminist historiography will become more clear. Such practices are bound to encounter three theoretical-institutional objections: those of historical positivism, literary formalism, and postmodern constructionism—all of which are engendered by the dominant paradigm of biblical studies.

I.

TEXT AND REALITY

Biblical critical studies approach the relation between text and history, representation and historical reality, in very different ways. Antiquarian positivism reduces texts to archival quarries for historical facts, understanding them as windows on the world which give us accurate information and "data" about the past. Positivist textualism, by contrast, insists that one cannot move beyond the text to historical reality, but that one can only decode and reconstruct the symbolic narrative world of the text.[3] Postmodern constructivism contends that the past is *only* textual. "Facts" are created by the narrative acts of coding history and by the choice of narrative strategy, interpretive models, selection, plot, and closure. In this view, the past is constituted as a domain of representation. None of these three interpretive strategies, however, is adequate for a feminist emancipatory historiography.

Dominant biblical discourses theorize the relationship between text and reality, between historical representation and history as event, between past and present, and between the ancient and the contemporary reader, either in terms of radical difference or in terms of radical identity. Yet, these models jeopardize our understandings of reality. A similar epistemological split can be observed in the study of women in the biblical worlds. On the one hand, insistence on the identity of historical texts with reality presupposes what still needs to be demonstrated. On the other hand, insistence on the radical difference between representation and reality renders the historical world irredeemably past and inaccessible to us.

Antiquarian positivism. As I have pointed out in Chapter 1, the predominant understanding of how history in general, and early Christian history in particular, is written holds that historians are scientists who give us an objective and unbiased account of the past. According to such an understanding, to know our history means to memorize both the dates of significant events and the names of important historical figures—nearly all of whom seem to have been white elite men. Accordingly, historians assemble historical facts and data drawn from authenticated sources in order to tell us with scientific objectivity what actually happened. However, if we were to believe that historiography objectively mirrored historical reality, then we would be forced to conclude that women and other nonpersons have seldom acted as historical agents or contributed to our common history.

Moreover, forms of empiricist scientism and antiquarianism insist on the radical difference between past and present. Their scientistic gesture represses the present and turns the past into an empirical object. Within the interpretive framework of historical objectivism and positivist antiquarianism, biblical studies understand literary texts and archeological "data" either as reflections of reality or as more or less clouded windows to historical reality. Historical events are transformed into given facts and hard evidence that can be distilled from textual or archeological sources.

The ethos of objectivist scholarship demands that the contemporary interests of the inquiring scholar must be eliminated as much as possible from historical research and description so that the strange and foreign world of the text can emerge. History is thus written to reconstruct past events and ideas as they actually occurred. Indeed, positivist historiography is written in such a way that historical factuality appears to have determined the organizational structure of historical representation. Scientific style and description create a realistic account as though historical narrative were an accurate reflection of the "natural" order of things.

Variant scholarly accounts of the same historical event are contested with reference to *facts* rather than to the rhetorical arguments that have transformed textual sources and historical events into data and facts. Objectivist scholarship does not require that the historian's narrative show *how* it is plotted, as though it were a factual transcript of what actually happened, for instance, to the daughter of the Syro-Phoenician woman and what Jesus actually said to her. In short, for the sake of the legitimating authority of factuality in historical work, both historical-critical and socio-cultural positivist studies insist that their work is scientific. As such it is value-neutral, detached, objective, and dispassionate. While extreme historical positivism has been widely abandoned by biblical scholars, it is still widespread in popular culture. As one of my students reports: "I was working on this paper over the Thanksgiving holidays and discussed with my relatives the ideas of history as a narrative or story which is constructed and they just could not, or perhaps would not, understand or accept the concept that fact does not equal truth nor is there such a thing as an objective History (with a capital H) of the world."[4]

Although biblical scholars generally subscribe to a modified positivist value-neutral stance and notion of biblical studies as "hard science," they do not articulate the constructivist character of their discipline. Instead, scholars eschew self-conscious, critical reflection on how "scientific" historical discourse is constructed by the historian who chooses from a multiplicity of traces of past events and turns them into historical facts. Claiming scientific disinterestedness, scholars overlook the ethicopolitical implications of their historical work by pretending to be oblivious to the theological-political interests and disciplinary pressures of the scholarly or popular interpretive communities for whom they write.

Scholars have developed various methods to access the historical-social reality which biblical texts are believed to reflect. They seek, for instance, to establish and then trace back the earliest traditions in order to arrive at the actual historical situation of the early Christian communities or to establish the "facts" which we can know about the historical Jesus. History of religions and of culture analyses also aim at an objective description of the cultural-religious environments of early Christians. Religious documents and archeological monuments are reflections of the cultures and religions of past peoples which reveal the alterity (otherness) of a past totally different from our own.

Historical and theological studies on women in the Bible, or on Jewish, Greek, or Roman women, assume that androcentric texts *about women* mirror *women's* historical reality. They do not pay sufficient attention to the marginalizing and silencing functions of androcentric records. Nor do they attend to the patriarchal politics inscribed in androcentric source texts and archeological reports. Moreover, by not problematizing the androcentric frame and patriarchal models of historiography in general and of early Christian history in particular, they cannot but reinscribe the historical marginality or insignificance of women.

Studies of the social and symbolic worlds of early Christianity utilize methods and models derived from the sociology of knowledge, sociology in general, and cultural anthropology. However, anthropological and sociological biblical studies also often understand their reconstructive work as objective, social scientific criticism that has universal truth claims. Therefore, they tend to take over sociological or cultural reconstructive models without problematizing their underlying theoretical frames and political implications. For instance, scholars have taken over Weber's and Troeltsch's notion of patriarchalism without taking any feminist sociological or sociopolitical analyses into account. Others take over scientific models such as Mary Douglas's group-grid construction, Wilson's typology of sects, or the system of honor and shame as an objective scientific given. Since these models have been allegedly "tested" by scientific anthropology, biblical scholars claim that such scientific models enable them to avoid androcentrism and ethnocentrism and to see things as people in the ancient Mediterranean world saw them. Adopting a Weberian or Durkheimian analysis, other scholars separate ideology or theology from political and social struggles in the Roman empire and confine themselves to individuals and their subjective choices. Others stress the importance of intuition and sympathy in accurately recreating the alienness of historical moments and cultures.

However, both classic norms of sociocultural analysis on the one hand, and sociological or anthropological theory as the reification of such classic notions on the other hand, have changed since the late 1960s.[5] Sociology, political theory, and cultural anthropology have been reshaping themselves in part because of what has been learned from conflicts about multicultural social reality and the "Western culture controversy" in higher education. In addition, feminist analyses have underlined the gendered character of theoretical concepts and scientific modes of investigation.[6] The South African biblical scholar Mosala, therefore, has aptly criticized the politics of social-scientific criticism in biblical studies:

> The politics of our sociological approaches are constantly symbiotic with the object of their criticism in the dead part of ancient biblical societies on the one hand, and the dead part of nineteenth century historical-critical methods on the other. The point of my argument is that in their present form the sociological approaches cannot serve as adequate tools of a black biblical hermeneutics of liberation. [7]

In short, the posture of scientific objectivism masks the extent to which the concept of objective social science and history is itself a theoretical construct. Historical scientific language is not objective and descriptive. It is metaphorical and constructive. Androcentric language is a nonreferential system of communication. It shapes reality in that it not only transmits but also promotes the values woven through the fabric of historical discourses and patriarchal societies.

Positivist textualism. Literary critical studies, by contrast, attend to language and text; but, in general, they suspect historical discourse. Such literary critical approaches in biblical studies take on many different forms and names, including narrative criticism, structuralist exegesis, anthropological structuralism, composition criticism, rhetorical criticism, discourse analysis, story-centered criticism, the study of biblical imagination, and the formalism of New Criticism with its conception of biblical writings as autonomous, internally unified literary works.

Over and against diachronic reconstruction, literary biblical critics emphasize synchronic analysis, plot and character development, conventions, rhetorical figures, genre, point of view, narrative coherence and unity, sender and receiver, narrator and narratee, narrative levels and rhetorical structure. By and large, however, literary critical and rhetorical studies retain their base in textual formalism and New Criticism. Even reader response critics of the gospels have focused on the textually defined universal reader. Both the "implied reader" and the ideal version of the author, however, are not only construed as textual functions. Actual readers also are understood as generalized, ideal, universal types, divorced from historical particularity.

In short, literary critics stress the distance between the world or story of the text and any possible real events to which the narrative may refer. Accordingly, historical "reality" does not exist beyond and beneath texts. Reality is not behind but in front of the text. Narrative fictionalizes the author and the audience in the sense that both are cast into a role inscribed in and prescribed by the text. Biblical literature is "fictive," not in the sense of false, but in the sense of produced in language. However, despite the tendency within literary criticism to reject critical historical analysis, the coherence, unity, and simplicity of biblical narratives can lead, for instance, to a reading of the gospels as realistic "historical" narratives. Such a reading seems to be more than just a neo-conservative abuse of literary criticism; it is also the result of textual positivism.[8]

As I have pointed out in the first chapter, feminist literary studies of the Bible charge that one commits the "referential fallacy"[9] by assuming that actual historical women are represented by the female characters in the biblical story. The women in the biblical text, they contend, are fictive characters who do not represent historical actors. According to this view, to equate the female followers of Jesus with a group of persons beyond the narrative world, for instance, is to reduce the metaphoric and imagistic story of Mark to allegory.[10]

However, a feminist literary criticism that eschews any historical diachronic reconstruction cannot but remain ensconced in the rhetorical world projected by the androcentric text. If there is no possibility of reconstructing a historical world *different* from the androcentric world construction of the text, or if it is impossible to take a reading position different from that engineered by the text, then feminist interpretation is doomed to reinscribe the reality construction of the grammatically masculine text. It cannot but reproduce the androcentric universe of the sacred text—a text which either marginalizes women, subsumes them under generic male terms, or eradicates their historical presence altogether through its androcentric inscriptions. By refusing to reconstruct a feminist memory and history, a feminist-positivist textualism only deepens the historical silence about women and all those who are absent or marginalized in historical records.

The experience and analysis of patriarchal colonization, however, tells us that women are and always have been historical subjects and agents. Women and other nonpersons have shaped culture and religion, even though androcentric records do not mention our existence and work. This silence is apparent, for example, in several articles that I have come across which chart the status of recent scholarly work on early Christian history. Although all of these articles are written by distinguished scholars in the field, and although they discuss socioanthropological models for the historical reconstructions of early Christian beginnings, none of them mention, much less assess, the feminist theoretical model of historical reconstruction I developed in *In Memory of Her*. According to the historical record of scholarship promulgated by these scholars, my work and that of others either does not exist, or is not deemed social-scientific and thus is not counted among "respectable" histories of early Christianity. Moreover, I recently pointed this out to one of my colleagues who was preparing a "state of the question" report on "social scientific criticism," only to discover that feminist social and historical criticism was not mentioned there either. One can only wonder whether a work is disqualified as unscientific because it utilizes feminist—rather than marxist or positivist—sociopolitical models, or because it is thought to speak merely about women.[11]

Recognizing the rhetorical control and marginalizing functions of androcentric texts and scholarship, feminist biblical criticism can not afford to perpetuate the patriarchal assumptions and silencing strategies of malestream biblical criticism. Instead, it must articulate a theory and method of interpretation which can integrate both sociohistorical and literary criticism. In doing so it has to guard against the dynamics of androcentric scholarly discourses, which either marginalize and eliminate women's reality from the historical record, seek to co-opt alternative historical models into the malestream as the same, or attempt to disqualify these models as "ideological," "deviant," "unscientific," and "other." In short, feminist biblical studies must critically assess the rhetorical discourses of biblical scholarship as well as the rhetorical strategies of the androcentric biblical text.

If biblical texts and scholarship construct at one and the same time both the reality which brought them forth and the reality to which they respond, then this reality is accessible to us not only in the world that the text displays but also in all that it represses or marginalizes. As critical rhetorical studies, biblical historical analyses must lay open the historical reality which the rhetoric of the text at once displays and hides. To do so, one cannot simply follow the directives for reading inscribed on the surface of the text. Rather one must interrogate both the power/knowledge relations structuring biblical texts and the contemporary discourses of biblical studies. To that end, a critical feminist biblical interpretation intersects with the analyses and strategies of what is loosely called postmodernism, or the "new historicism."

The New Historicism. So-called postmodern historical studies are preoccupied with language and representation, that is, with the free play of signifiers. According to this approach, the experience of the "world" as given in language and linguistic representation shapes human consciousness. One can only know the world through a network of cultural ideological practices and socially established systems of meaning which are all-informing. Insofar as postmodernism or the "New Historicism" assumes that subjectivity is constructed by various cultural codes, it stresses subjected-ness but not agency. The subject is summoned or interpellated, that is, brought into place, by specific ideological and discursive formations.

Because it rejects the possibility that there can be any unproblematic privileged position from which to speak, postmodernism cannot theorize agency for change. "Postmodernism manipulates but does not transform signification. It disperses but does not (re)construct the structure of subjectivity."[12] Whereas literary criticism's stress on the autonomy of the androcentric text tends to make the feminist biblical reader captive to the text's strategies, postmodern theory appears to foreclose any theoretical space for a critical feminist reading of liberation.

The various strategies of "postmodernism" insist that there is no transhistorical or universal human experience and essence. Human subjectivity is constructed by cultural codes which position and limit all of us in various and divided ways.[13] Postmodernist writers thus argue against universal abstract reason and the transcendental subject, positioned outside of time and space, who has privileged access to truth. They reject the traditional Western theory of abstract and universal truth as the correspondence between a proposition and a transcendental reality, replacing it with an understanding of truth as historically contingent and constructed in the process of knowing and doing.[14]

In an article entitled *History as Usual?*, Judith Lowder Newton has pointed out that while even feminist theorists give credit to "postmodernism" for articulating the "New Historicism," they tend to overlook the originating contributions of the women's movement and of feminist theory.[15] Whereas the interaction between feminist and postmodern theories is widely discussed in feminist scholarship, the opposite is not the case in the discussions of postmodern theorists. Feminist intellectual labor and theoretical creativity, Lowder Newton argues, remains either invisible in the discussions of postmodernist scholarship and its origins, or they are appropriated by male theory and are thereby robbed of their specific political strategies.

When one situates the problem of how to write all women and subordinated men back into ancient history within malestream biblical studies, one opens the door to the same marginalization and misappropriation of feminist historical reconstruction. Such a misappropriation is likely in an androcentric frame which only permits women's discourse either to be integrated into dominant male discourse as "the same," or to be constituted as the marginal discourse of "the Other." By contrast, my strategy here is to open up a theoretical space in which the contributions of feminist historical theory to the problem of how to write an emancipatory biblical history can be explored. The discursive practices and political aims of a critical historiography for liberation, I am arguing, can only be effective when situated within a feminist rhetorical paradigm of historiography.

II.
REALITY IN A CRITICAL FEMINIST HISTORIOGRAPHY

A comparison of postmodernist and feminist theory highlights crucial *differences* which are significant for a feminist rhetorical reconstruction of Christian beginnings.

Feminist theory emerges at points in history when women experience the contradictions between their real historical world and their own self-understanding. For such are the points at which women begin to articulate these contradictions and to engage in a struggle for change. Feminists experience a kind of alienation in being simultaneously participants and outsiders in both our cultural and religious traditions as well as in the communities that marginalize and oppress us. Critical feminism turns this experience of alienation into a positive vantage point from which to articulate a *different* reality on the basis of women's social experience as out-sider/insider, as resident alien. This different perspective sheds light on all dimensions of society, culture, and knowledge. Women describe such breakthrough experiences differently: as "the scales falling from my eyes," as an intellectual and emotional "click," or, in religious language, as a "conversion" which "splits the world wide open." Cultural "common sense," dominant perspectives, religious dogmas, and scientific knowledge are recognized as androcentric, male-biased, and therefore not sufficiently objective and "true." While this feminist recognition may lead to disillusionment and anger, such an awareness also carries in it a sense of possibility and power.

The Renaissance historian Joan Kelly expresses this experience of intellectual exhilaration:

> Before my intellectual life and personal life could cohere, I had to go through an exciting transformation of consciousness. Suddenly the entire world of learning was open to me. It had a new and compelling attraction and was utterly questionable at the same time. Most compelling and most questionable was everything I thought I had known about the Renaissance. The change I went through was kaleidoscopic.[16]

The insight that scientific theories and totalizing articulations of the world are not objectively true does not lead to feminist nihilism or resignation. Rather, such an insight creates a sense of empowerment and commitment to change. This "root experience" of feminism engenders the recognition that gender identity is neither biologically nor divinely ordained, but linguistically and socially constructed in the interest of patriarchal power relations.

The realization that we are ideologically "scripted" and implicated in power relations provokes the recognition that women also suffer from a "false" or "incomplete" consciousness. As long as we are interpellated in patriarchal structures of domination and live in a patriarchal world of multiplicative oppressions, feminists can never be fully "liberated." However, this insight must not lead feminists to argue that historical agency and knowledge of the world are not possible at all. Granted, the postmodernist critique correctly insists that our subjectivities are "scripted" and that the science and philosophy of elite Euro-American men have not known the world as it is but have created it as they wished it to be according to their own interest and likeness. Yet this recognition does not lead feminists to advocate a relativist pluralism. Rather, it compels feminist and other minority scholars to articulate a *different* knowledge and vision of the world, one that can inspire and sustain a liberating praxis.

In order to articulate such a different history, feminist scholars utilize women's experience of reality and struggle against patriarchal exploitation as a scientific resource and a significant indicator of the reality against which hypotheses are to be tested.[17] A feminist version of objectivity recognizes "the provisionality and multiplicity of local knowledges" as "situated and embodied knowledges." Yet, unlike postmodernism, it does not argue that historical reconstructions are totally relative. It maintains rather that "it is possible to give a truer, more adequate account of a 'real' world" and human history.[18] In short, once women have recognized ourselves as historical subjects and theological agents we can develop a hermeneutics of suspicion which recognizes the androcentric ideological construction of reality in language, texts, and other religious-cultural representations. Although we are scripted, contradictions and fissures in the script and between scripts make a reading "against the grain" possible. Feminist critical theory challenges the dichotomy between historical reality and text, past and present. It insists that while ostensibly stressing the alien character of the world of the text, historical narrative tells the story of ancient Greece or early Christianity by refracting the historical reality inscribed in the text into our own language and world.

In the process of such a refracting, historians shape their material not just in terms of a narrative framework but also through selection of "data," periodization, and ascription of significance. Models for historical reconstruction are metaphoric in the sense that metaphor is a way of describing something in terms of something else. For instance, whereas the conception of history as the search for causal laws to explain objective facts has a mechanistic root-metaphor, that of history as evolution is based on an organic biological metaphor.[19] Moreover, historians create time periods which reflect the root-metaphors of their approach.[20] Thus, the delineation of historical periods is actually retrospective symbolic constructions which were unavailable to the historical actors themselves.

Finally, as linguistic representation, history is narrative-laden insofar as scholars use theoretical metaphors or models to organize their materials into a coherent argument. Epistemologically, history cannot be a record of what has happened. Rather, as Hayden White has insisted, it is "a progressive redescription of sets of events in such a way as to dismantle a structure encoded in one verbal mode in the beginning so as to justify a recording of it in another mode at the end."[21]

A hermeneutics of suspicion interrogates the ideological functions of the ever new encodings of the androcentric historical text, commentary, and world construction in language. We are still able to disclose and unravel "the politics of Otherness" inscribed in and constructed by the androcentric text because feminists experience and theorize about a historical reality in which "the others" are present and active.

90

A critical feminist theory and rhetorical paradigm of history recognizes that all representations of the world are informed by our own historical-cultural position, by the values and practices shaped by our historical-cultural location as well as by the ways we are implicated in power-relations. Recognizing that the past is only known to us through textual traces "is not however the same as saying that the past is only textual as the semiotic idealism of some forms of poststructuralism seems to assert."[22] Historical representation gives *meaning*, not *existence* to past events. Although in epistemological terms we can know the past today only in and through historical discourse, past events have occurred. By underlining the fact that all cultural forms of representation are ideologically grounded and that access to reality is always mediated through language, one problematizes and denaturalizes references to the real. Such a demystification does not, feminist theory insists, excuse us from giving a more adequate account of reality, an account that does not deny or repress the historical activity of the subordinated "others." If feminism understands itself as social movements for changing patriarchal relations of domination and subordination in society and church, then feminist scholars in religion must develop a theoretical vision of the world and of history in which women appear and matter. As Chris Weedon[23] succinctly observes: "feminism is a politics, whereas postmodernism is not." Instead, postmodernism remains politically ambivalent.

The paradox in which "feminists find ourselves is that while we regard patriarchal discourses as fiction, we nevertheless proceed as if our position, based on a belief in the oppression of women, were somewhat closer to the truth."[24] Committed to a sociopolitical movement that works for change, feminist theory must resist being incorporated into postmodernism and go beyond it. By merely making ideological inscriptions explicit and deconstructing them in a never ending play of deferral, feminist theory can neither ignore nor condemn its heritage of patriarchal culture and religion. Instead, it must reappropriate emancipatory elements of the past so that it can *speak from within* Western society and biblical religions, although it simultaneously questions and indicts their patriarchal discourses.

Because of its commitment to change and transformation, a critical feminist theory for liberation takes an explicit ideological position. It does so in the full awareness that postmodernism's rejection of a privileged position equally constitutes an ideological stance. Hence a critical feminist epistemology that speaks from the vantage point of women struggling for liberation rests on the insight that

the "master position" in any set of dominating social relations tends to produce distorted visions of the real regularities and causal tendencies in social relations. . . . The feminist standpoint epistemologies argue that because men are in the "master position" vis-à-vis women, women's social experience—conceptualized through the lenses of feminist theory—can provide the grounds for a less distorted understanding of the world around us.[25]

Feminism, when understood as a social movement for change, generates a different historical "consciousness." It constructs history as a "conceptual vision," or a "vantage point,"[26] and then enables us to understand and change patriarchal reality. The critical articulation of the *ekklēsia* of women constructs such an "emancipatory vantage point" *within* Western society and biblical religions. This location within political and cultural struggles is "acquired by acknowledging one's commitment to projects for political and cultural transformation."[27] It is an adopted partisanship that grounds the articulation of philosophical stances, theories, and histories. In short, feminist theorizing and theologizing is rooted in sociohistorical praxis.

As a rhetorical communicative practice, feminist historiography does not seek to sunder text and reality, whether in an antiquarian or in a formalist fashion. Rather, its "texts" seek to reconstruct and construct a *different* sociohistorical reality. Consequently, the goal of feminist biblical interpretation is to empower women through the critical analysis and constructive narrative of a *different* reality.[28] Since we participate not only in the androcentric cultural discourses of marginalization and subordination, but also in the democratic "humanistic" discourses of freedom, self-determination, justice, and equality, feminist scholars can engage in a different historical imagination for reconstructing the past.

Nevertheless, insofar as this "humanist"[29] discourse has been constituted as elite Euro-American "male" discourse, the democratic reality to which it refers is at one and the same time historical masculine and egalitarian-utopian. As the democratic discourse of the *ekklēsia* it has to be "imagined" *differently*. Such "imagination" is not fictive fantasy. It is rather historical imagination, because the reality to which it refers has been at least partially instantiated in the historical struggles of "the subordinated others" who have refused to be defined by the patriarchal politics of inequality, subordination, and dehumanization.

III.
A FEMINIST MODEL OF HISTORICAL RECONSTRUCTION

In *In Memory of Her* I was not seeking to write early Christian women's history. Instead, I wanted to articulate a critical feminist model[30] for the reconstruction of early Christian beginnings in order to break the ideological hold of androcentric biblical texts on the historical representation of and imaginings about early Christian life and history. Since the lack of a written history is a crucial sign of oppression, such a reconstruction is not just an academic affair; it also seeks to empower the *ekklēsia* of women in the struggle for liberation.

Such a reconstructive historical model seeks to reshape our historical and theological self-understanding by displacing the androcentric reconstructions of early Christian origins that marginalize or eliminate women and other nonpersons from the historical record. It does so by interrogating the rhetorical strategies of androcentric biblical texts in order to subvert them. For it is in and through such an interrogation that the "reality" which the text marginalizes and silences is brought to the fore. Indeed, androcentric language and male-authored texts presuppose women's historical presence and agency; for the most part, however, they do not articulate it. The androcentric text's rhetorical silences, as well as its contradictions, arguments, prescriptions, and projections, its discourses on gender, race, class, culture, or religion, must be exposed as the ideological inscriptions of the Western politics of Otherness.

Furthermore, such a historical model, which is able to examine the rhetorical strategies of the androcentric text and its symbolic universes, provides means not only for exploring *what* the text excludes, but also for investigating *how* the text constructs what it includes.[31] Androcentric biblical texts mythologize, reverse, absolutize, and idealize patriarchal differences, obliterating or marginalizing the historical presence of the devalued "others."[32]

As rhetorical texts they create a world in which those whose arguments they oppose either become the "deviant others" or are no longer heard at all. Yet freeborn women and slave women and men were present in the early Christian movements—not only as victims, but also as historical interlocutors and agents. *In Memory of Her* reads early Christian androcentric texts in their Greco-Roman and Jewish contexts in order to reconstruct early Christian history in terms of social-ecclesial struggles and rhetorical arguments through which the "politics" of exclusion and submission unfold.[33] This "patriarchal politics of submission" did not originate with—but was mediated by—Christian Scriptures. Hence it was not invented by the Enlightenment but was first articulated in the context of the classical city-state.[34]

The rhetorical-historical situation in Athens was similar in some respects to that in which the Enlightenment "politics of otherness" was articulated. On the one hand, the classical, oligarchic "philosophy of otherness" was generated by the contradiction within the patriarchal social stratification of Athenian society. On the other hand, Athenian democracy claimed citizenship for all, but restricted its exercise to elite male citizens since freeborn women as well as slave women and men were excluded from electoral privileges.

This sociopolitical contradiction has produced philosophical justifications for restricting the circle of citizens to propertied male heads of households. In the analogical argument of Greek philosophy the chain "Greek-male-human" represents culture, whereas that of "barbarian-female-animal" represents nature, bestiality, and violence. The cultural anthropologist and historian Page duBois has argued that civil war, the increase in the slave population, and the widening social gulf between those who owned property and those who did not modified the fourth-century analogical articulation of the "philosophy of otherness" in two quite different ways.[35] Both modes of philosophical legitimization of patriarchal social stratification are still alive today.

Plato rearticulates the analogical argument in terms of his anthropology by turning it into the hierarchy of "the great chain of being." The narrative myth of the metals likens those who are fit to rule with gold, their helpers with silver, farmers with iron, and craftsmen with brass. All men who do wrong in this life become women in the second incarnation, then slaves, birds, animals on foot, worms, fish, oysters, and so on. Slavery becomes the model for social stratification on all levels.[36] The *logos* not only makes male citizens central, but reason places them on top of the ladder, with all other creatures subordinate and inferior by nature. Thus the dominance of the male citizen, the philosopher, is no longer justified in terms of *autarkeia* (autonomy) but in terms of his superior nature.[37]

Aristotle also argues for practices of patriarchal exclusion and subordination on the grounds of nature and reason. His rhetorical model, however, is not slavery but the patriarchal household in which wives, children, slaves, and property were owned by and at the disposal of the freeborn Greek male head of household. Only the male citizen who is ruler in his home over women, slaves, and children is capable of participating in the governing of the *polis* and elects his superiors to positions of power. In Aristotle's argument slavery is not a metaphor for all relationships; it is the link between human and animal. The subordination and exclusion of freeborn women and Greek-born slave women and men from citizenship, Aristotle argues, is justified because their natures do not make them "fit to rule."[38]

This classical contradiction between "the politics of patriarchal submission" and the "equality of all citizens" surfaced in the first century C.E. with the revival of Aristotelian philosophy which was directed against emancipatory movements. In *In Memory of Her*, this contradiction serves

94

as the historical paradigm for reconstructing Christian beginnings. On the one hand, early Christian sources still point to the sociopolitical conflicts between the early Christian "freedom" movements and their dominant patriarchal Greco-Roman and Jewish cultural contexts. On the other hand, these sources also testify to the rhetorical contradictions *within* early Christianity, the contradictions between the ethos of the *ekklēsia* as a "discipleship of equals," or as "equality in the Spirit," and the emerging patriarchal patterns of leadership and organization within segments of the Christian community. The patriarchal arguments for the "politics of submission" engendered not only the restrictions against women's leadership but also the acceptance of slave women's suffering. This leads to the reintroduction of the patriarchal division between the public and private spheres within the *ekklēsia*. It provides arguments for relegating (elite) married women to the private sphere, for restricting their activity to proper "feminine" behavior, and for accepting slavery within the Christian community and ethos.

However such a conflictive model of historical reconstruction would be misapprehended if it were read either in terms of linear development or in terms of rapid and uncontested decline from *ekklēsia* as the discipleship of equals to *ekklēsia* as the patriarchal household of G-d. Instead this model seeks to conceptualize early Christian history as a struggle that is still going on. Just like a Russian doll within which many smaller dolls fit, so my reconstruction in *In Memory of Her* of the historical struggles between patriarchy and *ekklēsia* in Greco-Roman society and early Christianity seeks to situate the religious history of women within early Christian history, within Jewish history, within Greco-Roman history, and within the history of Western society, rather than playing one of these against the others.

Such a rhetorical model of historical reconstruction can relate diverse texts to each other—texts about women's leadership, clues about the inclusive and egalitarian organization of early Christian communities, passages such as the baptismal proclamation of Galatians 3:28 and the list of names in Romans 16, the ethos of suffering discipleship rather than patriarchal adaptation, the notion of the *ekklēsia* as a community of friends. This model poses these as one side of the argument. The other side of the debate emerges through, for instance, Paul's incipient patriarchal rhetoric, or in the construction of early Christian beginnings by Luke-Acts. This side is also represented by both the household code texts requiring submission from wives, slave women and men, and young people to the *pater familias*, as well as by the ecclesial adaptation of the patriarchal "politics of submission," which was adopted by the Pastoral Epistles, the letters of Ignatius, 1 Clement, and later "patristic" and "gnostic" writings. A feminist rhetorical model of historical reconstruction is able to interrelate both sides of the tradition as an ongoing debate rooted in sociopolitical and ecclesial struggles.

Such a displacement of androcentric source-texts, and their reorganization in terms of the "contradiction" which has generated the politics of submission and rhetorics of otherness, reconstructs historical-social "reality" not as a "given fact" but as a plausible "subtext" to the androcentric text. This reconstruction in terms of the early Christian struggles and arguments about the "politics and rhetorics of patriarchal submission" also allows one to understand the cultural dependencies and effects generated by this early Christian debate and struggle. Such a feminist reconstruction has achieved its goal when it can make those whom the androcentric text marginalizes or excludes centrally present as historical actors.

IV.
A HISTORICAL-RHETORICAL READING

Placed within a rhetorical model of historical reconstruction, the different versions of the story of the Syro-Phoenician woman can be read in terms of the arguments about boundary constructions and transgressions within early Christian communities. The absence of this story in Luke's Gospel can also be explored in terms of such a rhetorical model. If the different accounts of the Gentile woman's story are understood as rhetorical discourses about who may and who may not claim the powers of the *basileia* and the rights of its citizenship, scholars no longer need to reduce the different historical interpretations to a single meaning; nor do they need to transform these differences into a single historical fact.

As I have pointed out in the concluding pages of the introduction, the gospels have two different but similar versions of this story.

1. In Mark 7:24–30 the woman's identity is marked through linguistic/cultural (Greek) as well as national/racial (of Syro-Phoenician origin) characterizations. She makes her way into "the house" and asks Jesus to liberate her daughter from demonic possession. Yet, the story does not center on the telling of the miracle but on the argument about *food—children—table—house dogs*. With this argument Jesus denies her and her child access to liberation because she is a cultural, religious, and national outsider. The woman takes up Jesus' insulting parabolic saying and uses it to argue against him. She wins the controversy because Jesus, convinced by her argument (*dia touton ton logon*), announces her daughter's healing.

An analysis of the transmission of this story in the gospel tradition makes it possible to reconstruct how rhetorical arguments have shaped this narrative. The story could have begun as a simple Galilean miracle story about a woman asking Jesus to exorcise her daughter, with Jesus granting her request. Such a story can still be traced in verses 25.26b.29b.30 of the Markan text. At a second stage of the tradition, verses 26a.27–29a might have been added. The Greek word *chortastēnai* (become satisfied) connects this story with the two (pre)Markan feeding miracle stories (cf. Mark 6:42; 8:4.8). This retelling of the story introduces the opposition between Syro-Phoenician—Greek—woman and Jesus—Galilean—male. It also brings in the parabolic saying about *food—children—table—dogs*, a saying which could play on an "ironic" double meaning if Jesus speaks of street dogs and the woman of house dogs. Thus this addition to the miracle story not only introduces the opposition between Jew and Gentile, but it also ascribes an offensive, exclusive attitude to Jesus, an attitude which the argument of the Syro-Phoenician woman challenges and overcomes. At a third stage, this story is taken over by Mark and tied into the gospel narrative through the introduction of verse 24 and the qualifying addition of "first" in verse 27.

In *In Memory of Her*, I have argued that the pre-Markan controversy story constructs a conflict between those who claim a saying of the "historical Jesus" to restrict the Jesus movement to Israel and those who argue for the extension of the movement to include non-Israelites. Although the Syro-Phoenician respects the primacy of the "children of Israel," she nevertheless makes a theological argument against limiting the Jesuanic inclusive table-community and discipleship of equals to Israel alone. That such a theological argument is placed in the mouth of a woman gives us a clue to the historical leadership of women in opening up the Jesus movement to "Gentile sinners" (Gal. 2:15). The story of the Syro-Phoenician makes women's contribution to one of the most crucial transitions in early Christian beginnings historically visible. Through such an analysis, the Syro-Phoenician can become visible again as one of the apostolic foremothers of Gentile Christians. By moving her into the center of the debate about the mission to the Gentiles, the historical centrality of Paul in this debate becomes relativized.

Such a reading of the story helps one to understand why Luke does not incorporate this story into his gospel. His reconstruction of early Christian beginnings acknowledges the problem of the Gentile mission but ascribes its solution to G-d and pictures the male apostle Peter and the Gentile missionary Paul as the central figures of early Christian mission and church. This Lukan historical model has no room for a story about an educated Greek woman, who as a religious and ethnic outsider argues with

Jesus for the Gentiles' share in the power of well-being. In short, Luke cannot incorporate a story about a woman who wins the theological argument against erecting narrow ethnic and religious exclusive boundaries.

Gerd Theissen contextualizes the story of the Syro-Phoenician not in terms of early Christian theological debates, but rather in terms of socioethnic Jewish conflicts. His close form-critical and sociocritical reading of the story emphasizes that the story's first tellers and audience were familiar with the tensions between Jews and Gentiles in the villages of the Tyrian-Galilean border regions. The description of the Syro-Phoenician as Greek characterizes her, according to Theissen, as an educated upper-class woman who asks Jesus for help. This characterization underlines the "social" clash between her and Jesus, who is portrayed, by contrast, as an itinerant preacher and exorcist from the backwaters of Galilee. In the context of such a sociocultural status difference, Jesus' retort must have been heard, according to Theissen, as follows: Let the poor people in the Galilean backwaters be satisfied. For it is not just to take away food from the poor people in the Galilean villages and to give it to rich Gentiles in the cities. This reading situates the story of the Syro-Phoenician not within an early Christian debate, but within a conflict between poor Galilean villagers and rich Gentile citizens, with Jesus expressing the resentment of the underprivileged population.

Whereas Theissen stresses a sociocultural contextualization, Sharon Ringe reads the story in terms of gender discourse. She sees the woman as widowed, divorced, or never married, as totally alone and isolated from family support. When we meet her she is left with only a daughter, who is a further liability in her society's terms. Nevertheless, for the sake of her daughter, the woman breaks custom and stands up to the visiting rabbi and miracle-worker.

Ringe rejects the interpretation of the original story in terms of either cultural or early Christian missionary conflicts. Instead, she argues that the story's significance is christological. The story could not have been invented by the church because of its shocking portrait of Jesus. Rather than inventing such a story, it is more likely that the early church tried to make the best out of a bizarre tradition which must have preserved the memory of an incident in the life of Jesus "when he was caught with his compassion down."[39] Only in the Markan retelling does the story, according to Ringe, become a story about Jews and Gentiles.

2. In Matthew's version (15:21–28) the two protagonists remain embroiled in the argument about *food—children—master's table—house dogs*, but both their characterization and the plot of the story changes. The woman is consistently rebuffed not only by Jesus but also by his (probably male) disciples. She is characterized with the archaic term "Canaanite,"

which reminds the reader not only of Rahab, who facilitated Israel's entry into Canaan, but also of Israel's long struggle with Canaan's cultic heritage. The woman not only enters the public domain, but she does so speaking loudly. The Greek word for her public outcry, *krazein*, also carries cultic overtones. Indeed, such ritualistic cries were directed toward the Gods, but the Gods were generally held by philosophers to be unworthy of them.

Gail R. O'Day has argued that Matthew's form of the story is the narrative enactment of a lament psalm, which has two major sections consisting of plea and praise. The woman's words constitute the section of petition, whereas Jesus' final words provide the movement from plea to praise:

Petition:	Have mercy on me
Address:	O Lord, Son of David
Complaint:	Daughter is severely possessed by a demon (v.22)
Address:	Lord
Petition:	help me (v.25)
[Response:	Yea, Lord]
Motivation:	For even the dogs eat the crumbs . . . (v.27)

O'Day summarizes her interpretation: "The Canaanite woman stands fully in the tradition of Abraham and Moses who were not afraid to bargain with God (Gen. 18:22–33; Num. 11:11–15); she is profoundly linked with all the broken and needy petitioners who sang Israel's songs of lament, with all those who cling to the faithfulness to the promise. She is not a Jew; she is, nevertheless, fully Jewish."[40]

According to Elaine Wainwright's analysis, on the other hand, the story of the Canaanite woman has the form of an encounter story which structures the following sequence: *introduction* (v.21), *petition* (v.22), *twofold difficulty* (v.23 "he did not answer," "send her away"), *difficulty* (v.24 prophetic commission only to Israel), *petition* (v.25), *difficulty* (v.26), *overcoming of difficulty* (v.27), *assurance* (v.28). According to Wainwright, two counter-traditions are inscribed in the pre-Matthean story: one is the conflict surrounding women's role, the other is the tradition against the mission to the Gentiles. By endowing the woman with "liturgical" speech, women's significant participation in the community is affirmed. By introducing the particularistic statements against her, the narrative implies that those who are against the mission to the Gentiles are also against women's active leadership in the community. Thus both the Matthean introduction (v.21) and the characterization of the woman as Canaanite tie the story into the various theological interests which are already unfolding in the overall gospel narrative. The affirmative closure in verse 28 indicates that the Matthean redactor has shared the community's traditional support for the active participation of women.[41]

3. A less-known version of the woman's story is found in the Jewish-Christian Pseudo-Clementine Homilies, which are thought to have been composed during the third and fourth centuries, but which probably incorporated older materials.[42] They tell the story of Clement of Rome who accompanied Peter on his missionary journeys. In their retelling of the story (Ps.Clem.Hom. II,19,1–3), the woman receives a name for the first time. She is called Justa, which means in Latin "just." Although the disciples also ask Jesus to heal her daughter, he refuses: "It is not permitted to heal the Gentiles who are similar to dogs in that they use all kinds of food and do all kinds of things, since the table in the *basileia* is given to the sons of Israel. But hearing this she wanted to participate in the table like a dog, namely in the crumbs from the table, abandoned her previous customs, in that she ate in the same manner as the sons of the *basileia* and achieved, as she desired, the healing of her daughter."

In a later chapter we are told that Justa, an honorable woman, has bought the two brothers of Clement free from slavery and has adopted them. Justa is said to have brought them up "very attentively in all the departments of Greek learning" (Ps.Cl.Hom. XIII,7,3). In this Jewish-Christian retelling, the Syro-Phoenician woman of Canaanite origin, now named Justa, is joined by the disciples in her supplication for her daughter. She does not persuade Jesus to change his prejudice but she is persuaded by Jesus to change her life style. Justa, who is characterized as a well-educated, upper-class woman, converts to Judaism. She becomes the righteous one.

In conclusion, within a rhetorical model of historical reconstruction, these different retellings of the story of Justa do not cancel each other out in the search for a single version that could tell us authoritatively what actually happened. Like the Baptist African-American "lining hymn," a rhetorical interpretation does not draw out a single melody in a linear fashion; rather, it amplifies and deepens the individual lines of interpretation. Although I have attempted here to trace a chronological development of the transmission of Justa's story, these different versions can also be read in a synchronic fashion, whereby each telling sheds a different light on the ongoing debates and conflicts about the formation of the *ekklēsia*, which stood in tension with the exclusive patriarchal prejudices and practices within and outside the Christian movements.

Whether such a rhetorical model of historical reconstruction, developed more fully in *In Memory of Her*, is adequate and "objective," must be judged by whether or not it develops sufficient interpretive power to undo the silencing strategies of the androcentric text, laying open the patriarchal "politics of submission" and "rhetorics of otherness" inscribed there.

Those who seek to disqualify such a feminist historical reconstruction of early Christian beginnings on the grounds that it is unscientific must develop an alternative model, namely one which has greater explanatory power both to make present the historical reality of those whom the text marginalizes or excludes and to do justice to all the information we find in our sources.

However, the deconstruction of the patriarchal "rhetorics of otherness and submission," as well as the reconstruction of the reality and voice of the silenced others, I submit, cannot be accomplished in any value-neutral paradigm of historical studies—whether antiquarian, empiricist-factual or literary constructivist. Rather, this deconstructive and reconstructive process must explicitly situate itself within a rhetorical and emancipatory paradigm of historiography, because only such a paradigm can theoretically acknowledge that historians reconstruct the past in the interest of the present and the future. Our search for history and roots is neither antiquarian nor nostalgic: it is political. It is political because our understanding of the present shapes our reconstructions of the past, while our reconstructions of the past shape present and future reality.

In a rhetorical-emancipatory paradigm, the objectivity of historical reconstruction is not achieved through objectivism. It depends, rather, on the explanatory power of the heuristic models and arguments generated to comprehend history as the reality not only of Western elite men but also of the subordinated and dehumanized others. To paraphrase Alfred Schutz, insofar as the experience of my predecessors was women's experience of reality in a patriarchal society, I can interpret it in the context of a feminist analysis of Western patriarchy as well as in the context of women's and other nonpersons' struggle for freedom, dignity, and self-determination.[43] Such an emancipatory reconstruction of our cultural and religious past is not a fictive creation out of nothing. It is rather a disciplined argument for a *different* historical consciousness and imagination.

A feminist theological reconstruction of Christian beginnings seeks to recover the past of women and other nonpersons as a heritage for the present and a vision for a nonpatriarchal future. The women who have shaped the early Christian movements are dead. After so many years we no longer can hear their stories and arguments. A feminist hermeneutics of remembrance desires to recover from historical silences the traces of their lives and faint echoes of their voices because of our need for a memory of women who have not only suffered and resisted patriarchal oppression, but who have also spoken and acted in the power of the Spirit-Sophia.

4
JUSTA –
CONSTRUCTING COMMON GROUND

Everybody But Me

I went to church every Sunday being a pious person and I heard the preacher talking about heaven and eating milk and honey and wearing long white robes and I felt the spirit and shouted out, shouted out that I wanted to be in the number too.

Suddenly I looked up at the wall, saw that all the folks gathered around Jesus had straw blond hair and sky blue eyes and there wasn't a brother among them. I knew again that they did mean everybody, Everybody, but me.

When I got home I was hurt to find that they really did mean everybody, Everybody, but me.

Well putting two and two together you and I can plainly see that those folks down in Washington have never been thinking of you and me, from here on I'm going to be thinking about me. I'm going to get together with you and my sisters and brothers black and white all over the country and over the world and we're going to put up a terrific fight until we win and we will and when we say peace and freedom for everybody it will mean Everybody, everywhere.

It will mean me.[1]

To Speak in Public:

A Feminist Political Hermeneutics

For the introduction to this chapter, I would like to recall the Syro-Phoenician or Canaanite woman again. According to the extracanonical tradition her name is *Justa*, the just or righteous one. According to Matthew's Gospel she does not enter the house and interrupt Jesus; rather she "comes out" and "shouts after" Jesus and his disciples. She is not characterized as a stranger but as someone "from this region" of Tyre and Sidon to which Jesus has come. The reader shares the (male?) disciples' embarrassment about her noisy behavior and wishes her to go away quietly. The story is not structured by the dualistic opposition inside/outside and hidden/open as it is in Mark but by that of private/public and woman/man.

In each version of the story the woman has broken all the rules of conduct. She has shown no proper feminine sensitivity at all. For modesty required not only that a woman not speak in public, but also that she not intrude upon men's company. Although Jesus does not address her directly, brushing away her request, she continues to insist that the boundaries between inside/outside, private/public, male/female must be crossed. Whereas in Mark's story readers are startled by the woman's audacity when she engages in an argument with Jesus, in Matthew their attention is focused on the woman's public speech and behavior. Concern for the well-being of her daughter, who signifies the future, impels the woman to enter the public domain of men, thereby claiming the privilege of a citizen.

Following Justa, the justice-seeking woman, a critical feminist biblical interpretation must position itself in the public-political center of church and academy, rather than on the boundaries of feminist sex/gender alterity-constructions. Such a positioning calls for a shared systemic analysis of patriarchy and the construction of a public feminist countersphere in which to theorize a critical model of reading. Such a rhetorical counterspace, I argue, can not be articulated within the logic of identity but must situate itself within the democratic paradigm and logic of the *ekklēsia*. Only a critical rhetorical space and vantage point outside the cultural-religious sex-gender system allows one to demystify that system, naming it as a cultural discourse of domination. However, the possibility for such a theoretical space, I would argue, depends on the existence of a social movement for change; and, in turn, the articulation of such a theoretical space empowers feminist movement.

If one wants to articulate such a theoretical rhetorical counterspace, one is forced to push towards the limits of everyday common-sense language. Such language at once constructs and mystifies patriarchal frameworks that are widely accepted as "given" and "common sense." Theoretical efforts to problematize such self-evident "commonplace" language are of necessity complex and difficult. They also fly in the face of a certain feminist rhetoric which insists that feminist texts must be written simply, clearly, and eloquently so that anyone can understand them without too much intellectual effort.

However, such a feminist assumption supports rather than breaks through "common-sense" patriarchal linguistic constructions of meaning. A simple "commonplace" statement such as "women are women and men are men" entails a host of theoretical assumptions and practical implications that must be analyzed in a critical process of conscientization. Christine Schaumberger,[2] for instance, has pointed out that women's groups are eager to reflect on their own experience and to tell their personal stories but that they are often unable or unwilling to engage in a systemic analysis of their experience. Yet without theoretical reflection and analysis, cultural and religious patriarchal frameworks remain "natural" and "common sense." This is especially true for cultural constructions of gender which are held to be "given" and "natural."

Insofar as a critical feminist paradigm of biblical interpretation for liberation seeks to empower women to become reading subjects and critical agents of interpretation who can claim the authority of struggle in evaluating biblical texts and discourses, it must pay attention not only to its sociopolitical location but also to the "systems of meaning" determining its readings of the Bible. A feminist biblical interpretation requires an engagement with feminist paradigms of reading, which are rooted in different systemic analyses of women's oppression. They seek to make the dominant symbolic "frames of meaning" conscious in order to empower women to participate as reading subjects in the construction of meaning while simultaneously becoming conscious of their process of construction.

Yet, what does it mean to read as a feminist? Does it mean to read *as* a woman, *like* a woman, or *like* a feminist? Does it mean to read from a woman's perspective, from a feminist standpoint, or from a womanist vantage point? Since the very meanings of the terms "woman" and "feminism" are continually contested, rejected, or reappropriated in feminist discourses, it is necessary to delineate one's theoretical framework of inter-pretation carefully.

Rather than summarize the by now well-known and well-worn typol-ogies of the different directions in the women's movements and their theo-retical constructions, that is, rather than engage in the ongoing debate between feminist existentialism and feminist constructivism, I will attend to the notion of patriarchy,[3] a term which I have employed throughout my narrative but whose critical elaboration has been deferred. Focusing on the notion of patriarchy allows one to differentiate between two theoretical feminist discourses: one which defines patriarchy as a sex-gender system in the context of the Western logic of identity, and one which constructs it in the context of multifaceted liberation struggles.

I.
THE PATRIARCHY: SEX-GENDER SYSTEM

While some feminist theorists reject patriarchy as an ahistorical, universal-izing concept, most regard it as a key theoretical notion for explaining the creation and maintenance of men's sexual, social, political, and ideological power over women. In feminist theory the definition of patriarchy is gener-ally no longer restricted to the power of the father over his kinship group, as it is in social theory. Rather, it is defined as the social structures and ideologies that have enabled men to dominate and exploit women through-out recorded history.

If patriarchy is defined in terms of male-female gender-dualism, then exploitation and victimization on the basis of gender and sex become the primary oppression. The difference between male and female is held to be the most basic and *essential* difference of humanity: the division between women and men is the origin and basis of all other divisions—of economic class, culture, race, religion, nationality, and age. In this view, the system of patriarchy—understood as men's domination over women and women's exclusion from politics, culture, history, and religion—has been total and ever present. Women were not only the objects and victims of male rule but also compliant agents who have desired to live for men's well-being.

Whereas feminists generally agree on the deconstructive move in socio-cultural gender analysis, they part company in their articulation of a posi-tive position of *alterity*. North American "radical" or "cultural" feminism argues that liberated women are, in essence, the better human beings since their nature has not been corrupted by patriarchal power drives. Whereas the masculine self is impersonal, violent, abstract, striving for conflict and domination, women's true essence is nurturant, intuitive, receptive, organic, and sensuous. Such an essentialist position can take a constructivist turn when it argues that binary masculine/feminine gender polarity is not biologically innate or divinely ordained but socially constructed. According to this understanding, ideological gender constructs keep patriarchal domination in place and make it appear "common sense" and "natural" to both women and men. Most feminists today subscribe to such a constructivist theory of gender. Yet there are still others who reassert some form of biological determinism of being female, or a philosophical essentialism of the feminine, or both.[4] In short, they argue that there are two sexes: Women are women and men are men.

The European "theories of the feminine" also seek to constitute an "alterity" which is not only epistemological but social, through the displacement and revalorization of female essence. The Italian feminist Cavarero expresses this theoretical position succinctly: "By essential and originary difference I mean that, for women, being engendered in difference is something not negotiable; for each one who is born female, it is always already so and not otherwise, rooted in her being not as something superfluous or something more, but as that which she necessarily is: female."[5] Quoting Cavarero, the American theorist Teresa de Lauretis concludes her discussion of the risk of essentialism: If one does not start from the basic assumption of essential and originary sexual difference, "the still necessary articulation of all other differences between and within women must remain framed in male dominant and hetero-sexist ideologies of liberal pluralism, conservative humanism, or goddess forbid, religious fundamentalism."[6]

Three basic strategic positions with respect to the feminine as alternative theoretical space have been developed in Euro-American feminist discourses: The first strategy appropriates and reformulates Jungian psychoanalytic theory that revalorizes the repressed feminine archetype.[7] The second position, most brilliantly articulated by Mary Daly, uses an ontological-linguistic strategy to articulate such an alterity. It is a process of be-coming instantiated by the Wild, Original, Self-actualizing woman who has made the leap from phallocracy into freedom, into the Otherworld of Be-ing. This strategy is actualized by the metamorphosizing woman, by the Crone and the Original Witch, by the Archaic Elemental metapatriarchally moving Woman. She is the one who represents a new species, an Original Race.[8]

The third strategy for revalorizing Woman and the feminine has recently gained high currency in U.S. feminist academic discussions. The theory of the maternal-feminine is an import from what is usually called "French feminism," but it generally refers only to the work of Kristeva, Cixous, and Irigaray.[9] Although American work on the "maternal" has on the whole concentrated on the sociohistorical critique of motherhood as an

106

institution, more recent multidisciplinary studies on maternal thinking[10] "repeatedly extol pre-oedipal unboundedness, relatedness, plurality, fecundity, tenderness, and nurturance in the name of the difference of female identity."[11]

Feminist scholars are careful to emphasize that the theory of the maternal-feminine seeks to subvert the assumed neutrality of logocentric and phallocentric principles, representations, and knowledge, destabilizing existing forms of writing and knowing in ways undreamed of before. Nevertheless, the American reception of so-called French feminist theory and its concern with the feminine as metaphor and construct tends to reinscribe the cultural feminine, especially in the popular reception of religious feminists: fluidity, softness, plurality, sea, nature, peacefulness, nurturance, body, life, Mother-Goddess, as antithetical to solidity, hardness, rigidity, aggressiveness, reason, control, death, Father-God. As a result, the theory of the maternal-feminine sometimes comes dangerously close to reproducing in the form of deconstructive language traditional cultural-religious ascriptions of femininity and motherhood, ascriptions all too familiar from papal pronouncements which have now become feminist norms.

In the 1980s, feminist theory, so the story is told, moved beyond the liberal feminist criticism of the sexism of knowledges and the structural critique of patriarchal theories to the critique of phallocentrism which represents both sexes in terms that are only appropriate to the male. "Radical" feminism moved from a theory that takes sexism and women as its center of analysis toward a critical feminist investigation of theory as hiding its masculinity. An open recognition of "the masculinity of knowledges is necessary to clear a space within the 'universal' " for women *as* women, a space where women's specificity can be articulated—or so we are told. "In exploring the language of femininity and autonomy, feminist theory has introduced the possibility of a dialogue between knowledges now accepted as masculine and the 'alien' or 'other' voice of women."[12]

Yet this historical narration of the rediscovery of the feminine does not mention that the major development in critical feminist theory during the 1980s was the emergence of many different feminist voices around the globe, voices which have questioned and rejected the essentialist understanding of woman and the feminine in Euro-American feminist theory. In this light, it is very disturbing that white feminist theory and theology in the United States have become increasingly fascinated with the European-American articulation of sexual difference and the valorization of the feminine precisely at the moment when major theoretical work, especially by African-American feminists, has emerged. For such work not only challenges the primacy of gender oppression, it also theorizes it differently.[13]

The conservative political underpinnings of the reception of so-called

French feminism in the United States become apparent when seen in such a global contextualization: "The knowledge offered here is not benign. It is that real shifts in world power and economic distribution have little to do with *jouissance*, the pre-Oedipal, or fluids and that the luxury of first-world feminism to dwell on such issues depends on the preservation of first-world abundance guaranteed by systematic underdevelopment elsewhere and by the postponement, by whatever means, of a political decentering."[14] In addition, the alignment of the masculine with rationality and of the feminine with poetry, mysticism, magic, and religion reinscribes the Western logic of identity. It is precisely this logic which has produced not only Western theories and theologies of the feminine, but also the colonialist constructions of the "native," the "noble savage," and "the Oriental."[15]

Feminist poststructuralist theory also understands "patriarchy" to refer to women's subordination to men. However, it understands the power relations between women and men as "structural," i.e., as existing in the institutions and social practices of society. Patriarchal structures *pre-exist* individual men and women. Since all meaning is constituted in language, and since discursive systems of meaning precede us, our subjectivity, the sense of who we are and the ways we relate to the world, is not a unique essence, but the product of our society, culture, and religion. Therefore, the subject is always the site of conflicting discourses. Biological sex differences do not have an "inherent" meaning but are negotiated and produced within a range of conflicting legal, medical, religious, and cultural discourses: "Discourses represent political interests and in consequence are constantly vying for status and power. The site of this battle for power is the subjectivity of the individual and it is a battle in which the individual is an active but not sovereign protagonist."[16] In this understanding, biblical literature, just as any other literature, becomes one specific discursive site where the meaning of gender as "natural" is constructed. Biblical texts offer their readers particular subject positions which advance particular meanings, pleasures, and values.

Feminist literary critics have developed several reading strategies within this feminist framework of patriarchy which understands women's gender oppression as primary and originary oppression. I would like to sketch two of them here in order to utilize them later in shaping an interpretive feminist framework within the logic of democracy. Neither proposal operates within the Western essentialist paradigm. Neither understands gender as an attribute of anatomy. Instead, both strategies understand gender identity as an effect of one's discursive positioning and strategies.

Firstly, Tamsin E. Lorraine argues that human subjects are not merely effects of the social codes and institutions which precede them but that they also shape these discourses in their attempt to construct meaning and to navigate these codes in a way that is subjectively satisfying.[17] The self is therefore not an essence or a given entity but a process of self-constituting activity. Moreover, this self-constituting activity is also world-constituting. Thus, persons with different self-strategies live in different worlds of meaning. Lorraine abstracts masculine/feminine self-strategies in order to analyze the self-constituting activity in the supposedly "gender-blind" philosophical texts of Kierkegaard, Nietzsche, and Sartre.

In Lorraine's model, gender categories are not substantive entities but heuristic concepts for mapping the effects that notions of gender have on the construction of meaning. She constructs two opposite and mutually exclusive poles representing "pure femininity" and "pure masculinity." The feminine pole is chaotic flux, beyond language, completely unique and unrepeatable. There can be no "pure" feminine self because such a self would be dissolved in the chaotic flux of life and unable to distinguish itself from the world around it. The feminine self-strategy seeks to maintain self-continuity through connectedness with others and through conformity to the self/other pattern set by another by responding to that other self's desire. In contrast, the purely masculine pole is changeless, self-sufficient, without conflict, confusion, or motion. Similarly, there can be no "pure" masculine self, because such a self would be fixed, changeless, and therefore without life. The masculine self-strategy seeks to maintain the self in and through opposition by assuming the pre-given self-slot within the cultural self-other pattern and seeks to develop a clear pattern in which everything has a "rational" place and order. The masculine self seeks out others who will confirm his self/other pattern by playing the "other" to his self.

Although both women and men must adopt masculine and feminine self-strategies for maintaining the self, cultural gender discourses summon individuals to position themselves closer to one or the other end of the spectrum. Lorraine does not seek to reify cultural gender categories but to deconstruct them by amplifying gender stories, filling in the contents of both sides of the dichotomy in such a way that readers can work through the gender notions that bind them: "Just as nightmares lose their power to terrify once we confront them, so may half-submerged notions of what it means to be masculine or feminine lose their power to control us once we recognize them. [My analysis] will free [readers] to explore alternatives in self-strategies rather than prompt them to adhere more rigorously to the one 'appropriate' to their sex."[18] Thus Lorraine seeks to open up her reading model for articulating the self-identity of individuals or groups not just in terms of gender-strategies. She advocates a reading that can integrate the fullest range of perspectives and self-strategies as mutually supportive and enriching of—rather than destructive to—a self-identity which is continually transforming.

Secondly, within the sex-gender system Teresa L. Ebert seeks to theorize a poststructuralist practice of reading in political, rather than individual, terms. She develops her model of interpretation not for reading philosophical texts, but for reading romance literature which plays on the desires of women readers. Ebert defines patriarchy as "the organization and division of all practices and significations in terms of gender and the privileging of one gender over the other, giving males control over female sexuality, fertility and labor."[19] Her work addresses the question of why patriarchy is successful in maintaining and reproducing the domination of one gender over the other by mapping the logical square of Greimas in terms of psychoanalysis and postmodern understandings of ideology.[20] Greimas's "logical square," which is familiar to biblical exegetes, maps the relations of meanings in texts in terms of binary oppositions. The constitution of meaning brings into play oppositional [← — — — — — →], contradictory [←—————————→], and implied or presumed relations [—————————→] between two terms or complexes of meaning. For instance, the logical relationship between the terms man and woman can be mapped as follows:

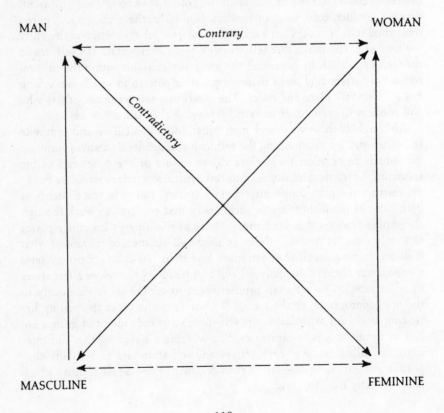

MAN   *Contrary*   WOMAN

Contradictory

MASCULINE   FEMININE

Since the semiotic square allows one to analyze the relations between oppositions, contradictions, and complementarities, it can serve as an analytic model for mapping the ideological relations in a text, particularly the ways in which ideological contradictions are repressed or disguised in textual features. Such a model can indicate how the dominant ideology seeks to repress its incongruities and to prevent those aspects which challenge its hegemony from being articulated.

Ebert defines the symbolic order of patriarchy or culture as "the set of discourses aimed at producing and circulating subjectivities in terms of prescriptions and prohibitions, and ideology as the agency that enforces these injunctions and thus secures those subjectivities."[21] A historical-political redescription of the logical square is thus warranted if one understands the symbolic order not as a logical-universal given, but rather as a historically produced process aimed at insuring the maintenance of patriarchy as the rule of men according to the Law-of-the-Father (phallocentrism). The symbolic order thus can be understood "as the site of social struggle over signification in which opposing significations are repressed and relegated to the imaginary, which is the space for what the symbolic excludes."[22]

To analyze the production of gendered subjectivity in patriarchy one needs first to identify its fundamental injunction, the Law-of-the-Father, or the phallus as the primary cultural signifier. Subsequently, one needs to demystify the representation of the phallus as natural, as anatomical organ. And finally one needs to map how individuals are compelled to line up on the side of having or not having the phallus, or how they are "interpellated" into the prescribed gender-position. Since patriarchal ideology operates to secure a stable relation between the phallic signifier and the individual, it represents the phallus as a given—rather than a culturally constructed—signifier.

In the process of reading, women do not simply identify with the images of the text or internalize its norms; rather, they assume their place in the symbolic order by inserting themselves into the subject-position which ideology articulates: "Signifying practices in patriarchy, such as romance narratives, participate in the representation of the phallus as already given and natural, thereby tying the phallus securely to anatomy and enjoining individuals to line up *only* on the side of having the phallus or of *not* having the phallus ideologically bound to their anatomy, thus producing the subject positions of male and female."[23] Biblical readings that take the male gender of G-d and Jesus as given similarly function to stabilize cultural patriarchal self-identities. Such an ideological naturalization of gender differences, as well as the en-gendering of the subject in patriarchal texts and through reading, can be mapped onto the semiotic square in a composite fashion to reveal the elementary structures of signification as follows:

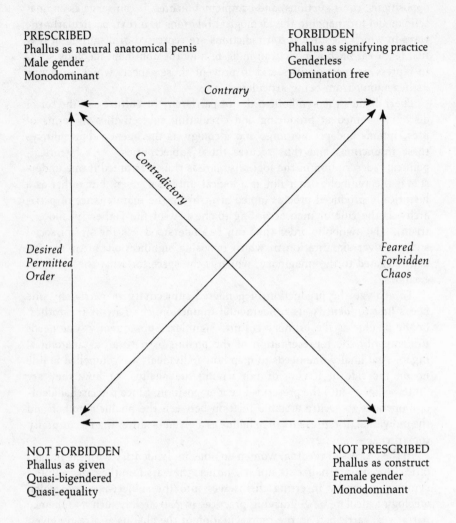

PRESCRIBED
Phallus as natural anatomical penis
Male gender
Monodominant

FORBIDDEN
Phallus as signifying practice
Genderless
Domination free

Contrary

Contradictory

Desired
Permitted
Order

Feared
Forbidden
Chaos

NOT FORBIDDEN
Phallus as given
Quasi-bigendered
Quasi-equality

NOT PRESCRIBED
Phallus as construct
Female gender
Monodominant

In short, patriarchal ideology is a *misrepresentation* not because it stands in opposition to truth or is a false version of an original "real." Rather, it is a misrepresentation insofar as it organizes signifying practices in such a way that the struggle over signification is suppressed. It does so by representing the relation of signifier to signified as a fixed dyadic correspondence which in turn is "naturalized." Dualistic gender differences are thus represented as natural, biological, universal "givens," although they are in reality merely signifying practices. Readers must recognize that texts and representations are not reflections of the "real" but are ideological constructions. There is no place outside ideology from which one can critique ideology. One can only critique an ideology by locating oneself in another one, or by using the contradictions within a single ideology to uncover its disjunctures and opposing relations.

For doing so, Ebert suggests two strategies to engender change and resistance in the counterpatriarchal struggle over signification: on the one hand, feminist analysis has to unmask the ideological contradictions which patriarchal ideology conceals, and, on the other hand, it must articulate the unsaid, the forbidden, the ungendered other, which patriarchal signification suppresses. Such a discursive space cannot be totally separate from existing sociopolitical reality; nor can it understand itself as independent of capitalist patriarchy.

However, it must not be overlooked that Ebert's mapping of patriarchal ideology considers patriarchy synonymous with phallocentrism and understands it as the organization of all cultural signifying practices in terms of the privileging of male gender over its Other, female gender. Still, such a mapping remains within the terms of the sex-gender system constructed by androcentric language and patriarchal ideology. Woman is not only subsumed under male terms, but Third World women as the Others of the Other are doubly invisible in androcentric language structures. If ideology conceals not only its own inconsistencies and contradictions but also its very own construction, then it becomes important to destabilize even further the illusion of a unified, stable subjectivity that patriarchal hegemony constructs. This must be done, I suggest, by specifying patriarchy not just in terms of gender but also in terms of race, social status, and civilization.

Oppositional discourses, such as feminist theory or theology, are never independent of their dominant discourses and patriarchal societies or institutions. On the contrary, they are inextricably and inevitably intertwined with them insofar as they labor under the terms of those dominant discursive formations. Theories of the feminine are still implicated in patriarchal ideology that "naturalizes" biological sex differences, giving such differences the same significance for all women. In collusion with dominant patriarchal ideology, such oppositional discourses on the feminine make us think that, like race, sex/gender is a "natural category." Thus both gender and race differences become "common sense" and they "feel real" for most people. They do so by taking "biological" differences and infusing them with deep symbolic meanings that affect all our lives rather than by seeking to denaturalize and demystify them as sociopolitical constructions.

Instead of universalizing and essentializing white elite *femininity* as a natural gender category, a feminist interpretation for liberation, I argue, must seek to clear a discursive space where women as a political collectivity can define themselves without needing to suppress patriarchal structural divisions among us. Rather than constructing capitalist patriarchy as an all-encompassing totality from which no one can escape, feminists need to conceptualize a different critical site from which to speak. This must be done, I suggest, in sociopolitical rather than simply anthropological dualistic terms.

II.
PATRIARCHY:
PYRAMID OF MULTIPLICATIVE OPPRESSIONS

The mainstream feminist articulation of women's oppression primarily in terms of gender domination has been problematized for years by socialist-marxist feminists, as well as by Third World feminists.[24] They have pointed out, on the one hand, that women are oppressed not only by sexism but also by racism, classism, and colonialism.[25] On the other hand they have rejected the mainstream feminist definition of patriarchy, which holds that men are the oppressors and women the victims and that culture, history, and religion are man-made. Instead, women of color have argued consistently that women of subordinated races and classes are often more oppressed by elite white women than by the men of their own class, race, culture, or religion. As a result of this contradiction in feminist discourse, neither the interconnection between the exclusion of Euro-American women and all other "subordinates" from citizenship, nor its ideological justification in terms of reified "natural" sexual/racial/class/cultural differences, has been given sufficient attention. Such a connection is completely neglected by feminist thinkers who construe the feminist intellectual history of the past thirty years as a contrast between the feminists of the 1960s and 1970s, who were committed to the struggle for equal rights, and postmodern feminists of the 1980s and 1990s, who problematize the sex-gender system and valorize the feminine.[26]

Whenever mainline liberal, radical, or socialist-marxist feminists do pay attention to the objections of Third World feminists, however, they tend to adopt an "adding on" approach of listing oppressions in feminist discourses. This method ignores the fact that systems of oppression criss-cross and feed upon each other in women's lives. Such an "adding on" method conceptualizes the patriarchal oppression of women not as an interlocking, multiplicative, and overarching system, but as parallel systems of domination that divide women against each other. To list parallel oppressions, or to speak of a "dual system oppression" (patriarchy and capitalism),[27] or even of the triple oppression of women in patriarchal societies, obscures the *multiplicative* interstructuring of the pyramidal hierarchical structures of ruling which affect women in different social locations differently.

Indeed such an "adding on" feminist analysis disregards the historical interstructuring of race, class, gender, and nation as forms of stratification which develop together out of the same set of circumstances and which therefore need to be changed simultaneously.[28] "Simultaneous oppressions are not just multiple but multiplicative: racism is multiplied by sexism multiplied by ageism, multiplied by classism multiplied by colonial exploitation."[29] Consequently, women of color have challenged white feminists to join them in recasting feminism as a theory and practice that can conceptualize "the intermeshed oppression of class, race, ethnicity and gender as unacceptable," thereby redefining "women's liberation as part of a struggle against all these forms of oppression."[30] Such a reconceptualization of feminist theory and practice seeks to make women's *differing* experiences of multiplicative oppression central to all feminist discourses.

Challenged by black feminists in religion, I have sought to articulate for the past decade or so a critical feminist theology of liberation that does not understand patriarchy just in terms of the binary gender system. Such a delineation of patriarchy does not take gender oppression as its primary frame of reference in which "sexual difference constitutes the horizon" (Irigaray) of our theorizing. Instead, I have sought to reconceptualize patriarchy as a key heuristic category of feminist theology and biblical interpretation in such a way that it can make visible the complex interstructuring of the conflict-producing oppressions of different groups of women that are obscured by the ideology of patriarchy as binary sex-gender system.

Rather than identifying patriarchy with binary male-female domination, I have argued, one must construe the term in the classical sense, specifically, as a complex pyramidal political structure of dominance and subordination, stratified by gender, race, class, religious and cultural taxonomies and other historical formations of domination.[31] Such a critical feminist theory does not construe patriarchy as an essentialist substantive concept, but as a heuristic category, or as a diagnostic, analytic instrument that allows one to investigate the multiplicative interdependence of gender, race, and class stratifications, as well as their discursive inscriptions and ideological reproductions. Rather than trace the different historical formations of patriarchy in Western societies[32] and biblical religions, I direct attention here to the classic and modern formation of democratic patriarchy and its legitimating discourses.

The classical form of patriarchal democracy was both androcentric and ethnocentric. It drew its boundaries in terms of dualistic polarities and analogies between gods/humans, Greeks/Barbarians, male/female, human/beast.[33] The boundaries of citizenship were constituted through civilization,

115

war, and marriage. The difference between radical democracy and the patriarchal *ethnocentric* form of Greek democracy can be sketched as follows:

GREEK DEMOCRACY

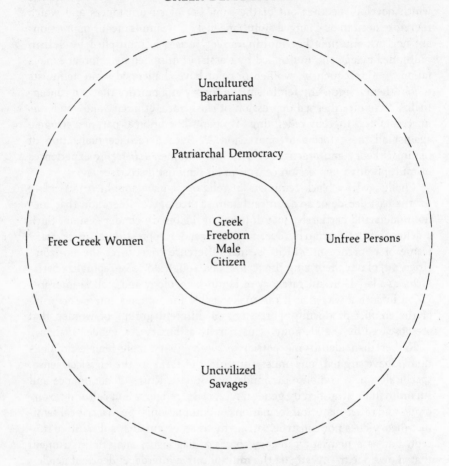

In the classical Greek understanding of patriarchy, the democratic state is structured and sustained by the pyramidal model of the patriarchal household in which the propertied male head, the father of the household, had legal power over his wife, offspring, kin, servants, slaves, and other dependents.

The structuring dividing lines run between those men who own property and those women and men who are owned, between those who rule and those who are ruled, between those who as superiors command and those who as subordinates obey, between those who are free from manual labor and have leisure for philosophical and political activity and those who are economically dependent and whose labor is exploited. In the tradition of patriarchal Greek democracy, Western society and family are not just male, but they are patriarchal (rule of the father) or, more accurately, *kyriarchal* (rule of the master or lord), because elite propertied men have power over those subordinate to and dependent on them. The patriarchal democracy of the Greek city-state then can be mapped as follows:

PATRIARCHAL GREEK DEMOCRACY

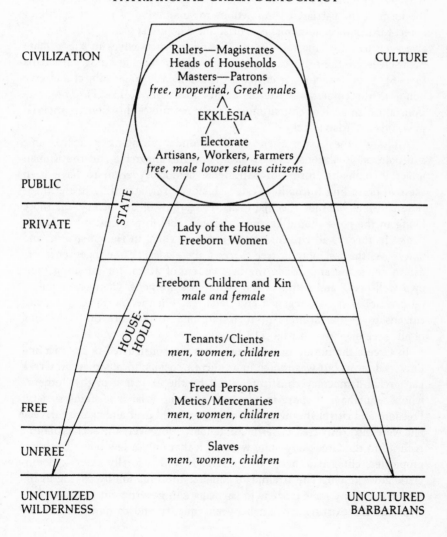

117

This mapping of classical democratic patriarchy as an overarching system of domination must not be misconstrued as a universal, ahistorical "master paradigm," however, since, unlike modern political theory, Greek political thought is not interested in articulating a universal political order. Rather it understands itself as a concrete reflection of the sociopolitical situation and the common good of the Athenian city-state.

The Roman imperial form of patriarchal rule exemplifies the monarchical pyramid of the patriarchal household, but it also incorporates elements of democratic practices. This model of power was legitimated by Neo-Aristotelian philosophy, which found its way into Christian Scriptures in the form of the patriarchal injunctions to submission. The first Epistle of Peter, for instance, admonishes Christians who are servants to be submissive even to brutal masters (2:18–25) and instructs wives to subordinate themselves to their husbands, even to those who are not Christians (3:1–6). Simultaneously it entreats Christians also to be subject and give honor to the emperor as well as to his governors (2:13–17). The post-Constantinian ancient church most closely resembles this Roman imperial pyramid in Christian terms.

Although they have been modified under changing socioeconomic and political conditions, the Greek aristocratic/oligarchic and the Roman imperial/colonialist forms of patriarchal democracy seem to have been the two prevailing forms in Western history. Yet, according to the theoretical vision, but not the historical realization, of democracy, all those living in the *polis* should be equal citizens, able to participate in government. In theory, all citizens of the *polis* are equal in rights, speech, and power. As the assembly of free citizens, the *ekklēsia* came together in order to deliberate and decide the best course of action for pursuing their own well-being and securing the welfare of the *polis*. Democratic political practice is not disengaged and detached. On the contrary, it enables citizens to be the arbiters of their fate and to promote the well-being of all. (See diagram on page 119.)

In Greece the notion of democracy was not constructed in abstract and universal terms but was rooted in a concrete sociopolitical situation. Greek patriarchal democracy constitutes itself by the exclusion of the "others" who do not have a share in the land but whose labor sustains society. Freedom and citizenship were not only measured over and against slavery but were also restricted in terms of gender. Moreover, the socioeconomic realities in the Greek city-state were such that only a few select freeborn, propertied, elite, male heads of households could actually exercise democratic government. The attempt to equalize the situation by paying insufficiently wealthy male citizens to participate in government could not balance out the existing tension between equality and community. Actual

FULL DEMOCRACY—EKKLĒSIA OF WOMEN

AS DEMOCRATIC VISION

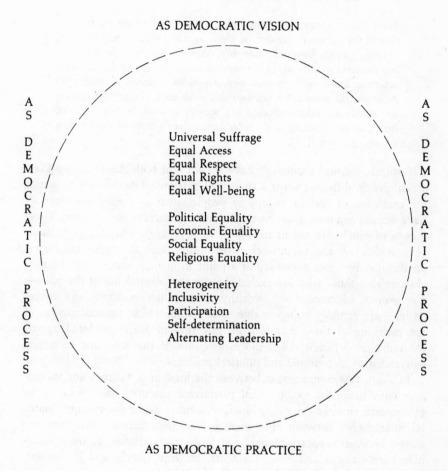

A
S

D
E
M
O
C
R
A
T
I
C

P
R
O
C
E
S
S

Universal Suffrage
Equal Access
Equal Respect
Equal Rights
Equal Well-being

Political Equality
Economic Equality
Social Equality
Religious Equality

Heterogeneity
Inclusivity
Participation
Self-determination
Alternating Leadership

A
S

D
E
M
O
C
R
A
T
I
C

P
R
O
C
E
S
S

AS DEMOCRATIC PRACTICE

participation in government remained conditional not only upon citizenship but also upon the combined privileges of property, education, and family status as a freeborn male. Nevertheless, there are still traces which intimate a different understanding of ancient democracy. As Page duBois has succinctly pointed out: "The ancient democracy must be mapped as an absence. We have only aristocratic, hostile representations of it . . . The *demos*, the people themselves, have no voice in history; they exist only figured by others."[34] Plato and Aristotle, our main sources for the political

119

theory of democracy in antiquity, are philosophers who are critical of the democratic vision and practices of the *polis*:

> While Plato preserved the transforming power of the *polis*, the foundation of the Athenian democratic ideal, by a hierarchical restructuring of society which dissolved autonomy, Aristotle preserved the Athenian commitment to self-rule at the expense of the power of political interaction to shape ordinary men into responsible citizens. According to Aristotle, the good life is not available to all men, because the good is not simply an order embodied in a society as a whole, but a way of living, of contributing to an order rather than simply of constituting a fragment of it.[35]

Feminist political theorists[36] have shown that both Aristotle and Plato articulated in different ways a theory of patriarchal democracy to justify the exclusion of certain groups of people, such as freeborn women or slave women and men, from participation in democratic government. These groups of people are not fit to rule or to govern, they argue, on grounds of their deficient natural powers of reasoning. Such an explicit ideological justification becomes necessary at a point in history when it has become obvious that those who are excluded from the political life of the polis— free women, educated slaves, wealthy metics (alien residents), and mercenaries—are actually indispensable to it. Philosophical rationalizations of the exclusion of these people from government are engendered by the contradiction between the democratic vision of the *polis* and its actual patriarchal socioeconomic and political practices.

In short, this contradiction between the logic of democracy and its tension with historical sociopolitical patriarchal practices has produced the kyriocentric (master-centered)[37] logic of identity as the assertion of "natural differences" between elite men and women, between freeborn and slaves, between property owners and farmers or artisans, between Athenian born citizens and other residents, between Greeks and Barbarians, between the civilized and the uncivilized world.

As the work of Elizabeth Spelman has underlined, the articulation of "natural" gender difference applies in the classical philosophy of Plato and Aristotle solely to Athenian freeborn elite men and women. Strictly speaking, slave women and alien resident women are not *woman*. They are "gendered" not with respect to slave men or alien resident men, but with respect to their masters. They are subordinated to and therefore "different in nature" from not only elite men but also elite women. As a result, the patriarchal pyramid of dominance and subordination engenders not only male-female and male-male but also female-female "natural differences."[38]

III.

MODERN CAPITALIST PATRIARCHY

The assumption of "natural" differences operates in a similar fashion to justify the exclusion of certain peoples from the emergent modern democracies. A similar contradiction between democratic vision and sociopolitical reality becomes evident again with the emergence of modern democratic politics in the West, which has articulated itself as *fraternal* capitalist patriarchy.[39] This contradiction is engendered by the tension between capitalism and democracy as John McGowan has pointed out: "Capitalism's legitimacy rests not only on an economic framework and effective production of goods but also on its nondisruption of certain key liberties that characterize democratic politics in the West."[40]

Since modern capitalist democracy is modeled after the classical ideal of patriarchal democracy, it perpetuates the contradiction between patriarchal practices and democratic self-understandings inscribed in the discourses of democracy in antiquity. At first, modern democracy excluded propertied and all other free women, as well as immigrant, poor, and slave men and women, from the democratic right to elect those who govern them. "Property" and elite male status by birth and education, not simply biological-cultural masculinity, entitled one to participate in the government of the few over the many. In addition, modern patriarchal democracies have taken over the patriarchal procedures of Athenian democracy in which those elected to office govern, whereas those who are citizens have the right to elect their rulers.

It must not be overlooked, however, that this institutionalized contradiction between the ideals of radical democracy and their patriarchal actualizations has also engendered movements seeking full self-determining citizenship. In the past two centuries the emancipatory struggles for equal rights have gained voting and civil rights for all adult citizens. Since these movements could not overcome the patriarchal stratifications that continue to determine modern constitutional democracies, however, they merely made the democratic circle coextensive with the patriarchal pyramid, thereby reinscribing the contradiction between democratic vision and political patriarchal practice.[41] In turn, liberal theorists of democracy have sought to reconcile this contradiction through procedures such as periodic voting, majority rule, representation, and procedural resolution of conflicts. In the process, democratic liberty is construed merely as the absence of coercion, and democratic process is reduced to the spectacle of election campaigns.

In short, the philosophical logic of identity, which in antiquity articulated the asymmetric binary dualisms of human/animal, male/female, and free/slave as "natural" differences in order to legitimate patriarchal rela-

121

tions of domination and subordination, is also inscribed in the discourses of modern Eurocentric political philosophy and theology. Modern democracy perpetrates many of the ideological practices found in ancient political philosophy, insofar as it claims that its citizens "are created equal" and are entitled to "liberty and the pursuit of happiness," while it retains "natural" patriarchal, sociopolitical stratifications. This classical patriarchal discourse was inscribed in Christian Scriptures,[42] rearticulated in Christian theology, and reproduced in modern political science. This discourse emerges in various ways: it manifests itself in the Enlightenment philosophers' construction of the "Man of Reason,"[43] it surfaces in Euro-American racist discourses on the "White Lady," and in the Western colonialist depiction of "inferior races" and "uncivilized savages." Indeed, like the "White Lady," Christian religion was considered to be a civilizing force among the savages.

This political, philosophical, and religious rhetoric of domination and "natural" differences serves to exclude the "Others" of white, elite, propertied Eurocentric Man from democratic government, citizenship, and individual rights. White, Euro-American, privileged Man has defined not only elite white Woman as his "Other" but also subordinated peoples, classes, and races as his "Others," exploiting them under the guise of modern Western democracy and civilization.[44] It is Euro-American elite educated Man, the Western "Man of Reason," who has produced knowledge and science and insisted that his interpretation of the world is true and objective. In short, knowledge is not just gendered but also racial, class-dominated, and Eurocentric.

In this light, the political philosopher Joan Cocks argues that modern political thought elaborates upon two aspects of masculine power: one seeking to secure species reproduction, the other sexual gratification. In the first place, patriarchal or father-right operates on the side of the hierarchical order, wielding control over wives, children, tenants, and wealth while exercising public rule and the punitive force of law. In the second place patriarchal power as masculine power has articulated itself as phallic right over the objects of its desire. It is based on male physique, on a particular type of body, on the penis representing masculinity: "Phallic right openly shows what patriarchal right had shrouded under so much spiritual drapery: that the regime of Masculine/Feminine, which enabled fathers to claim the position of master as rightfully theirs in the first place, founds itself at base on brute bodily difference."[45]

Since she takes father-right to be based in the family, Cocks argues that in modern capitalist societies father-right is diminishing, whereas phallic right is in the ascendancy. Although I agree with her insistence that the two aspects of the kyriocentric regime—namely patriarchal and phallic power—must be distinguished, I do not agree with her restriction of the patriarchal logic to the family. Instead, I would suggest that patriarchal power as *kyriarchal* power operates on an institutional-structural level, while phallic power functions on a linguistic-ideological level. However, the two modes of kyriarchal power are not equivalent.

Kyriarchal power operates not only along the axis of gender but also along those of race, class, culture, and religion. These axes of power structure the more general system of domination in a matrix- (or better, patrix-) like fashion, or in what bell hooks calls the interlocking systems of oppression. This "politics of domination" refers to "the ideological ground that they share, which is a belief in domination, and a belief in notions of superior and inferior . . . For me it is like a house, they share the foundation, but the foundation is the ideological beliefs around which notions of domination are constructed."[46] When one shifts the analysis for investigating the axes of power along which the matrix (or patrix) of domination is structured, one can map not only how these systems of oppression form the kyriarchal social pyramid, but also how they criss-cross the subject-positions that the politics of domination offers to individuals.

These contradictions between patriarchal and democratic ideology inscribed in modern capitalist patriarchal democracies can be diagrammed as on page 124. Such a mapping of patriarchal relations not in terms of gender, but of race (class, property, culture, or religion), can illuminate the alignments, contradictions, and oppositions between women and women.

In light of this analysis, feminist discourses must recognize that the universalist kyriocentric rhetoric of Euro-American elite men does not simply reinforce the dominance of the male sex, but it also legitimates the "White Father," or, in African-American idiom, the "Boss-Man," as the universal subject. By implication, Euro-American feminist theory and theology that articulates gender difference as the primary and originary difference not only masks the complex interstructuring of patriarchal dominations inscribed *within* women and in the relationships of dominance and subordination *between* women, it also masks the participation of white elite women and of Christian religion in patriarchal oppression, insofar as both have served as the civilizing conduits of patriarchal knowledge, values, religion, and culture.

In short, when one takes into account that the Western symbolic order not only defines woman as "the Other" of the Western Man of Reason but also maps the systems of oppression in opposition to the democratic logic of radical equality for everyone, then the semiotic analytical square can be drawn as on page 125. To be sure, the inclusion of women and the functional equivalents of slaves and foreigners in the ancient world into

PRESCRIBED
Male
Elite
Dominant
Propertied
Monodominant

FORBIDDEN
Radical democracy
Ekklēsia of women
Domination free
Self-determination
Well-being of all

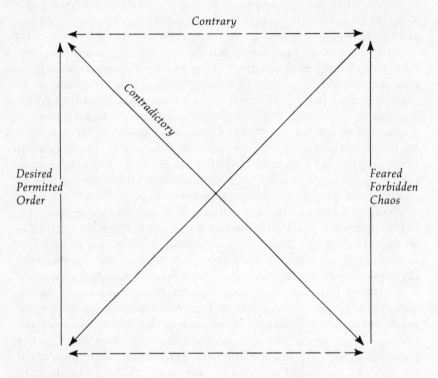

Contrary

Contradictory

Desired
Permitted
Order

Feared
Forbidden
Chaos

NOT FORBIDDEN
Patriarchal democracy
Quasi-equality
Quasi-self-determination

NOT PRESCRIBED
The Others
Gender, race, class, culture
Monodominant

modern procedural democracies has deepened the contradictions inherent in patriarchal democracy. Such an inclusion makes it possible to problematize kyriarchal systems of oppression by situating a critique between the gaps and interstices of the patriarchal and democratic paradigm. A feminist biblical interpretation for liberation must consequently locate itself in such an oppositional democratic imagination.

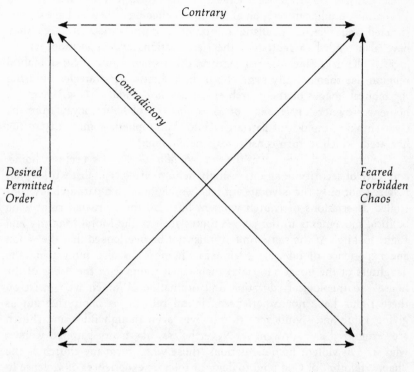

White Man   Black Man

Contrary

Contradictory

*Desired
Permitted
Order*

*Feared
Forbidden
Chaos*

White Woman   Black Woman

IV.
THE EKKLĒSIA OF WOMEN:
A FEMINIST RHETORICAL SPACE
FROM WHICH TO SPEAK

Although feminist theory has analyzed and always criticized androcentric dualism and asymmetric binary gender constructions, its own discourses have nevertheless tended to remain caught up in the kyriocentric logic of identity. Following this logic, they have continued to reproduce dualistic taxonomies which they construe as exclusive alternatives: either reformist or radical, socialist or liberal, private or public, equal rights or liberationist, insider or outsider, psychoanalytic or sociopolitical, essentialist or constructivist, European or American, First or Third World feminisms.

Feminist studies in religion and feminist theology likewise have deconstructed and rejected dualistic androcentric frameworks, although they have also tended to reproduce the classifications and oppositions of the logic of identity. Since the last century, the women's movement in biblical religion has theologically symbolized these discursive strategies by using the biblical images of the church either as "*household of God,*" home/at homeness/ownership/*Heimat,* or as *exodus* out of Egypt, away from the cigar-smoking moloch of patriarchy into the prophetic community of the liberated, which in turn constitutes a new home.[47]

The image of the church as the *household of God*[48]—as a refuge, home, and place of security in an increasingly dehumanized capitalist world—has inspired not only the advocates of true womanhood and patriarchally controlled associations of church women, but also the Christian right-wing political movements in the United States such as the Moral Majority and Right-to-Life. At the same time it must not be overlooked that the vision and experience of biblical religion as "home" has also motivated "the daughters of the house" to claim their equal rights with the "sons of the house" to theological education and ordination. Women who insist on these rights have not experienced biblical religion as oppressive but as giving value and significance to our lives even though Bible and church are recognized as androcentric. Nevertheless, like many battered women who stay in violent home situations, those who affirm the church as the "happy family" of God tend to deny or tolerate experiences of violence in order to "safeguard" religious survival and identity.

Conversely, feminists who call for an exodus out of biblical religions into the "promised land" of feminist community and Goddess spirituality do so because they have experienced the violence of institutionalized patriarchal religion and will no longer deny or tolerate it. They set out to create communities of women in the "other-world," a space in which those who have made the "leap into freedom" (Mary Daly) can experience their own power as the power of the Goddess (Carol Christ), celebrating their own rituals, creating their own gynecentric spirituality, or formulating a God in woman's image, a God who together with the masculine God can occupy a heaven, in a process of "becoming gods together" (Luce Irigaray).

Such a "liberated" community situates itself either as post-biblical and pagan or as a feminist base community in a dialectical relationship to the patriarchal church (R. Radford Ruether). Yet constructions of a liberated space, community, or religion of women tend to repress their own implication in patriarchal structures and mind-sets. Explicit recognition of such an implication would have to acknowledge that feminist gatherings do not constitute a "liberated community" or "home." As long as women live in a patriarchal world and society, feminist discourses cannot escape complicity in the patriarchal ideologies, structures, and power relationships from within which they speak. Like the wider feminist movement in society, so also the feminist movement in religion has difficulty dealing constructively with the patriarchal contradictions, conflicts, and divisions within women-church, because it tends to assume that women-church communities occupy a liberated religious space. Whenever such communities base their self-understandings on the idea of sisterhood, or on an oppositional community of women as women, rather than on a vision of alliances between different communities of women, they tend to attract women whose cultural-religious experiences and identities are alike. Mirroring other mainline feminist groups, women-church has basically remained a homogeneous white women's movement, often restricting itself to oppositional articulations of identity, spirituality, and liturgy within the paradigm of the logic of identity.

In my own work I have searched for a different biblical metaphor and rhetorical image that could mediate between the dualistic feminist alternatives of "church as home" and "exodus into a new, liberated home-space," while allowing for an open discussion of different feminist theories and practical strategies. In response to objections by feminists of color against the universalizing notion of patriarchy as gender oppression of all women by all men as a class or a caste, I have searched for an image that could "gather" and bring together different feminist interest groups in biblical religion rather than split us along lines of patriarchal divisions. Consequently, I thought it necessary to articulate a different biblical image and theoretical space from which to speak, since neither the affirmation of church as home nor the call for an exodus articulates biblical religion as a public site of feminist political struggles.[49]

In the context of the Roman Catholic women's movement in the United States I coined the expression *ekklēsia gynaikōn* as a counterterm to patriarchy in order to assert that, although silenced by the patriarchal church, women are church—*ekklēsia*—and we have always been church. The translation of *ekklēsia gynaikōn* as "women-church" by Diann Neu was adopted by a coalition of Roman Catholic women's groups in the United States for their first common conference in 1983 and has been embraced as a self-designation by ecumenical gatherings, conferences, and movements, especially in Europe, Australia, and Asia.[50]

In each context the notion of women-church is interpreted and deployed differently. Yet, because of R. Radford Ruether's far-reaching—although often misunderstood—interpretation, *women-church* is often conceived of in terms of *exodus-base* communities or alternative feminist spirituality

127

groups which tend to replicate the function of the hegemonic church as liturgical and spiritual "service" station. As the alternative spelling *woman-church* indicates, women-church also is often construed in essentialist feminine terms. Whereas some women-church groups understand their work as a form of pastoral ministry providing a "spiritual home" for women within organized religion, others exhibit sectarian tendencies in their disaffiliation with the institutional church.[51] In short, the notion of women-church has not been able to dislodge itself from the *home-exodus* alternative. Rather, it remains caught up in the dualistic logic of identity and consequently is often co-opted into one pole or the other.

Some object that the expression women-church is "too churchy" and "too Catholic,"[52] or that it falls back into the liberal strategy of the movement for equal rights. Such objections are usually raised either by women who are not affiliated with any church institution, by "low church" white women, or by African-American women whose loyalty is to the Black Church. They are also advanced by "gender-system" feminists who see in the project a further adaptation and co-optation of women's religious energies.

The indictment of the concept of women-church as too churchy or as too "confessional" seems justified insofar as the translation of the term and the practices of "women-church" tend to lose the radical democratic political meaning of the Greek word *ekklēsia*, which describes the political decision-making congress or assembly of full citizens. For while the expression women-church makes the connection between the notions of women and church, it is not able to hold together the notion of *ekklēsia* as both democratic assembly and as church. As a result, the term's intended political valence is lost.[53] Yet the purpose of qualifying and defining church/*ekklēsia* with the term "women" was precisely to bring into public awareness the fact that neither church nor society are what they claim to be: *ekklēsia*, a democratic congress of self-governing citizens.

Moreover, the aim of this neologism was to connect women's struggles in biblical religion with religious and political movements for freedom and equality. These movements have emerged again and again throughout the centuries because of the disparity between the professed democratic vision and actual patriarchal reality. However, the notion of the *ekklēsia of women* can only gather political power when one problematizes the gendered construction of the relation between public-political and private-religious spheres, while simultaneously naming both religious and civic patriarchy as sites of political-ideological struggles.

The second objection to the notion of women-church understood as the discipleship of equals is that the term falls into the pitfalls of liberal feminism. In an essay entitled "Equal to Whom?," which is ostensibly a review of *In Memory of Her*, Luce Irigaray poses the alternative: either equality or divinity. She misreads my understanding of equality as women's parity and equal access to church traditions and structures. Arguing against such an understanding of equality, she contends that a theology of women's liberation must seek for "an equal share in the divine. This means that what I [Irigaray] see as sexual liberation is God made a couple: man and woman and not simply God made man."[54] Therefore Irigaray asks, "What does equal mean as far as religion is concerned? Does it mean being equal to the other disciples or to God? And how can woman be equal to that other when he is another sex?"[55] Because of the short shrift I give the divinization of sex, she wonders whether the tendency to "neutralization" and its concomitant wish to become man are secretly at play in my work.

In short, Irigaray takes issue with the notion of the *ekklēsia* of women because it is not articulated in terms of feminine identity and ontology. Pointing out that all sociological analyses, models, and techniques fail to provide access to feminine identity, she flatly states: "But sociology quickly bores me when I'm expecting the divine."[56] At stake in this critique is not just that Irigaray and I utilize two different discourses. Nor is it the false dichotomy of "equality versus divinity."[57] Rather, at issue here is the feminist theoretical shift from the logic of identity to that of democracy. Emancipatory movements, including the women's liberation movement, do not struggle for equal rights in order to become masculine and the same as men. They struggle in order to achieve the rights, benefits, and privileges of equal citizenship which are legitimately theirs but which are denied to them by the patriarchal and kyriarchal regimes of Western societies and religions.

Emancipatory movements create discursive communities based on shared assumptions and values which define boundaries and validate claims to authority. In the past two decades the feminist movement in society in general and biblical religions in particular has offered one of the most dynamic examples of such a counterdiscourse. It has constituted an oppositional public arena in which to generate critical analysis of patriarchal oppression and to articulate feminist interests and visions. Still, insofar as the feminist movement has projected itself as a single oppositional front in terms of the sex/gender system, generating a universalizing critique of sociopolitical structures from the standpoint of (Euro-American elite) *Woman*, it has tended to constitute its feminist counterpublic as a hegemonic sphere of privileged, white Euro-American women.

Recent feminist work that does not position itself within the Western logic of identity, but rather within the ethical-political space of the democratic paradigm,[58] seeks to theorize such a public feminist space from which to speak. To get away from essentialist notions of Third World feminist struggles, Chandra Talpade Mohanti has suggested the notion of the "imagined community" of Third World oppositional struggles to be the kind of space which provides

> political rather than biological or cultural bases for alliance. Thus it is not color or sex which constructs the ground for these struggles. Rather it is the way we think about race, class and gender,—the political links we choose to make among and between struggles. Thus, potentially, women of all colors (including white women) can align themselves and participate in these imagined communities.[59]

Within the logic of radical equality one can theorize the *ekklēsia* of women as a site of feminist struggles for transforming societal and religious institutions. Such a theoretical frame can displace the feminist alterity-construct *woman* as the theoretical space from which to struggle and replace it with the democratic construct of the *ekklēsia* of women, which is at once an historical and an imagined reality, already partially realized but still to be struggled for. Historically and politically the image of the *ekklēsia* of women, in the sense of the democratic assembly or the congress of women, is an oxymoron, a combination of contradictory terms for the purpose of articulating a feminist political alterity. Establishing women-church as such an alterity identifies Christian community and biblical interpretation as important sites of feminist political-intellectual struggles to transform Western patriarchy.

Situating feminist theorizing and theologizing within the logic of equality rather than of identity allows one to contextualize so-called natural binary sexual arrangements together with those of race, ethnicity, or class as sociopolitical ideological constructions. Women live in structures that are not simply pluralist. Rather, "they are stratified, differentiated into social groups with unequal status, power, and access to resources, traversed by pervasive axes of inequality along lines of class, gender, race, ethnicity, and age."[60] Consequently, feminist theories must take care not to reinscribe such patriarchal status *divisions* as positive pluralistic *differences* among women. Rather, a feminist political discursive practice of liberation must "denaturalize" patriarchal racial, gender, and cultural status inscriptions.

As the intersection of multiple public feminist discourses and the site of contested sociopolitical contradictions, feminist alternatives, and unrealized possibilities, the *ekklēsia* of women requires a rhetorical rather than a scientistic positivist conceptualization of feminist biblical interpretation. Taking the *ekklēsia* of women as its discursive frame of reference, feminist biblical interpretation can move back and forth between different rhetorical strategies of interpretation, rather than constructing them as fixed positions that exclude each other. In such a way, the *ekklēsia* of women can make available polyglot discourses through which individual women can shape their own stories in conversation with the stories of other contemporary, historical, or biblical women.

Such discourses must render those women who have remained invisible even in feminist discourses visible again. By insisting in its own discourses on the *theoretical* visibility and difference, for instance, of black, poor, colonial, lesbian, or working women, feminist theory and theology make it clear that "women" do not have a unitary essence but represent a historical multiplicity not only as a group but also as individuals. Feminist discourses must also take care not to portray one group of women, e.g., lesbians, as monolithic, essentialist, and undifferentiated with no competing interests, values, and conflicts.[61]

Feminist discourses, then, are best understood in the classical sense of "deliberative rhetoric," which seeks to persuade the democratic assembly and to adjudicate arguments in order to make decisions for the sake of everyone's welfare. In the space of the *ekklēsia* of women, feminist biblical interpretation does not derive its criteria for such a "discerning of the spirits" from appeals to the universal divine feminine, to women's female nature, or to saving sisterhood. For such a process of discernment it can only utilize insights derived from women's specific historical-political-religious struggles against the systems of oppression operating on the axes of class, race, gender, ethnicity, and sexual preference among others.

Such a theological deliberation from within particular struggles and political coalitions acknowledges the multiple discourse locations of feminist voices manifesting a diversity of intellectual constructs and competing interest groups. To the extent that different feminist discursive publics articulate feminist analyses, proposals, and strategies differently, it becomes necessary to adjudicate between competing feminist definitions of the world and alternative constructions of symbolic universes. And yet, such competing feminist analyses of patriarchal reality and divergent feminist visions are not simply right or wrong. Thus they must not be construed as dogmatic positions but as strategic practices.

If it is historical experiences and struggles against patriarchy—and not sexual difference—which mark the "qualitative threshold" (Irigaray) that constitutes feminist identity formation in the *ekklēsia* of women, a feminist rhetorics and ethics of biblical interpretation must attend to how we read biblical texts, how we construct their worlds of vision, how we tell women's biblical stories and construct women's agency in biblical times, and how we choose the biblical values and visions that inform our struggles.

Such feminist rhetorical strategies are, firstly, the *rhetorics of liberation,* which can make the oppressive structures and power relations inscribed in biblical texts visible and which can interrogate "common-sense" assumptions in biblical interpretation that naturalize, theologize, and mystify kyriarchal relations of subordination, exploitation, and oppression. Secondly, the *rhetorics of differences* (not just of difference) must read biblical texts from different subject-locations, amplifying and valorizing not only "feminine" identity strategies but also those elaborated on the basis of race, culture, class, and religion. Thirdly, the *rhetorics of equality* does not understand biblical truth and revelation as given but rather as constituted in and through the practices of the "democratic" vision of the *basileia* which spells well-being for all. Its deliberative discourses of interpretation cannot assume a detached posture but must engage the particular sociopolitical locations and concrete desires of biblical readers. Finally, the *rhetorics of vision* cannot position itself within postmodern theories that understand postindustrial capitalist society and culture as a "system without an author," or as a "subjectless, self-transcending, economic mega-machine" and which reject the Enlightenment discourses of human rights, emancipation, equality, and democracy.[62] Rather, it must interrogate biblical texts for religious visions that foster equality, justice, and the logic of the *ekklēsia* rather than that of patriarchal domination.

By constantly engendering debate, the *ekklēsia* of women seeks for better strategies and visions in order to construct a different reality and to avoid orthodox patriarchal divisions. Clarifying and adjudicating contested concepts and proposals, it seeks to engender biblical interpretation as a process of moral deliberation and practical solidarity in the midst of diverse and often competing struggles for liberation. Its criteria of assessment and evaluation, however, must privilege the theories and strategies of feminists who speak from the experience of multiplicative patriarchal oppression.

5

SOPHIA –
DISCERNING THE SPIRIT

Spirit Flowers

Spirit flowers are our lives,

We move in the
promise of the future.
We watch the ones
born unto us
walk, talk, dance, sing
grow into the futures we've dreamed.

Sometimes losing faith
we bemoan
the wind which blows too strongly
losing our perfection.
We berate the sun
which shines too brightly
baking us black.
We deny love
tormenting our waking hours.
We kill the dream
leaving goals unattended.

But then the gentle breeze blows;
The sun breaks open our smiles;
The dream is reborn
Our love blossoms and
we are fulfilled.
The blue sky and warm sunshine
caress our shoulders
and wrap us in security
making us believers again.
We create
and what we create
is our future.
Spirit flowers we are.[1]

Because of Her Faith:

A Critical Theological Hermeneutics

A feminist biblical hermeneutics is often equated with a feminist theological hermeneutics. In this second part of the book I seek to distinguish between a historical, political, and theological hermeneutics. In the two preceding chapters I have argued that the *ekklēsia of women* is the hermeneutical space where a feminist reconstructive and constructive rhetorics has to position itself. In this chapter I seek to explore such a critical rhetorics in terms of ideological,[2] cultural, and religious constructions of meaning.

I.
DEBATED ISSUES

Any articulation of a religious-theological hermeneutics must guard against three sets of feminist misunderstandings: In the first place, the task of a feminist theological hermeneutics must not be limited "to doing what the theological tradition has always done, which is to read the text and retell the story in light of contemporary experience and as an affirmation of values and worldview."[3] While biblical scholars in general agree that philological, archeological, historical-critical, and literary critical studies are integral to the discipline, some reject hermeneutical reflection and theological or ideological discussion as a part of their task. Yet, such a scientific disavowal of biblical theological inquiry serves to maintain the patriarchal religious-cultural power of the Bible insofar as it does not critically assess the symbolic world-constructions of the text. Historical-literary scholars, rather than theologians, now assume the mantle of biblical authority insofar as they decide the correct meaning of the text. The drive to scientific certainty and authority often aligns itself with or replaces the theological drive to doctrinal unity and authority in biblical science. Yet a critical evaluative theological/ideological hermeneutics seems essential to a discipline that situates its practices in the canonical space of the Bible—a text which has taken center stage not only in Christian communities, but in the broader Western culture.

Even if it does not understand itself as theological, but only as cultural biblical criticism, feminist hermeneutics must address religious/theological issues. Insofar as the patriarchal politics of Otherness and arguments for systemic domination have been passed down in Western cultures through the medium of Christian Scriptures, a feminist biblical interpretation can not restrict itself to scientific, allegedly impartial analysis and description. Even when rejecting biblical faith and community, it must critically assess the meaning and values promoted by androcentric biblical discourses: it must explore the sociopolitical functions and contemporary authority claims of sacred texts within hegemonic cultural discourses.

Secondly, a critical feminist-theological re-visioning of biblical discourses and a pragmatic[4] re-claiming of women's theological agency must not be misconstrued in an "essentialist" way. Such a misconstruction is unavoidable if a theological biblical hermeneutic is understood either to be making universalist truth claims or to be ascribing an ontological essence to biblical texts and religion—whether a patriarchal or feminist essence.[5] As I have stressed in the preceding chapters, biblical texts and interpretations must be seen as rhetorical discourses. Like all rhetorical discourses, so also feminist theological interpretations are perspectival, historically and socially conditioned, "embodied" discourses. As such they do not make absolute—but, rather, relative—truth claims. Nevertheless, they do not subscribe to a thoroughgoing relativistic nihilism. Instead, they privilege emancipatory discourses over and against patriarchal dehumanizing ones. To quote Carol P. Christ:

> In my life and in the life of most feminist thealogians and theologians, commitment to feminism does not have the same status as commitment to patriarchalism. My passion for feminism is shaped by my felt experience, tempered by reflection, that it is more true to believe that women and men are equal and that women's contributions to the human community have been and are as important as men's than to believe the opposite.[6]

Conversely, a theological hermeneutics also should not be reduced to biblical apologetics. Since the sociopolitical location of a feminist theological hermeneutics determines the philosophical theoretical underpinnings of its arguments, such an apologetics does not interrupt the patriarchal sex-gender system; it reinscribes it.

In the tradition of the *Woman's Bible*, feminist theological apologetics

135

has focused on what men have said about woman, on male injunctions regarding woman, on the biblical teaching on womanhood, on the great women of the Bible, and on biblical symbolic constructions of woman and the feminine. The biblical site for such an apologetic discourse on woman is the patriarchal tradition of submission, which has cultural political roots both in the Middle East and in the classical philosophical tradition of Greece. Theologians such as Augustine, Thomas, or Luther, and thinkers such as Kant, Nietzsche, or Freud (to name a few!) have espoused a negative theology or theory "of woman."

In the face of the gradual changes brought about by the first and second women's movements in society and religion, this theology of women's subordinate status on grounds of their inferior nature has changed to a "separate but equal" position. Feminist essentialist theories or theologies of femininity, whether their godfathers be Goethe, Schleiermacher, Jung, Tillich, Lacan, Derrida, Teilhard de Chardin, or Pope John Paul II, have valorized Woman—body, sexuality, maternity, nature—as feminine archetype, essence, or divinity. Yet in their attempt to construct an oppositional discourse on Woman, these theories or theologies of the feminine have kept in circulation the discourse of classical Western philosophy and theology on gender-asymmetry, gender-polarity, or gender complementarity—a discourse which understands Man as the subject of history, culture, and religion, while it sees Woman as the Other.

Still, this essentialist Euro-American discourse on Woman as Man's Other has not only been interrupted by feminist theory but has often also been incorporated by it. In turn, the white Western feminist theory of Woman as the Other is being challenged by the emerging feminist movements around the world which dispute universalist claims about woman's common, essential nature and her otherness from man. If feminist theology seeks to displace the "politics of Otherness," these voices insist, it can no longer construct women's identity as unitary and universal, and no longer establish it in terms of either the exclusion and domination of the Others or as the Others' self-negation and subordination. In short, the emerging feminist movements around the world insist on the specific historical-cultural contexts of women and on the subjectivity as well as the plurality of women.

By deconstructing the ideological construct Woman, such global feminist discourses elucidate how the identity of women, of subordinated races, classes, cultures, or religions is constructed as "Other" of the "Other," as a negative foil for the feminine identity of the "White Lady." For instance, in her analysis of lynching, Ida B. Wells has elucidated the patriarchal manipulation of race and gender in the interest of political terrorism, economic oppression, and sexual exploitation.[7] The insights on the interaction between race, gender, class, and culture articulated by emerging feminist discourses around the globe thus enjoin middle-class feminists in the First World not to reduplicate the "whitemale"[8] universalistic discourse of gender dualism. At the same time they caution middle-class feminists of the Two Thirds world not to reproduce the colonial discourse on Woman and femininity. Such an injunction must be heeded by feminists engaged in articulating biblical-theological discourses.

Thirdly, a critical feminist theological rhetoric does not seek to fashion theological arguments to explain why it is important for feminists to read the Bible or to remain Christians. Instead, it critically explores the socio-symbolic worlds of the Bible and their theological meanings and moral values, because countless women still read and value the Bible as sacred Scripture. As Elizabeth Cady Stanton pointed out already in the last century, women themselves have internalized patriarchal biblical texts and injunctions as the "Word of G-d," rather than reading them as the "words of men."

Feminist scholars who reject a critical theological hermeneutics argue that women engaged in biblical religions suffer from a "false consciousness" and therefore should be encouraged—if not compelled—to abandon the Bible and biblical religions. On the one hand, by forcing women in biblical religions to choose between biblical faith and feminism, such a feminist stance cannot respect the religious experience of women that has enabled them to reject patriarchal cultural expectations. Nor is it able to articulate feminist strategies for becoming critical of the biblical discourses of domination and for envisioning a positive transformation of women's religious-biblical identities.

On the other hand, scholars who argue that feminists should not challenge conservative women's acceptance of patriarchal biblical texts because the Bible gives religious meaning to the lives of countless women are equally unable to fashion critical tools and interpretive religious strategies for liberation and transformation. To enable such transformations, a critical feminist hermeneutics must explicitly problematize the theological claim that the Bible speaks with divine authority and is normative for Jewish or Christian identity. It must do so *not* because it seeks to reconstruct the feminist essence and truth of biblical faith, and not because it means to justify patriarchal constructions of religious meaning by women. Rather, a critical feminist theological hermeneutics is necessary because of the historical function of biblical-theological authority claims in sociopolitical struggles for emancipation.

Throughout the centuries the Bible has been invoked as a weapon against women and other subordinates in their struggles for access to citizenship, to public speaking, to theological education, or to ordained ministry. The opposing sides in these often bitter debates have cited biblical normativity and revelatory authority not only for and against women's full ecclesial participation and religious leadership, but also for and against the full citizenship of freeborn women, for and against the emancipation of slave women and men, for and against the rights of lesbians and gay men, as well as for and against economic equity for poor women and their children. Both sides in this debate have appealed to—and continue to appeal to—the Bible as the Word of G-d for legitimating their arguments for and against women's and other unpersons' civil and religious emancipation. As a result of its social location in these political-religious struggles, a feminist *theological* hermeneutics has centered around the question of scriptural authority.

In short, the Bible functions in Christian discourse not only as a resource for critical insight and hope in the liberation struggle. It also constitutes an authoritative means for reinforcing a Christian identity formation based on the patriarchal exclusion and subordination or vilification of "the others." Hence, it not only becomes important to scrutinize contemporary patriarchal arguments which cite the Bible against movements of emancipation. It also is necessary to deconstruct the patriarchal politics of otherness that is not only inscribed in the pages of the Bible but also permeates the modern discussion on biblical normativity and authority.

II.
BIBLICAL NORMATIVITY AND AUTHORITY

In her article "Speaking in Tongues," Mae Gwendolyn Henderson argues that black feminist critics seek "to configure a tradition of black woman writers generated . . . by an emancipatory impulse which freely engages both hegemonic and ambiguously (non)hegemonic discourse."[9] She contrasts this tradition with "the anxiety of influence" which Harold Bloom attributes to male writers.[10] This whitemale tradition is shaped by an adversarial dialogue between fathers and sons. Henderson also distinguishes the tradition of black women writers from the tradition of "anxiety of authorship and authority" which Gilbert and Gubar attribute to white women writers.[11] While white men have written about themselves and their world, white women and black men have tended to write about white men, in relation to whom they have defined themselves.

A cursory review of hermeneutical discourses on the status of the Bible in modern theology indicates that the tradition of whitemale biblical hermeneutics also suffers from the modern "anxiety of identity and influence," whereas the emerging discourses of white feminist hermeneutics

138

tend to define themselves in relation to Eurocentric male biblical hermeneutics. This seems one of the reasons why feminist hermeneutics has
focused on the normativity and authority of the androcentric sacred text
which has been formulated in dominant whitemale theology.

Beginning with Paul (cf. 1 Cor. 11:2–16 and 1 Tim. 2:9–15), Christian
thinkers have legitimated patriarchal discourses of subordination with reference to scriptural authority. The theopolitical appeal to the normativity
and authority of the Bible has remained throughout the centuries one of
the major strategies for maintaining the Western cultural politics of otherness and of patriarchal submission. Scholars have shown that modern
biblical criticism originated in the context of political-philosophical debates
in England, debates in which arguments were drawn from the arsenal of
Scripture. During the sixteenth, seventeenth, and eighteenth centuries,
cultural-political discourses still assumed the traditional Scripture principle,
although, in the long run, such discourses completely undermined the
traditional understanding of the Bible "as the authoritative source of all
human knowledge and understanding."[12]

Thinkers such as Hobbes, Spinoza, Locke, Boyle, and Newton "continually sought [their] models and arguments within the Bible, and the approach of each particular thinker in question provided the real criterion
for the analogies drawn between the reconstructed biblical model and the
principles which were normative for shaping the society of his time."[13]
The principles of rationalist humanism which the English deists adopted
as the criterion for their biblical criticism greatly influenced both the Constitution of the United States, through figures like Paine, Franklin, and
Jefferson, on the one hand, and the German Enlightenment, as well as the
development of historical-critical exegesis, on the other.[14]

Insofar as historical biblical criticism has not only brought to the fore
the rich diversity and often contradictory character of biblical texts, but
has also adopted the rationalist and humanist critique of the Bible's historical and moral discourses, it has underlined the fact that, taken as a whole,
the canon cannot constitute an effective theological norm. Therefore it has
become difficult to sustain even the modern reformulation of the traditional
Scripture principle, a reformulation which no longer construes the Bible
as a literary or historical unity and source for *all* knowledge, but which
simply maintains its "doctrinal unity possessing equal authority in all its
parts, with theological inconsistencies ruled out in principle."[15]

Such an apologetic attempt to articulate an authoritative theological
canon shares in the Western philosophical "logic of identity," which "consists in an unrelenting urge to think things together, in an unity."[16] Feminist political philosophers have criticized Eurocentric modern political theories for construing the civic male public as expressing the "impartial and

139

normative point of view of normative reason," which stands in opposition to the private sphere of the family, the sphere encompassing particularity, emotion, religion, and women. Reason (*ratio*) as the "logic of identity" consists in the drive "to formulate an essence," to eliminate all uncertainty and unpredictability, and to construct total systems which subsume otherness (alterity) in the unity of thought.

The impartial reasoner expresses this "logic of identity" by eliminating otherness. The "Man of Reason"[17] treats all situations according to the same rules, which can be reduced to the unity of one rule or principle. The "logic of identity" strives to eliminate both the differences among moral subjects and the specificity of particular situations. The transcendental subject can establish such an essence only by assuming a G-d's eye view of reality—a theological Archimedean point amid the sea of historical relativity from which the subject can comprehend everything by reducing it to a synthetic unity or principle. The modern theological search for a *normative* canon shares this drive to formulate an essence that brings the concrete particulars of diverse biblical texts into theological unity.

Contemporary theological hermeneutics[18] has sought to deal with the crisis of the traditional "Scripture principle" by articulating a theological normative essence in various ways. Scientific biblical criticism can no longer reason out the authority of the Bible for all of life and appeal to the normativity of all biblical texts. Still, it seeks to maintain scriptural authority for the sake of Christian identity by articulating a canonical center and authoritative norm. The theological "logic of identity" postulates a material principle or textual center as *the canon within the canon,* that is as the essential and controlling element and norm in the Christian canon. In turn, such a "canon within the canon" becomes the authoritative key for the interpretation of biblical writings and the norm for their theological evaluation. This hermeneutical approach looks for theological criteria and norms within the Scriptures themselves, claiming that it can derive from Scripture what this *canon within the canon* should be. Some of the major suggestions for articulating such a canon include the following.

1. *The historical Jesus*[19] was the norm proposed by nineteenth-century liberal theology, and it continues to be used as such a norm today, for instance by Latin American liberation theologies. However, the historical Jesus has been seen in contradictory ways as representing the highest consciousness of G-d (Schleiermacher); as having proclaimed G-d's reign as a moral kingdom of love and justice (Ritschl); or as having been on the side of the poor and the oppressed (Sobrino).[20] From different perspectives, Edward Schillebeeckx and Hans Küng likewise appeal to the historical Jesus and his proclamation as the normative center.[21]

In the last two centuries, the "quest for the historical Jesus" has instantiated the Western "logic of identity," especially in its search for a unifying center of Scripture. The urge to reach the actual historical words and events in the life of Jesus seems to be the raison d'être for much of historical critical research. Curiously enough, although the futility of this quest for the historical Jesus and what he actually said and did has long been recognized, scholars have not abandoned it. On the contrary, they "resurrect" it again and again.[22] The motivating force behind this search for the historical Jesus is not simply historical but rather theological. Indeed, the driving force behind the theological quest for the historical Jesus is the attempt to secure Christian identity in terms of the Western "logic of identity." This search for the life and message of Jesus follows this logic by reducing the multiple images of Jesus to a singular historical one, namely an image which authoritatively constitutes the center of Christian identity. Needless to say, different scholars construe such a center, and therefore the "historical Jesus," according to their own values and beliefs.

2. Other proposals replace the historical Jesus as a criterion for Christian identity with the notion of the *earliest apostolic witness*. Schubert Ogden, following Willi Marxsen, appeals to the earliest apostolic witness as the criterion that provides the singular norm for the theological evaluation of biblical texts. Some have interpreted my feminist theological reconstruction of Christian origins in *In Memory of Her* along these lines, and it has been suggested that I have produced a feminist variation of the "myth of innocence" as a normative criterion. Yet, a careful reading of the first three methodological chapters of my book can establish that this is not the case. I do not propose that the earliest apostolic witness and practice—either that of the Jesus movement or that of the pre-Pauline missionary movement—is a historical "given" fact and authoritative canon. Rather, I argue that early Christian origins are to be (re)constructed from a feminist perspective. Such a feminist theological perspective, positioned in the rhetorical space of the *ekklēsia gynaikōn*, provides the critical norm and criterion by which all biblical traditions and writings must be assembled into a historical model.

3. A third variation on the "logic of identity" paradigm in biblical studies finds expression in the search for *a liberating theological principle* or essence which can be derived from the Bible. Some have appealed to the prophetic principle or tradition as the "canon within the canon." Such an appeal was perhaps most strongly elaborated within neo-orthodoxy. As one of the most powerful theological movements, neo-orthodoxy reacted against liberal theology's emphasis on religion as the highest human cultural expression. With its critique of religiosity, such a neo-orthodox her-

meneutics has severely indicted the development of institutional structures within the later writings of the Christian canon. Its understanding of the church as an "eschatological" community, or as an "exodus community," has provided a contrasting image to the concrete historical development of the church.

The Pauline-Lutheran doctrine of "justification by faith" can function in a way that is similar to the prophetic principle and its use as a unifying central criterion. R. Bultmann, for instance, makes use of "justification by faith" as the theological criterion over against any objectification of the Christian kerygma through myth. Thus, justification by faith provides the theological criterion for his program of demythologization. Another way of articulating a "canon within the canon" distinguishes between the theological *essence* of biblical texts and their time- and culture-bound *forms*. Yet such a reduction of particular biblical texts to a theological principle, theological essence, or ethical norm not only cuts down the rich pluriformity of biblical discourse to abstract principle and norm, it then goes on to claim that such a theological principle is the inspired and revealed Word of G-d. Hence, such a reduction of the pluriform biblical narrative to a singular universal moral principle masks the accountability of the theological interpreter for the articulations of such ontological principles, theological essences, or moral norms.

4. Following the same logic of identity, the theological method of *correlation*[23] in turn seeks to establish a *critical correlation* between such a "canon within the canon"—however formulated—and a contemporary norm, be it disclosure experiences, the feminist principle of the "full humanity of women," or other liberatory goals. Such a *hermeneutical* correlation not only obfuscates its own sociopolitical location, intellectual agency, and dependency on contemporary frameworks in formulating the norms or principles to be correlated, it also follows the "logic of identity" insofar as it jettisons the need for specific analyses and critical theological evaluations of particular texts. A theological hermeneutics which utilizes the method of correlation cannot but reduce the richness of biblical texts and traditions to one particular text, tradition, or principle. Just as the "canon within the canon" model is reductive, so also the method of critical correlation or critical confrontation separates form and content and then formalizes and universalizes them into a equivocal principle. Although Paul Tillich criticized Karl Barth's dialectical method, his own method of correlation is still motivated by the apologetic drive, in that it engages in a critical dialogue of "yes and no" between contemporary culture and biblical religion in order to end with an affirmative "yes" to biblical religion.

In short, in its search for a "canon within the canon," for the "unity" of Scripture, or for a single theology of the Bible, I argue, theological hermeneutics enacts the Western "logic of identity," which eliminates both the irreducible particularity of historical texts and their social contexts, as well as the theological differences among biblical writers and contemporary interpreters. To the extent that historical critical interpretation has elaborated the pluriform and often contradictory meanings of biblical texts, it has refuted the possibility that the canon as a collection of diverse historical and theological writings can constitute a unitary norm. A theological hermeneutics must therefore seek to understand biblical authority in a different way.

5. More recent approaches to the question of biblical authority and normativity in malestream theology have therefore shifted their focus away from the text to the constitutive agency of the religious community in fashioning the biblical canon. They argue that biblical writings did *not* become canonical Scriptures because they were believed to be uniquely inspired but because the church found them useful. Early Christian writings, for instance, were acknowledged as canonical on the basis of the theological criteria of apostolicity, catholicity, orthodoxy, and traditional usage, which were used in a variety of combinations. "In particular the principles of apostolicity, catholicity, and orthodoxy were less the reasons for canonical recognition than means of legitimizing the authority that attached to certain documents in virtue of their longstanding use by the church."[24] This pragmatic understanding of Scripture also informs a contemporary *functional* hermeneutical approach which starts from the actual use of Scripture in biblical communities. Like a cultural classic, the Bible has *de facto* authority in the churches because it functions to shape Christian life and identity.

The *canonical* approach in turn focuses on the transmission and reinterpretation of the originating biblical events and traditions in the light of new situations. This process of continual reinterpretation was constitutive for the formation of canonical ecclesial identity and for the authority of Scripture. A *third approach*, moreover, seeks to integrate the functional and the canonical approach by stressing that "the authority of the Scriptures does not rest on a single meaning that is received and then interpreted, but rather that the meaning of the Scriptures is construed in relation to the integrity of the events and traditions expressed in the Scriptures along with the ongoing process of reception of these interpretations."[25]

This approach construes the authority of Scripture not as that of a classic, but as that of a constitution—the constitution of an ongoing community understood not as a set of laws, but "as a set of interpretive practices that provide basic paradigms of Christian identity."[26] Indeed, all three of these hermeneutical approaches no longer seek to locate scriptural authority within the canon, but instead shift its location to the interpretive practices of the Christian community in the past and in the present. They do not, however, explicitly address the issues of power and control embedded in discourses of authority.

III.
A FEMINIST CANONICAL HERMENEUTICS

Not unlike the dominant articulations of a canonical hermeneutics, a feminist canonical hermeneutics seems to remain caught up in the Christian Western "logic of identity." To achieve theological unity, feminist theological hermeneutics also tends to reduce the historical particularity and contradictory pluriformity of Scripture to a feminist "canon within the canon," a liberating "organizing principle," or a normative center of Scripture. Feminist biblical and liberation theological scholarship has inherited both its search for an interpretive key and its "logic of identity" from the dominant discourses of historical criticism and theological hermeneutics. Just as these discourses have developed because of the relativizing results of biblical historical criticism and the modern challenge to the normative authority of the Bible, so also a feminist theological hermeneutics has originated amid controversy.

Although malestream theological hermeneutics also has its roots in religious-political debates, feminist hermeneutical discourses are situated in *different* religious-political struggles. They are not concerned with justifying a certain form of government or church on biblical grounds. Rather they seek to argue on biblical grounds against those who use the Bible against women or other nonpersons.

Several feminist hermeneutical positions have crystallized in confrontation with those who claim biblical authority to legitimate patriarchal subordination. The *first* position rejects the Bible because of its patriarchal character. The Bible is not the word of G-d but that of elite men justifying their patriarchal interests. An opposite argument insists that the Bible must be "depatriarchalized" because, correctly understood, it fosters the liberation of women. Finally, a middle position concedes that the Bible is written by men and rooted in a patriarchal culture but nevertheless maintains that some biblical texts, or at least the basic core of the Bible, are liberating and stand in critique of patriarchy.

A feminist biblical apologetics. A Christian feminist apologetics asserts that the Bible, correctly understood, does not prohibit, but rather authorizes the equal rights and liberation of women. This approach usually focuses on "key" passages about women such as Genesis 1–3, the biblical laws with regard to women, or Pauline and post-Pauline statements about women's place and role, in order to show that they have been misunderstood or misused by those arguing against women's dignity and rights. A feminist hermeneutics, therefore, has the task of elaborating the correct understanding of such texts so that their biblical authority can be claimed for women's rights.

However, not all texts used against women and others who are subordinated in their liberation struggles can be proven to be willful misinterpretations. The rich diversity and contradictory character of the Bible elaborated by historical critical scholarship has proven that, taken as a whole, the canon cannot provide an uncontested theological norm. In light of such scholarship, it becomes difficult to sustain the traditional doctrine that the canon forms an inerrant unity which in principle rules out theological inconsistencies. Nevertheless, feminists belonging to conservative churches still subscribe to this doctrinal understanding of canonical authority as inherent in biblical texts. They propose three different hermeneutical strategies to solve the problem.

1. A loyalist feminist hermeneutics argues that biblical texts about women can be explained in terms of a hierarchy of truth. Whereas anti-feminists argue, for instance, that the household-code texts require the submission and subordination of women and that Galatians 3:28 must be understood in light of them, evangelical feminists hold that Ephesians 5 requires mutual submission and that the injunctions to submission must be judged in light of the canonical authority of Galatians 3:28. The overarching principle of equality and mutuality expresses G-d's intention and revelation. According to this theological reasoning, statements about patriarchy are not theologically prescriptive but only descriptive.

2. A second strategy is *universalist* and *essentialist*. This approach makes a distinction between historically conditioned texts that speak only to their own time and those that speak with authority for all times. For instance, the injunctions of 1 Corinthians 11:2–16 to wear a headcovering or a certain hairstyle are seen as time-conditioned, whereas Galatians 3:28 pronounces the equality of women and men for all times. However, in order to decide which texts are valid for all times, this strategy needs to borrow the criterion developed in the first approach, namely, that of an overarching truth according to which all subsequent truths may be evaluated.

3. A third approach is *compensatory*. It challenges the overwhelmingly androcentric language and images of the Bible either by pointing to the stories about strong women in Scripture or by tracing the allusions to feminine images and language for G-d that are found throughout the

sacred writings of Judaism and Christianity. By gathering the remaining egalitarian texts that are often overlooked in traditional exegesis, it seeks to address and to respond to the feminist indictment of biblical religion as patriarchal. Such a strategy embraces the divine female figure of Wisdom, for instance, or the feminine character of the Holy Spirit, in order to legitimate the use of feminine language for G-d and the Holy Spirit today. This approach, however, does not address the contention of feminist scholars[27] that the biblical belief in transcendent masculine monotheism has served as a justifying concept and image for the triumph of patriarchy.

4. A fourth apologetic strategy uses a *method of contrast*. It insists that the Bible must be studied on its own terms in its sociohistorical context. At the same time, this strategy deepens the chasm either between biblical communities and their surrounding historical cultures or between biblical times and our own. For example, to compare the unjust patriarchalism of Abraham consigning Sarah to possible rape with the insights of modern feminism on rape is to compare not just apples and oranges, but apples and camels. In the interest of constructing a cultural gap between the past and the present, this approach either downplays or neglects entirely the emancipatory movements and ideologies in the biblical worlds. Because of the increasing criticism of Christian feminist anti-Jewish tendencies in biblical interpretation, this approach tends to be less and less used vis-à-vis Judaism, while it seems to be expanding with regard to Greco-Roman women's situation.

5. Finally, a fifth apologetic strategy seeks to *"depatriarchalize"* Scripture or to redeem Scripture from patriarchal confines. The feminist reader observes the plight of women in ancient Israel or early Christianity. She does not deny that evidence abounds for the patriarchal subordination, inferior status, and abuse of women. Instead, she combines feminism and biblical criticism to shape a method of reinterpretation that seeks to redeem the past and the present of Scripture from imprisonment in patriarchy. Such a method of reinterpretation stresses the contradictions inscribed in biblical texts and emphasizes the "pilgrim character" of Scripture, which has maintained a dialogue with generations of readers. Such a feminist hermeneutics of "redemption" gathers those texts that show signs of female strength and retells patriarchal texts as memory of the victims.[28]

A feminist canon. Recognizing the pervasive androcentric character of biblical texts, other feminists seek explicitly to isolate an authoritative essence or central principle that biblically authorizes equal rights and liberation struggles. Such a liberation hermeneutics does not aim to dislodge the authority of the Bible. On the contrary, it seeks to reclaim the empowering authority of Scripture in order to use it over and against conservative right-wing biblical antifeminism.

1. A first strategy here seeks to derive its norm from the Bible and to identify an authoritative canon within the canon, a central principle or *the* "gospel message." Since feminist studies generally recognize that the Bible is written in androcentric language and rooted in patriarchal cultures, such a normative center of Scripture allows one to claim biblical authority while enabling one simultaneously to reject the accusation that the Bible is an instrument of oppression. Although feminist biblical interpretation which recognizes the ideological character of androcentric language and texts has questioned the unifying drive of the "logic of identity" of malestream scholarship, its hermeneutical discussions nevertheless have tended to adopt the theological strategies of "whitemale" biblical scholarship. To salvage scriptural authority and normativity, feminist theological interpretations have reduced the historical particularities of biblical texts to an abstract feminist principle, yet feminist biblical and liberation theological scholarship has inherited rather than initiated this search for an authoritative "canon within the canon" from historical-theological exegesis, which recognizes the pluriformity of Scripture but nevertheless wants to maintain the normative unity of the Bible.

In short, although liberationist biblical discourses have rejected the value-neutral, objectivist, apolitical rhetoric of academic biblical scholarship, they have not rejected its "drive to unity and essence." Just as male liberation theologians stress G-d's liberating act in history, singling out the Exodus as "canon within the canon" and focusing a "new reading of the Bible" on the liberating "biblical recollection and regathering of G-d's salvific deeds" (Croatto), so also feminist liberation theologians have sought to identify a liberating theme, tradition, text, or principle as the hermeneutical key and authoritative norm of the Bible, which is recognized as an androcentric-patriarchal book. Letty Russell, for instance, has suggested "G-d's promises for the mending of creation"[29] as one such hermeneutical key.

2. A debated problem in feminist liberation theological hermeneutics remains the question of whether such a feminist critical hermeneutical key or normative principle must be derived from, or at least be correlated with, the Bible so that Scripture will remain the normative foundation of feminist biblical faith and community. A mediating second position argues that the Bible becomes authoritative in the hermeneutical dialogue between the ancient world that produced the text, the literary world of the text, and the world of the modern reader. Such a position, as articulated for instance by Sharon Ringe, rejects any criteria extrinsic to the biblical text

itself for evaluating the diverse and often conflicting biblical voices. Instead, it maintains that the Bible contains its own critique. It points, for instance, to the vision of a transformed creation in Isaiah 11:6–9 as the criterion intrinsic to Scripture. The principle of "no harm"—they shall not hurt or destroy in all my holy mountain—becomes the normative criterion for assessing biblical texts. However, this approach does not reflect critically on the fact that it is the interpreter who *selects* this—as opposed to some other—criterion, thereby giving it normative canonical status.

3. A third strategy within the "feminist canon" approach recognizes that such a feminist critical norm is not articulated by the biblical text. Rosemary Radford Ruether, for instance, has shifted her hermeneutical perspective in the course of feminist discussions. Whereas in her earlier work she had proposed the prophetic text or tradition as such a "canon within the canon," in her contribution to the discussion of feminist biblical hermeneutics edited by Letty Russell she shifted to a hermeneutics of correlation:

> The Bible can be appropriated as a source of liberating paradigms only if it can be seen that there is a correlation between the feminist critical principle and that principle by which biblical thought critiques itself and renews its vision as the authentic Word of God over and against corrupting and sinful deformations. . . . This biblical critical principle is that of the prophetic-messianic tradition.[30]

Radford Ruether articulates such a feminist critical principle in universalist terms as "the full humanity of women." This feminist critical principle of women's full humanity is to be correlated with the prophetic-messianic critical principle or dynamic found in the Bible. Radford Ruether insists that a *correlation* can be established between this feminist critical norm and the "principle by which the bible critiques itself and renews its liberating vision over and against corrupting deformations." Such a feminist strategy positioning itself within a hermeneutics of correlation, however, reduces the particularity and diversity not only of biblical texts, but also of feminist articulations, to an abstract, formalized principle or norm. In short, such an approach fails to see that biblical texts and interpretations are the site of competing discursive practices and struggles which should not be reduced to an abstract norm.

4. A fourth hermeneutical strategy proposes that women-church must create a feminist *Third Testament* that canonizes women's experiences of G-d's presence as a new textual base. Revelatory breakthrough experiences inspire women to write new poems and tell new stories which are given authority by the base communities of women-church. Feminist theology

authenticates these stories and thereby "creates a new textual base, a new canon," a "Third Testament" that can speak about the experience of G-d's presence in the lives of women. "Women must be able to speak out of their own experiences of agony and victimization, survival, empowerment and new life, as places of divine presence, and out of these revelatory experiences write new stories." Just as the androcentric texts of the First and Second Testaments reflect male experience, so also the stories rooted in women's experience constitute a Third Testament which deserves canonical status.

While this hermeneutical insistence on women's experiences of struggle and survival as places of divine presence resembles my own hermeneutical proposal, I would not want to give these stories rooted in women's experience a fixed canonical status alongside the canonical First and Second Testaments. I would not want to do so, because such a canonization of women's stories would reinscribe the cultural-theological male/female dualism as *canonical* dualism. Moreover, like male experience, women's experience is embedded and structured by patriarchal culture and religion. Consequently, it too needs to be subjected to a process of critical evaluation.

Instead of reducing the historical richness of the Bible to an abstract principle, timeless norm, or ontologically immutable archetype which is to be repeated from generation to generation, a critical hermeneutics of liberation seeks to reclaim the whole Bible as a formative root-model, that is, as a historical-ecclesial prototype. To read the Bible not as an unchanging archetype but as a structuring prototype is to understand it as an open-ended paradigm that sets experience in motion and makes transformation possible. To be sure, the experiences which the biblical root-model generated are not always liberating. They often can be oppressive, and not simply because of unfaithful or false interpretations and receptions. Biblical texts and writings reinscribe relations of oppression not only because they are androcentric; many also have been formulated in their original contexts in order to maintain patriarchal sociopolitical structures and religious identity formations.

In short, the question of scriptural authority has taken center stage in the discussions of a feminist theological hermeneutics. Since the last century, feminist biblical hermeneutics has agonized and argued about what kind of authority the Bible can claim in the lives of women. Today, feminist biblical discourses appear still to be caught up in this apologetic debate which seeks to show that the Bible, or at least parts of it, is *either* liberating—and therefore has authority for women and other nonpersons—*or* totally patriarchal and must be rejected.

Feminist hermeneutical discussions engendered by the first and second women's movements in the United States continue to share in the white female anxiety about authority, centering as they have around the question of how the Bible as an androcentric and often patriarchal book can be authoritative for feminist theology and emancipatory struggles. In white feminist liberation theological discourses the Bible as the authoritative and authorizing "word of God" has occupied center stage. Accordingly, the articulation of the feminist subject of biblical interpretation or that of a theological model of reading as a critical praxis for liberation has been neglected and deserves more attention.

IV.
THE THEOLOGICAL AUTHORITY
OF THE *EKKLĒSIA* OF WOMEN

To minimize the possibility of feminist biblical interpretation being co-opted in the interests of the Western patriarchal "logic of identity," feminist biblical hermeneutics, I have argued in *Bread Not Stone*, must conceptualize its act of theological interpretation as a moment in the global praxis for liberation. Just as recent malestream theological hermeneutics locates the authority of the Bible within the church's practices of biblical interpretation, so my proposal seeks to situate that authority within the *ekklēsia gynaikōn* as the discipleship of equals. The main task of a feminist theological hermeneutics in the rhetorical space of women-church is not to defend biblical authority. Rather it is to engender critical discourses which can claim the theological authority of the "others" to engage in a deliberative process of biblical interpretation. Such a critical feminist interpretation for liberation, as developed in *Bread Not Stone*, can be further theorized when one situates it within the Western paradigm of the logic of democracy rather than that of identity.

Firstly, a critical feminist hermeneutics must explicitly shift its interpretive practices from the canonical paradigm articulated by the "logic of identity" to that of the "logic of democracy" articulated by the *ekklēsia* as the democratic assembly of free citizens who gather to decide their own affairs. This paradigm shift engenders a different notion of biblical authority and truth. Examining ancient Greek legal, philosophical, and literary texts on torture, Page duBois argues that the Western "logic of identity" in classical Greek philosophy has developed the concept of truth as something hidden—something to be excavated or extracted by the torture of slaves. "This logic demands a closed circle, an other, an outside, and creates such an other. And in the case of the Greek city, the democracy itself used torture to establish this boundary, to mark the line between slave and free, and to locate truth outside."[31]

The Man of Reason as the Western philosophical subject understands truth as something that is not known, but buried, secreted in the earth, in the body, in the woman, in the slave: something that must be extricated through torture or sexual violence. In a similar fashion, biblical revelation has been understood in traditional theology as an uncovering of a hidden mystery which is located in the unknown and in the beyond, and which is made known only to a select few. The "canon within the canon" approach, for instance, seeks to uncover, to distill or extract, such a universal truth or authoritative norm.

According to Page duBois, in the Western tradition this "logic of truth" coexists with the "logic of democracy," understood as the "notion of equal power among members of a community," a notion which "required the radical distribution of wealth, the elimination of social and political hierarchies. For some ancient thinkers, even slavery itself was eventually called into question."[32] This Western paradigm of the logic of democracy produces a different notion of truth. It does not understand truth as a hidden metaphysical given but as a multiple, polyvalent assembly of voices. Truth is not the discovery of what is hidden or lost, but rather a public "creation in democratic dialogue." The truth of democracy is produced in struggle and debate as an alternative discourse to torture. In this paradigm, truth is best understood as an "absent presence," a moment in a political process, a progressive extension of rights and equality to all members of an expanding community.

Within the paradigm of democracy, scriptural truth is to be constituted in and through communicative practices. Moreover, I suggest, the question of Christian identity can be reformulated within the Western paradigm of the logic of democracy, although this paradigm has left only traces in the historical, cultural, and religious representations produced by the Western Man of Reason. Likewise, the theological discourses of the *ekklēsia* as the discipleship of equals have been submerged in dominant theological articulations. Nevertheless there are still traces inscribed in Western cultural and religious discourses that allow for such a reconceptualization.

A feminist biblical hermeneutics which no longer positions itself within the Western paradigm of the "logic of identity" but is articulated within the "logic of democracy," I suggest, can overcome the *either* (accept the authority of the Bible) *or* (leave biblical religions) alternative that has determined feminist discourses on religion and the Bible. It can do so, however, only when it positions itself in the discursive space of the *ekklēsia gynaikōn*, created and sustained by the emancipatory struggles and radical democratic movements around the globe.

And yet, such a feminist rhetorical positioning is misunderstood if it is construed as the Roman Catholic attempt to develop an alternative "magisterium" to be compared and contrasted to the Protestant canonical principle which insists that not the church but only Jesus Christ can be the normative canon for a Christian feminist theology.[33] The attempt to construe an individualistic "Protestant" reader as an alternative to the "Catholic" conception of women-church remains equally caught up in the Western paradigm of the "logic of identity."[34] Such a misapprehension not only reinscribes man-made confessional controversies, it also turns the *ekklēsia gynaikōn* into a site of competing confessional discourses, rather than understanding it as a rhetorical space from where to assert women's theological authority to determine the interpretation of Christian scripture, tradition, theology, and community.

In turn, a feminist apologetic hermeneutics runs the danger of prematurely foreclosing a critical rhetorical analysis and feminist theological evaluation of particular biblical texts and traditions by passing them over in silence. It thereby tends to neglect biblical interpretation as the site of competing discursive practices. At the same time, it does not sufficiently appreciate that the Bible is a cacophony of interested historical voices and a field of rhetorical struggles in which questions of truth and meaning are being negotiated.

Secondly, positioning itself within the rhetorical space of women-church, a feminist theological interpretation continually can call into question and assess biblical texts and their worlds in light of contemporary liberation struggles. The hermeneutical insights and theological challenges of the heterogeneous voices emerging from the feminist movements of liberation around the world are central to such a critical process of biblical interpretation in the rhetorical space of the *ekklēsia*.

Mae Gwendolyn Henderson has pointed out that African-American women, free from both the elite male "anxiety of influence" and white women's "anxiety of authority and authorship," have no need to define themselves in relation to elite white men—to write about them or to become like them. The following comparison can illustrate what she means.

In the nineteenth century, Matilda Joslyn Gage had asserted not only women's right to biblical interpretation but also women's authority to engage in it. In 1878, at the annual meeting of the *National Woman's Suffrage Association*, she introduced the following resolution:

> Be it resolved: That the fundamental principle of the Protestant reformation, the right of individual conscience and judgment in the interpretation of Scripture, heretofore conceded to and exercised by men alone, should now be claimed by woman and that in her most

vital interests she should no longer trust authority but be guided by her own reason.[35]

The following year, after four women were expelled from the Congregational Church because of their activities on behalf of woman's suffrage, Gage introduced another resolution at the annual meeting:

> Whereas, By false interpretation of Scripture, woman is held to duties, not rights; responsibilities not power; and is deemed to be an appendage to man, created for his benefit and happiness.
> Whereas, This interpretation has nourished in man, love of dominion, selfishness, and sensuality, and has humiliated and degraded woman and humanity;
> Therefore, Resolved: That woman was created a free, responsible human being, equal to men in rights, powers, duties, and obligations, that among her rights is an equal right with man to a private interpretation of Scripture, to self-development and self-government in home, church, and state.

Indeed, we may marvel at Gage's critical insights over a century ago. And yet, even this articulation of women's authority to engage in biblical interpretation still defines itself in terms of the Enlightenment ideal of the Man of Reason and relegates interpretation of Scripture to the private sphere.

In contrast to that of elite white women, the point of departure for African-American women in the nineteenth century was not primarily the struggle for "private" interpretation of Scripture and self-development. Rather, African-American women heard and read the Bible in the context of their experience of slavery and liberation.

Since slaves were prohibited from learning to read and write, their biblical interpretation did not focus on the exegetical explanation of texts, but freely engaged the stories and images of the Bible to illuminate their sociopolitical experience. "Interpretation was therefore controlled by the freeing of the collective consciousness and imagination of the African slaves as they heard the biblical stories and retold them to reflect their actual situation as well as their visions for something different."[36]

Moreover, African-American women such as Sojourner Truth, Amanda Berry Smith, Jarena Lee, Julia Foote, Maria Stewart, or the Quaker Elizabeth (of whom we know only her baptismal name) derived their authority for biblical interpretation and preaching first of all from a mystical experience in which they encountered G-d or Jesus directly. It was this confidence in the privileged nature of their relationship with the Divine that compelled

African-American women to transcend the limits imposed upon them by the patriarchal gender-race system.

Like white suffragists and black men, African-American women evangelists sought valorization and authentication from the Bible. However, unlike white women and black men, African-American women spoke from a doubly disadvantaged location. As blacks, they had to address white audiences who doubted the human capacity of African-Americans for learning and religious salvation. As women, they had to address audiences, black and white, who questioned both their ability to exercise authority and the legitimacy of their speaking in public.

Thirdly, the critical interplay between "spiritual" experience and authorizing interpretation of Scripture leads to an implicit privileging of sociopolitical experience. In her famous speech at the Akron Convention on Women's Rights, Sojourner Truth, who was illiterate and a former slave, argued for women's theological authority and civil rights with reference to her own experience of slavery. The much quoted statement of Howard Thurman's grandmother, a freedwoman who could not read or write, similarly articulates experience as a criterion for assessing Scripture:

> During the days of slavery, she said, "the master's minister would occasionally hold services for the slaves. Always the white minister used as his text something from Paul. 'Slaves be obedient to them that are your masters . . . , as unto Christ.' Then he would go on to show how, if we were good and happy slaves, God would bless us. I promised my Maker that if I ever learned to read and if freedom ever came, I would not read that part of the Bible."[37]

The womanist ethicist Katie Cannon has stressed that in the last century racial slavery was the sociopolitical context not only of African-American but also of white hegemonic biblical interpretation. She identifies the three ideological constructs that made it possible for white Christians to justify chattel slavery. As *property*, slaves were seen as not fully human; as *Africans* they were classed as heathen savages to be saved through enslavement; and as *Christians*, white or black, they were expected to believe that slavery was divinely willed in the Bible.[38] Within this context, Africans used the Bible as a "matrix" for the transformation of meaning. Such an Afrocentric reading of the Bible incorporates texts that affirm the dignity of the African person in the face of dehumanization, rejecting those texts that can be used to legitimize slavery. Read in the rhetorical space of the struggle for liberation from slavery, the Bible offered enslaved Africans dignity, equity, and citizenship. "Redemption and salvation incorporated economic and political empowerment and a restoration to civil status."[39]

Writing from a Chinese feminist perspective, Kwok Pui Lan focuses on the colonialist contextualization of biblical interpretation. Reading the Bible in a non-Christian world, Christian Asian women question both whether the biblical canon contains all the truth and whether it is rigidly closed. They challenge the universal truth-claims of Western biblical interpretation and measure the authority and meaningfulness of the Bible by the praxis of the Christian community. Kwok Pui Lan proposes a process of "dialogical imagination" as an Asian feminist hermeneutical model. Such a model uses Asian cultural and religious traditions and sacred texts as the context for biblical reflection, and the social biography of the people as a hermeneutical key for biblical interpretation.[40]

Chung Hyun Kyung likewise argues that Asian women's theology must locate G-d's revelation in the lives of Korean peoples if it wants to overcome the Bible's colonizing function in perpetrating the cultural dependency of Asian Christians on Western biblical interpretation. "The texts of G-d's revelation was, is and will be written in our bodies and our peoples everyday struggle for survival and liberation. . . . Our life is our text, and the Bible and church tradition are the context which sometimes becomes the reference for our own ongoing search for G-d."[41] She insists that Asian women theologians of the second generation should not spend their energies fighting colonial legacies and an oppressive clerical male system. Instead they must get in touch with the power of the history and struggle of their people in order to articulate a "survival-liberation-centered syncretism" as a new model for doing theology.

In turn, mujerista theology points to the intersection of feminism, Hispanic culture, and women's struggles for survival and liberation as the context of biblical interpretation. Ada Maria Isasi-Diaz argues that the Bible has not played a major role in the popular religiosity of Hispanic women. Rather their religiosity centers on the saints. However, Hispanic women's acculturation to the dominant bibliocentric Anglo-Protestant culture of the United States amid their struggles for survival makes it necessary for them to use the Bible as a weapon to defend themselves. Thus, in such a context, the Bible can no longer be ignored but must be used. "Mujerista theology deals with the specific situation of survival, and in every given situation the Bible should and must be submitted to a Hispanic, feminist, liberative canon. . . . Hispanic women's experience and their struggle for survival, and not the Bible, are the sources for mujerista theology, a liberative praxis."[42]

Fourthly, a feminist theological hermeneutics positioning itself within the Western cultural and religious paradigm of the logic of democracy does not work with the theological notion of a hidden divine reality or truth revealed in canonical texts. Rather, a feminist critical rhetorics of liberation engages the notion of inspiration as the divine breath of life invigorating all and everyone. Both a feminist "canon within the canon" approach and a "hermeneutics of correlation" strategy locate authority formally (if not always materially) in the Bible, thereby obscuring their own processes of finding and selecting theological norms and visions either from the Bible, tradition, doctrine, or contemporary life. In contrast, a critical evaluative hermeneutics, situated in the rhetorical space of the *ekklēsia gynaikōn*, derives its theological authority from the experience of G-d's liberating presence in today's struggles to end patriarchal domination.

Such divine Presence is at work today, for instance, when people realize and acknowledge the oppressive and dehumanizing power of the patriarchal interstructuring of sexism, racism, economic exploitation, and militarist colonialism. Moreover, such a Presence is at work when Christians name these destructive systems theologically as structural sin and heresy. Indeed, we will find many resources for this process of naming, not only in the Bible but in various other religious, cultural, and intellectual traditions. The authority of inspiration is not restricted to a select few but is given to the whole church. All are believed to be enlivened and empowered by the life-giving breath of Sophia-Spirit.

IV.
THE AUTHORITY OF SOPHIA-SPIRIT

Inspiration—the life-giving breath and power of Sophia-Spirit—does not reside in texts: It dwells among people. She did not cease once the process of canonization ended. She is still at work today. Such a theological understanding of the authority of Scripture does not require obedience to and acceptance of biblical texts; rather, it calls for a critical process of discerning the presence of the Spirit in the *ekklēsia* of women: the people of Sophia-G-d who are women. The central theological question of a feminist theological hermeneutics is not the rationalist problem of whether G-d exists, but the rhetorical inquiry as to what kind of G-d Christians believe in and proclaim.

Firstly, the African-American "sisters of the Spirit"[43] of the nineteenth century wrote not only in the North American tradition of the Puritan and black spiritual narrative, but also in the prophetic-mystic tradition of biblical women. Maria Stewart explicitly acknowledges the spiritual legacy of this tradition. Referring to the leading Hebrew, Greek, and Roman women of ancient times, as well as to those of the thirteenth and fifteenth century, she asserts: "The religious spirit which has animated women in all ages . . . has made them, by turns, martyrs, apostles, warriors, and concluded in making them divines and scholars."[44]

Because of their confidence in their privileged relationship with G-d, both the African "sisters of Wisdom" and their medieval European predecessors seized their religious authority for rejecting their societies' gender, class, and race stereotypes. They derived their remarkable sense of authority, self-worth, self-confidence, and power from their spiritual experience. This spiritual self-reliance enabled them to step outside their appointed place in the patriarchal order. Although they were often not literate and only trained as servant-girls, they stood up to ministers and defied excommunication and attacks. Their spiritual autobiographies enact the "logic of democracy":

> None of these women thought of herself as a visionary or social reformer of institutions . . . Nevertheless, through their autobiographies, all three women implicitly identify themselves with an inchoate community of the Spirit that transcends normal social distinctions in the name of a radical egalitarianism. Their life stories bear witness to a framework of values and a view of experience that not only help to describe the guiding "spirit" of that community but also help to bring it into being by exemplifying its ethos in both the subject matter and the style of their writing.[45]

Whereas the Western logic of identity separates reason from emotion, desire, affectivity, passion, and imagination for the sake of impartiality and objectivity, the logic of democracy requires passionate involvement, respect, and recognition of the other, desire for justice, recognition of needs, zest for life, the capacity to relate to others, and especially the vision of a different community of equals. Whereas the logic of identity creates dichotomy and oppositions, the logic of democracy seeks to integrate inside and outside, public and private, politics and religion, reason and imagination.[46]

A critical feminist hermeneutics that articulates itself within the logic of democracy must be grounded in a spirituality of vision and imagination. Any exercise of freedom demands that one be able to imagine a different reality. Throughout the centuries the "sisters of the Spirit" could only proclaim the "gospel of freedom" and challenge ecclesial male leadership because they pursued their vision of a different church. In the authority of the Spirit, they could struggle against racial prejudices, educational and social disadvantages, and overcome gender limitations because they had a vision of a radically different society and world. As Graham Shaw has written, "Without such a critical and creative use of the imagination to transcend the limitations of the actual, there is no possibility of change or freedom. . . ."[47]

A critical interpretation for liberation or a spirituality of vision is not compelled by the modern question of whether G-d exists, as liberation theologians have pointed out. Rather it is moved by the question of what kind of G-d Christians imagine and how they speak about the Divine in a world of alienation, injustice, exploitation, and suffering. Mystical-sapiential theology does not understand G-d as the totally transcendent unmoved mover, the heavenly and almighty patriarch who makes, orders, and controls the world from on high. Rather, as incarnational theology, the spirituality of vision stresses the mutual indwelling of the world in G-d and of G-d in the world; the saving collaboration between Christ and the believer; and the Spirit of G-d, Divine Wisdom, as a living fountain, a festal "dance of blazing love."

The medieval abbess and mystic Hildegard of Bingen, for instance, envisions G-d Sophia as creative power and atmosphere enfolding and quickening in ceaseless motion and dance the world from within. She describes G-d-Sophia-Sapientia-Wisdom as follows:

> O power of Wisdom
> You encompassed the cosmos
> encircling and embracing all
> in one living orbit
> with your three wings:
> one soars on high
> one distills the earth essence
> and the third hovers everywhere.[48]

Yet, spiritual vision becomes illusion when it refuses to be challenged by and confronted with reality. When, for instance, the authority of the Bible is used to inculcate obedience and to avoid confronting the reality of oppression and injustice, biblical interpretation becomes a continuing exercise in illusion.

Secondly, a critical feminist theological hermeneutics of liberation therefore must attempt to reconstruct the traditional spiritual practice of "discerning the spirits" as a deliberative rhetorical practice. Such a spiritual practice must displace the Western totalizing "logic of identity" inscribed in the discussion of biblical authority and unity for the sake of a careful critical interpretation and theological evaluation of particular biblical texts.

As theological subjects, Christian feminists must claim their spiritual authority to assess both the oppressive and the liberating imagination of particular biblical texts. They must do so because of the patriarchal functions of authoritative scriptural claims that demand obedience and acceptance. By deconstructing the totalizing patriarchal rhetorics and politics of subordination, critical feminist discourses can generate new possibilities for the communicative construction of biblical identities and emancipatory practices. The "canon" for such a critical reading and evaluation of biblical texts may be echoed in the Bible, but it cannot be derived from it. The theological criteria which allow us to test out how much biblical texts and symbols perpetrate patriarchy are informed by biblical experiences but not abstracted from them.

Instead, the "canonical standard" for discerning biblical texts and imagination must be articulated in a systemic analysis of reality and confrontation with contemporary struggles to end patriarchal oppression. It is from these struggles that we gain the perspective with which to approach the religious visions of the Bible and to discriminate among its diverse theological tendencies. Whereas the traditional Scripture principle rests on the identity of the divine and androcentric Word, the understanding of the biblical canon as a formative root-model generates a plurality of readings and experiences.

Mae Gwendolyn Henderson's theory for reading black women writers, I suggest, again is helpful for critical discernment and evaluation in biblical interpretation. Such a theory is based on the "simultaneity of discourse," signifying "a mode of reading which examines the ways in which the perspective of race and gender and their interrelationship structure the discourse of black women writers. Such an approach is intended to acknowledge and overcome the limitations imposed by assumptions of internal identity (homogeneity) and the repression of internal differences (heterogeneity) in racial and gendered readings of works by black women writers."[49]

Utilizing Bakhtin's "dialogics of discourse" and Gadamer's "dialectics of conversation," Henderson demonstrates how the dialectics/dialogics (public competitive/familial testimonial discourse) of a black and female subjectivity structure black women's discourse. She chooses "speaking in tongues" as a trope for the "discursive diversity, or simultaneity of discourse." She argues that in the Scriptures there is a link between the gift of *glossolalia* (i.e., the privileged communication between the charismatic and the divine), *heteroglossia* (i.e., speaking in diverse known languages), and *hermeneia* (i.e., the gift of interpreting divine communication):

> I propose, at this juncture, an enabling critical fiction—that it is black women writers who are the modern day apostles, empowered by experience to speak as poets and prophets in many tongues. With this

159

> critical gesture, I also tend to identify a deliberate intervention by
> black women writers into the canonic tradition of sacred/literary
> texts. . . . Might I suggest that if black women writers speak in tongues
> it is we black feminist critics who are charged with the hermeneutical
> task of interpreting tongues.[50]

I would like to use Henderson's interpretive model somewhat differently. The feminist biblical interpreter, I suggest, is also positioned in a rhetorical space defined by the "simultaneity of discourse." As a feminist theological subject she participates in the emancipatory discourses of the *ekklēsia gynaikōn,* of women-church, which seek to establish identity and freedom. As a woman in an oppressive culture, traditional male profession, and patriarchal religion, she participates as citizen/believer, minister/priest, or professor/scholar in the hegemonic discourses of patriarchal church and academy that reinscribe the structures of oppression. In addition, the inscription of such a "simultaneity of discourse" characterizes biblical literature itself and its interpretations. In short, the intervention of feminist theological interpretation into hegemonic biblical discourses is at one and the same time *contestatory,* in disrupting the conventional canonical stories and androcentric biblical discourses, and *re-visionary,* in re-reading and rewriting one's self and one's history.

A cursory re-reading of the story of the Syro-Phoenician woman in Mark 7:24–30 and its interpretations can serve as an example for such a process of critical disruption and re-vision. This story is *theologically* difficult because of the saying of Jesus in verse 27: "Let the children be fed, for it is not right to take the children's bread and throw it to the dogs." As we have seen in the previous chapters, it is likely that this story is pre-Markan and that Mark softened Jesus' saying by adding *proton:* Let the children be fed *first.* Whereas Luke's Gospel does not have this story at all, Matthew changes its theological dynamics in significant ways: He adds the saying, "I was only sent to the lost sheep of Israel," introduces the disciples as those who want to get rid of the woman, deepens Jesus' rejection, and stresses the woman's faith (*megalē sou hē pistis*) rather than her argument and teaching (*dia touton ton logon*).

Two theological emphases are found in the reception history of the Matthean story[51]: One underlines the aspect of salvation history, the other stresses the virtuous example of the woman. The *salvation historical* interpretation utilizes the allegorical method of interpretation. The healing from a distance corresponds with the situation of the pagans, the dogs of verse 26 are analogous to the Gentiles, the children represent Israel, the bread of the children is the gospel, the table is sacred Scripture. Such allegorical interpretations spiritualize and theologize the story in such a way that it can be read in a salvation historical sense. The woman is seen as a proselyte who intercedes for the salvation of the Gentiles, who are saved not through the encounter with the historical Jesus but through his word. Whereas the Jews were the children and the Gentiles were the dogs in the days of Christ, now in the time of the church the opposite is the case: the Jews who have killed the prophets and Jesus have become dogs. Thus the salvation historical interpretation is closely intertwined with an anti-Jewish reading.

While the salvation historical reading is anti-Jewish, the exemplary paraenetic reading seeks to shape Christian identity. This *paraenetic* reading focuses on the paradigmatic behavior of the woman, especially her exemplariness, which is differently understood in different denominational historical contextualizations. Interpretations of the early church, medieval times, and the Catholic Counter-Reformation understand faith as a virtue that is expressed as modesty, perseverance, reverence, prudence, trust, and especially meekness and humility. According to this interpretive strategy, the woman's humbleness comes to the fore, especially in verse 27, where she does not reject Jesus' calling her a dog but accepts it, saying, "Yes Lord." Whereas medieval exegetes ascribed "masculine" virtues to her behavior, modern exegesis stresses that her humble acceptance of grace expresses her "feminine soul." In contrast, the Reformation interpretation stresses the woman's faith rather than her humility, and the story becomes a doctrinal discourse on the topic of faith. Faith consists in the unconditional trust in the Lord, which expresses itself in repeated intercessions and persevering prayer. It consists in the recognition that the self is nothing except for its trust in Jesus, the Lord.

Modern commentators on the story are troubled by the negative statement made by Jesus in verse 26. Exegetes either declare this "Jesus saying" historically unauthentic, or they seek to explain away its religious-ethnic prejudice and exclusivity by resorting to features of the Matthean version or to anti-Jewish or folkloristic considerations. They argue, for instance, that Jesus does not intend to insult the woman but only wants to test her faith; that he rebukes her because he needed his meal and rest; that he was instructing his disciples and not the woman; that he muttered this harsh word under his breath; or even that it was the woman who first mentioned dogs, knowing how Jews regarded her people, so Jesus was merely responding to her word. Others suggest that the saying might have roots in rabbinic oral teachings or reflect a Jewish proverb dictating who eats first in a Jewish household. Others argue that Jesus used the diminutive of "dog" (*kynarion*) in order to soften this widely known Jewish label for Gentiles. All these arguments seek to diminish the prejudicial character of the saying on the lips of Jesus by giving good reasons for Jesus' insulting words. In short, rather than critically assessing and ethically evaluating

161

the patriarchal politics of the text for Christian identity formation, they try to explain away its offensiveness.

In *In Memory of Her* I have argued that because of the title *Kyrios* the historical setting of this story is not the life of Jesus but the Galilean missionary beginnings. I have thus historically contextualized this story in terms of the early Christian argument for the mission to the Gentiles: "The Syro-Phoenician woman whose adroit argument opened up a future of freedom and wholeness for her daughter has also become the historically still visible advocate of such a future for Gentiles. She has become the apostolic "foremother" of all Gentile Christians."[52] In a previous chapter I have shown that such a historical reconstruction is still plausible. Nevertheless, I also need to point out here that such a historical reconstruction should not be misused to justify the prejudicial religious world-construction of the text. That is to say, it should not be used to deflect a critical theological discussion and ethical evaluation of the prejudice and discriminatory stance ascribed to Jesus.

When trying to assess whether this story advocates patriarchal values and visions, feminist students usually disagree. Those who argue that the narrative is not patriarchal point to the fact that the woman is the major protagonist in this pronouncement story, that her argument convinces Jesus, and that her daughter was healed. But at what cost, other students ask. The woman does not challenge the ethnic-religious prejudice of Jesus but confirms it with "Yes Lord." She does not argue for equal access; she begs for crumbs. Thus she accepts second-class citizenship which she herself has internalized. She acts like a dog who is grateful even when kicked. Hence it is not surprising that commentators praise her for her humble submission. This is indeed a sacred text that advocates and reinscribes patriarchal power-relations, anti-Jewish prejudices, and women's feminine identity and submissive behavior.

In a class meeting, when we came to this impasse in the discussion, an African-American Baptist student chided us for not taking seriously the woman's powerlessness and the ironic cast of her words. A Hispanic woman countered that according to Theissen the woman was upper-class, urban, and well-educated. Nevertheless, the first student persisted: Even as a privileged, educated woman she remains a religious outsider, a despised foreigner, and a female who dares to disrupt the discourse of men. If she wants to achieve what she has come for, she needs to "play the game." Readers miss the irony of the story if they do not see that the woman humors the great religious man to get what she wants. The woman from Syro-Phoenicia wins the argument, her daughter is liberated. The stress on the "great faith" of the woman in Matthew's Gospel must not be read as reinscribing patriarchal submissive feminine behavior, but rather

162

in terms of Mark's contestatory discourse. Feminists engaging in biblical interpretation as theological subjects must problematize and reject a "feminine" or anti-Jewish inscription of Christian identity. Instead, we must re-vision Christian faith as a combative, argumentative, and emancipatory praxis that seeks the well-being of all.

Reflecting on our debate, Laurel Schneider, another student, rewrote and re-visioned the story of the woman seeking liberation:

> A feminist biblical re-visioning can embrace this woman, not for her submission to a sadistic faith-test, but for her resilience in the face of violent rejection. That same critique can lift up the truth of her "humiliation." She has been lauded through the centuries by male patriarchal scholars for humbly persisting in her right to "crumbs." The implication is that none of us is worthy of more than crumbs, but the miracle is that the crumbs under the table are sufficient.
>
> A feminist hermeneutic can no longer accept such interpretations as life-giving to women and must denounce the oppression which makes of a crumb on the floor too much to ask, or which makes of a crumb sufficient nourishment in the face of abundance. This is the abiding reminder of the story of the Syro-Phoenician woman. She persisted in the face of overwhelming rejection and was herself made lame in the struggle. In the end, however, she achieved the laying of a new table to which all are invited, under which none must grovel. And by this act, for this teaching, she went her way.[53]

Once again, the challenge is to set liberating praxis against the word that dehumanizes and excludes.

In conclusion: In discussing the story of the Gentile woman whose daughter was possessed I have tried to indicate how a critical process of feminist interpretation for liberation works. However, such a process of critical reading for spiritual discernment can only be liberating if it is accompanied by feminist consciousness-raising and the affirmation of women's authority to rearticulate biblical authority as empowerment and inspiration given for "our"—i.e., women's and all non-persons'—salvation and well-being. Inspiration must not be understood as a reified given in biblical texts but as inherent in the practices of a critical interpretation for liberation. The life-giving breath and creative power of Sophia-Spirit has not ceased with canonization. It still continues to empower women to engage in the struggle for dignity, justice, and liberation.

PRACTICES OF
BIBLICAL INTERPRETATION

P A R T

6

PRISCA –
TEACHER OF WISDOM

The Song of Questions

Mother, asks the clever daughter,
who are our mothers?
Who are our ancestors?
What is our history?
Give us our name. Name our genealogy.

Mother, asks the wicked daughter,
if I learn my history
will I not be angry?
Will I not be bitter as Miriam
who was deprived of her prophecy?

Mother, asks the simple daughter,
if Mirian lies buried in sand,
why must we dig up those bones?
why must we remove her from sun and stone
where she belongs?

The one who knows not how to question
she has no past,
she has no present,
she can have no future
without knowing her mothers,
without knowing her angers,
without knowing her questions.[1]

Feminist Theological Education:

Discourse of Possibility

Like the woman from Syro-Phoenicia who enters the house where Jesus stays and breaks through the cultural "masculine" tendency to separate and isolate, to draw exclusive boundaries, so women have entered the house of theological education and teaching from which we were excluded for centuries. Yet, women's theological silencing and exclusion is only one side of the story. The other side is a "dangerous memory" of women prophets and teachers in the early Christian movements. Both sides of the story must be recalled if women are to find their theological voice today.

The Greek woman outsider who moves into the house in order to engage Jesus, the teacher, in a debate about inside and outside for the sake of her daughter's welfare emerges as a paradigm for the feminist educator in religion. According to Mark 3:31–35, the boundaries are drawn between Jesus' natural family, who are outside the house, and the new kinship community of disciples, which consists of sisters, brothers, and mothers (but not of fathers) who are inside the house gathered around him.[2] In the early Christian movement the house is the place of teaching and instruction in discipleship. In the house-church, public and private space are not yet separated.[3] The sociopolitical location of the early Christian movement is the *ekklēsia* in the house.

Mention of the house-*ekklēsia* calls forth the name of another early Christian teacher of Wisdom: Prisca, as she is called by Paul (1 Cor. 16:19; Rom. 16:4; 2 Tim. 4:19), or Priscilla, the diminutive given to her in Acts 18:2–4, 18.26.[4] Prisca, one of the most eminent missionaries and founders of house-churches, spread the gospel together with Aquila. Like Paul they were Jewish Christians, traveling missionaries who were financially independent of any local church and supported by their trade. Prisca and Aquila were missionary co-workers of Paul but, like Barnabas and Apollos, they did not stand under Paul's authority.

Since Prisca and Aquila are always mentioned together, it is generally assumed that they were married, although nothing is said about their family status in the Pauline tradition. Their patriarchal status as a married couple is only asserted in Acts, probably for apologetic reasons. Both Prisca and Aquila were well-known leaders in the early Christian movement, of which their house-*ekklēsia* in Corinth, Rome, and Ephesus was a center. Their example indicates that the house-*ekklēsia* was fashioned after the organizational form of private associations rather than patterned after patriarchal household structures. Not only Paul but the entire gentile church had reason to give thanks to them.

Acts mentions one important incident in their work but does not elaborate on it. Prisca together with Aquila taught Apollos, one of the great missionaries of the early Christian movement of whom we know very little. Apollos was a cultured Jew from Alexandria, a theologian well versed in the Scriptures, who had been baptized with the baptism of John and knew the teachings of Jesus (Acts 18:24–19:1). After Prisca and Aquila heard him preach they instructed him more "accurately in the way of G-d." According to Acts 19:1–9, John's baptism of repentance did not mediate the Holy Spirit in ecstatic experiences. This context suggests that Priscilla's more accurate teaching could have entailed the gospel about Sophia-Spirit. The content of Priscilla's instruction might have been similar to the christological formula used in 1 Corinthians 1:24, which calls Christ "G-d's Power and Sophia," or that of 1 Corinthians 1:30 referring to baptism: "You however are in Christ Jesus, who has become for us Sophia from G-d."

Priscilla is also the name of one of the Montanist women prophets who were active in the second, third, and fourth centuries.[5] While asleep, "Christ in the form of a female figure" appeared to this prophet, "caused Wisdom to sink into her breast," and gave her a revelation about the future (Epiph. Her. XLIII.1.3; XLVIII.14.1). Since the Montanists' opponents could not refute the movement on doctrinal grounds, they attacked it by slandering it for its prophetic women leaders. According to Origen, "those disciples of women, who choose as their master Priscilla and Maximilla, not Christ" appeal to the succession of women prophets in Scripture to authorize women's leadership. Origen seeks to refute their claim by arguing to the contrary that the biblical women prophets did not speak in public or in the *ekklēsia* but only in private.

The names of other women prophets like Priscilla which have survived in antiheretical patristic records indicate that women were recognized teachers and preachers in many Christian communities. Like the medieval mystics and the African-American "sisters of the Spirit" in the nineteenth century, however, they recorded their spiritual teachings in books, which did not survive. For instance, the books of the Montanists were burned by imperial decree in 398 C.E. Around the same time, Hypatia, a philosopher, scientist, and professor at the university who was not a Christian, was lynched by a Christian mob in the streets of Alexandria (c. 370–415 C.E.).[6] Any discussion of women's theological education must position itself within this still visible although fragmentary tradition of women as teachers, prophets, and intellectuals. It must be faithful to the "dangerous memory" of women who dared to speak and to act in the power of Sophia-Spirit.

In the preceding chapters I have told the story of feminist biblical interpretation in terms of the diverse emerging feminist rhetorical strategies and of a critical historical, theological, and political hermeneutics that understands itself as a rhetoric of liberation. The subtext of this exploration has been feminist theory and theology. Rather than construing feminist biblical interpretation in individualistic spiritual terms, I have sought to theorize and position it within emancipatory feminist struggles to overcome patriarchal silencing and to speak from a public/political site.

In this chapter I will explore the issues facing women who pursue theological education, once an exclusively male domain. Since the institutional location of theological education is that of the male academy, I seek to construct a different feminist discursive space for a pedagogical practice of liberation. When one becomes conscious of women's sociopolitical location as "resident aliens" in theological education, it becomes apparent what is at stake in the theoretical construction of such a discursive position. Feminists who engage in theological education in order to transform the patriarchal discourses of church and academy can do so only if we become qualified residents and remain foreign speakers at one and the same time.

The explosion of women's studies in general, and of feminist studies in religion in particular, has generated theoretical and practical discussions regarding the frameworks, categories, presuppositions, foundations, and methods of academic disciplines which call for a reconceptualization of theological education. Although scholarship claims not to take sides in political struggles, feminist analyses have unmasked its claim to be socially neutral, objective, and value-free and have shown that in reality it expresses the subjective values of an elite male Eurocentric ethos. Feminists have therefore called for an overhaul of educational theory and practice, which would include articulation and analysis of experience, critical thinking, interdisciplinary and transdisciplinary learning, cooperative work and antihierarchical, democratic leadership. Paolo Freire's model of education as conscientization has had a far-reaching impact on the discussions of critical education and feminist pedagogy.[7]

In comparison to the numerous publications on feminist education in general, the literature on feminist theological education, although very significant, is limited. Even though new courses and educational programs have provided models of feminist theological education, these developments have not been discussed and documented in major studies. In addition to the study of the Cornwall Collective, which details feminist alternatives in theological education that were generated during the 1970s,[8] and a collection of essays on feminist courses in religion in colleges,[9] only one major work on feminist theological education has appeared in the past ten years.[10] The Mud Flower Collective discusses issues of difference, race, class, cultural and sexual location, and the possibility of feminist collaboration in theological studies, but it does not explore questions engendered by the institutional location and disciplinary structures of theological/religious studies.[11]

I.
INSTITUTIONAL LOCATION OF
PROFESSIONAL THEOLOGICAL EDUCATION

Postmodern feminist theory has made us conscious that the way we frame our texts and choose our rhetorical strategies involves issues of power which need to be made explicit. Hence, feminist discourses must render visible the historical and institutional structures from within which they speak.[12] The place from which a critical feminist reading of the Bible begins its intervention is not only the women's movement in biblical religion and society. The space from within which it speaks is also the interpretive community of academic and religious institutions that claims to be scientific, value-neutral, and objective.

The number of women studying theology and enrolling in seminaries has increased drastically in the past ten years or so, but no equivalent change in institutional practices has taken place.[13] Consequently, women entering biblical and religious studies still have to adopt the language and discourse of those clerical and academic communities that have silenced us, have excluded us as the "Other" of the Divine, marginalized us as the "Other" of the scientific Man of Reason,[14] and relegated us to the status of social, religious, and intellectual nonpersons.

It is a well-known fact that until very recently women were explicitly barred from theological studies and from seminary education. In this country, for instance, Roman Catholic women could not receive a theological doctorate until the 1960s. In my native country, Germany, which prides itself on its theological *Wissenschaft*, to this day not one Roman Catholic feminist has been appointed as a regular professor on a traditional theological faculty that educates future priests, university teachers, and ministers.[15] This is not an historical accident but the result of ecclesiastical control and patriarchal academic prejudice. If one recognizes the exclusiveness of the clerical academic paradigm, one realizes that women cannot simply be incorporated into this paradigm of theological education by an "add and stir" approach. Rather it becomes imperative to change not only patriarchal institutional structures but also the pedagogical practices of theological education.

As long as the public-political locations and interests of biblical-theological scholarship and education are not recognized, women and other theologically muted persons will continue to encounter great resistance in seminary and church and remain excluded from theological and biblical discourses in the academy. For women to enter into the dominant theological discourses as equals, both the systemic interrelation of theological-biblical knowledge and global oppression must be made clear and the "gendered character" of biblical studies rendered explicit.

The dominant paradigms of theological education must therefore be scrutinized critically for their emancipatory pedagogical aims and for their impact on the formation of critical consciousness. According to Stanley Fish, readers are always constrained by the frame of reference provided by the interpretive community to which they belong.[16] If the dominant interpretive community acts somewhat like a police force, defending against unacceptable interpretations, then it becomes important to reflect on the social institutional location of a critical feminist interpretation for liberation in departments of religion and schools of theology. For whenever liberation discourses are displaced from their social location in emancipatory movements and become integrated into the institutional practices of church or academy, they become subject to the disciplinary pressures and requirements of these interpretive communities.

Like white male students, women and other outsiders who enter theological schools have to undertake a *double agenda* of professionalization: they are to be socialized both into "scientific" theological thinking and into professional training at once. Like male students, women students must undergo a transformation from "lay" person in the religious and educational sense to a theological professional one. Such a transformation requires not only that students become familiar with the methods, literature, and technical procedures of biblical disciplines but also that they transform their intellectual theological frameworks. Students enter biblical studies for the most part either because they highly value the Bible and its history or because as future ministers they have to preach regularly on biblical texts. In any case, their intellectual frame of reference is a theology that accords the Bible intrinsic canonical authority or significant cultural value. Academic biblical scholarship, in contrast, is rooted in the critical questioning of biblical authority. To undertake such a double agenda of professionalization in biblical studies then entails a change of discursive frameworks from a discourse of acceptance of the Bible as a cultural icon, or from a discourse of obedience to it as the word of G-d, to a critical academic discourse that assumes the authority of inquiry and scholarship in challenging the cultural and doctrinal authority of the Bible.

ACADEMIC PROFESSIONALIZATION

Professionalization means for students *first* of all to become socialized into the ethos of biblical studies as a scientific academic discipline. Florence Howe has pointed to the crucial shift in the ethos of college education after the Civil War.[17] For almost 250 years college education in the United States was understood as a "discipline" for the training of elite white men in "religious and moral piety." After the Civil War, the new model for the production of knowledge and higher education became that of German scientific research. This transformation of the curriculum replaced religion with science as a rational philosophy claiming to account for the entire universe and resulted in a galaxy of separate "disciplines" and "departments" that accredit persons for a particular kind of professional work. The unifying ethos of objective method, scientific value-neutrality, and disinterested research in the emerging scientific academy unseated the centrality of the Bible and religion.

Hand in hand with this side-lining of the Bible and religion in college education is the professionalization of academic life and the rise of the technocratic university. The impact of this scientific positivist ethos was felt not only in religion, but in all disciplines within the university. The study of literature was compartmentalized under the headings "philology," "the scientific study of modern languages," and "the historical approach to literature." History as a discipline ostensibly sought to establish "facts" and "data" objectively, free from philosophical considerations or political interests. It was determined to hold strictly to evidence, not to sermonize or to moralize but to tell the simple truth—in short, to narrate things as they really happened.

Despite such claims to professional objectivity, virtually every academic discipline operates on the unexamined assumption of academic discourse that equates male reality with human reality. Intellectual histories and other "canonized" cultural and academic texts have generally assumed that "natural" differences exist between women and men and have defined women and other colonized peoples as rationally inferior, marginal, subsidiary, or derivative. Women and other colonialized intellectuals who have shown leadership and claimed independence have been judged as unnatural, aggressive, and disruptive figures. As Adrienne Rich puts it: "There is no discipline that does not obscure and devalue the history and experience of women as a group."[18] A similar statement could be made about working

173

class, women of color, or colonialized peoples. The recourse to biological determinism and gender differences is still frequent today in scientific debates that seek to defend the androcentric framework of academic disciplines as "objective and scholarly."[19]

This positivist ethos of value-free science also has provided the institutional context for the development of academic biblical studies as "hard" theological sciences. Just as the developing academic disciplines of literature and history sought in the last quarter of the nineteenth century to model themselves on the natural sciences, so also did biblical studies. Since in the United States the rhetoric of biblical studies as "science" was developed in the political context of several heresy trials at the turn of the twentieth century, its rhetoric of disinterested objectivity continues to reject all overt religious, sociopolitical, or theological engagement as unscientific. The aspiration of biblical studies in particular and religious studies in general to "scientific" status within the academy and their claim to universal, unbiased modes of inquiry denies their hermeneutic-theoretical character and "androcentric" optic. It also masks their sociohistorical location, as well as their sociopolitical or ecclesiastical interests.

Ministerial Professionalization

Students who belong to biblical communities of faith are taken up into a *second* agenda of biblical professionalization, which reproduces the conflict between the academic-scientific and the doctrinal-religious paradigm of biblical studies. Especially for students who want to become ministers, priests, or teachers of religion, professionalization entails taking up conflicting subject-positions.

Since historical-critical biblical studies came into being in conflict with the ecclesiastical doctrinal model of biblical interpretation, and since they still struggle against ecclesiastical or neoconservative biblicist interferences, they tenaciously cling to the ethos of scientific objectivity, value-free research, and freedom from all interest in contemporary questions of relevance. While systematic theologians and students of religion vigorously discuss hermeneutics and questions raised by epistemological discussions, critical historical-biblical education often equates "theological" with "apologetic" in order to insist on a value-free, disinterested inquiry about historical data.

This contradiction between the scientific value-neutral ethos of biblical studies and their status as *biblical*, i.e., theological canonical studies, comes to the fore especially in the tension between the commitments of ministerial students and the claims of value-neutral scientific descriptive exegesis. It surfaces as a practical question of how to "apply" the scientific results of historical critical studies to contemporary pastoral practice and preaching. The numerous commentaries on the lectionary, as well as the countless popularizations of biblical scholarship, testify to this discursive contradiction in biblical studies.

At the root of this contradiction is the presumed opposition between objective scientific inquiry and religious-ecclesial commitment. This contradiction has engendered the division of labor between biblical scholars, on the one hand, and ministers/preachers on the other. Disciplined historical-critical scholarship is said to restrict itself to the task of philological, archeological, historical, cultural, and literary analysis. Ministers and church authorities in turn have the task of applying the normative teaching of the text to the contemporary situation, but they are not to interfere in questions of scientific historical-critical scholarship.

Most American graduate departments which train future teachers for colleges and theological schools operate within the ethos of historical-descriptive, value-neutral biblical studies. They train students to analyze biblical texts as historical sources, as information about ancient history, or as literary artifacts. Consequently, future teachers and scholars do not learn to theoretically reflect on their own sociohistorical location and theological interpretive frames and are not trained to articulate their own prejudices and commitments. Since they have not learned in a methodological fashion to scrutinize the implicit frameworks and interests of scholarly, popular, or ecclesiastical interpretations of the Bible, they often approach teaching and theological education without engaging in disciplined ideological reflection. Insofar as professors in biblical studies, who as academic professionals now teach in theological schools, have been trained in graduate departments subscribing to the notion of positivist, disinterested, scientific scholarship, they tend to import their own doctrinal convictions and sociotheological assumptions into their teaching and to declare their selective research as "objective scholarship" that has universal validity. Consequently, their students are left to bridge the gap between biblical interpretation and their own religious self-understanding and political commitments, between the exegetical-historical and the public-religious task of biblical interpretation. The ethos of the discipline does not compel students to ask how theology or biblical interpretation as a discipline is constructed and how scholarship is conditioned by personal experience and social location. Nor does biblical education challenge them to articulate the political functions and ethical implications of dominant scholarship.

In short, the teaching of biblical studies as a given disciplinary field with scientific methods and objective modes of inquiry does not allow for problematizing *how* and *to what end* biblical studies as a scholarly or ministerial inquiry are constructed in certain circumstances and serving particular interests. Consequently, students are exposed, for instance, to the deconstructive impact of historical-literary critical methods but are not taught explicitly how to engage in critical sociotheological deconstruction and reconstruction. I remember, for example, entering theological education with a biblicist understanding that identified biblical texts with G-d's word and took the Gospels to be accurate accounts of what Jesus really taught and did. It took me more than two years and a crisis of faith to move from this biblicist understanding to one that valued the theological freedom to read biblical texts as a human witness to G-d and the ministry of Jesus. Whereas my teachers made us aware of extrinsic doctrinal censure and ecclesiastical pressures, they did not critically lay open for reflection and discussion how we as students and faculty had internalized the doctrinal model. They also did not introduce any critical reflection and evaluation of the methods, assumptions, and ethos of historical-critical studies.

Ministers in turn attempt to bridge this gap in their education either by extending the university model of historical criticism into their pastoral work or, more likely, forgetting what they have learned in seminary and falling back into the psychologizing, literalist or dogmatist mode of biblical interpretation. Since ministers have learned a methodological procedure that consists of value-neutral, descriptive, historical exegesis as a first step, and theological-pastoral application as a second step, which is methodologically not mediated, they are prone to relinquish critical historical and theological inquiry for the sake of ready-made piety. Women and others who have traditionally been excluded from theological education and the articulation of theology are often instinctively critical of this dichotomizing dualism in biblical education and reject it as "whitemale" scholarship. However, in doing so they are in danger of depriving themselves of critical analytic skills, biblical resources, and historical imagination that are essential to a liberation ministry or teaching that could have public significance.

II.
THEOLOGICAL EDUCATION
AS A CRITICAL RHETORICAL PRACTICE

When asked during a lecture tour in Germany why he has frequently addressed the questions of women and anti-Judaism in the New Testament, Krister Stendahl pointed to his concern with what he termed "the Public Health Department in biblical studies." If there were such a "Public Health Department" in biblical studies, scholars more frequently would address questions such as:

176

> What are the theological issues for an interpretation that does not
> produce a harmful fallout, to use the metaphor from atomic power. . . .
> There has never been an evil cause in the world that has not become
> more evil if it has been possible to argue it on biblical grounds. I think
> it is pretty clear that slavery in the western world would have been
> overcome considerably more quickly, had slavery not been part of the
> landscape in the Holy Book.[20]

Although dominant biblical scholarship has never followed up on this
suggestion and explicitly theorized such a "Public Health Department" in
biblical studies, liberation theologies of all colors have addressed this question. They have maintained that the goal of biblical interpretation is not
only explanation and understanding but ultimately a new and different
praxis.[21] As Gustavo Gutierrez has pointed out, the point of departure for
liberation theologies is not the question of the modern *nonbeliever*, the
question of faith and reason, but the struggle of the *nonperson* for justice,
liberation, salvation, and well-being. The basic methodological starting
point of all liberation theologies is the insight that all theological discursive
practices—knowingly or not—are by definition engaged for or against the
oppressed. Intellectual neutrality and value-free objectivity are not possible
in a world with a history of exploitation and oppression.

Hence, the discourses of liberation theology challenge theologians, ministers, and the entire Christian community to articulate their theological
assumptions, commitments, and interests in relation to the liberation
struggle of those who suffer from patriarchal—i.e., racist, sexist, colonial,
economic, militarist, and ecological—exploitation. To minimize its co-optation in the interest of Western patriarchy, a critical feminist biblical
interpretation, I have argued in the preceding chapters, must reconceptualize its act of critical reading as a moment in the global praxis for liberation.
In order to do so, it needs to de-center the dogmatic authority of the
androcentric biblical text, to deconstruct the politics of otherness inscribed
in it, and to consciously take control of its own readings before it can
retrieve biblical visions and possibilities for liberation.

Such a critical self-understanding and commitment, I have argued, requires a rhetorical approach to biblical studies and education.[22] In the past
years, I have begun to develop a model for critical theological reflection in
biblical studies that seeks to address the problem of the relationship between scientific inquiry and public responsibility, as well as ministerial
commitment, in terms of a feminist theology of liberation. Any retrieval,
reconstruction, and construction of Christian identity is implicated in sociopolitical and religious systems of domination. Theological inquiry must
therefore begin with a radical hermeneutics of suspicion and apply it to

177

biblical texts and theologies, as well as to the whole of Christian history and theology.

A hermeneutics of suspicion must begin with the deconstruction of the historical "master" paradigm of Christian-Western society and culture. Before it can move toward the reconstruction of Christian identity in concrete historical-political situations, such a deconstruction of dominant biblical discourses must be attentive to the traditional patterns of domination and subjugation in society, church, and academy. These patterns of exclusion and domination must first become the object of critical reflection and theological analysis before we can reconstruct "the heritage that shapes our identity." If self and identity "are always grasped and understood within particular discursive configurations, then consciousness is never fixed, never attained once and for all, because discursive boundaries change with historical conditions."[23]

A reconceptualization of biblical education in rhetorical-democratic terms therefore requires a different construction of the discipline of biblical studies and its professional ethos. Not only the immanent discourse of biblical scholarship but also the discourses of biblical education must be laid open for critical scrutiny in such a way that all students can participate in their own professional education as speaking subjects. Exploring with students the theoretical assumptions and conceptual constructs of "scientific" exegesis or theological interpretive frameworks can help to overcome professional self-alienation and foster theological creativity.

Moreover, it can enable students to engage with biblical historical and literary criticism as one important but historically and culturally conditioned approach in biblical interpretation. Pedagogical reflection must subject to disciplined scrutiny the origin of scientific biblical criticism within modern Eurocentric struggles of Enlightenment scholarship against dogmatist patriarchal church control. In doing so, it can displace students' fundamentalist and literalist identity formations by showing that it is not primarily a religious but a cultural patriarchal identity formation that is at stake here. At the same time, a critical pedagogy can appreciate biblical interpretations which have been developed in sociocultural locations different from those of white elite church- or university-men. Introductions to the study of the Bible would then focus not just on the development of scientific biblical criticism but also on approaches in biblical interpretation that have been developed in oppressed communities such as the Black Church or in emancipatory struggles. Finally, by analyzing the function of the Bible and biblical interpretation in political discourses of oppression, such a particularization of "scientific" introductory courses to biblical studies could make visible the collusion of biblical scholarship and preaching in sustaining an antidemocratic or colonialist mind-set and public ethos.

In such a critical theological model of education, students begin with the exploration of their own experience,[24] commitments, and questions, as well as with a critical analysis of their theological presuppositions and frameworks. They learn to analyze the theological interests of contemporary biblical interpretations as well as of biblical writers in order to discuss the sociopolitical implications of biblical texts and their interpretations. They not only acquire exegetical skills and study methods of literary analysis and historical reconstruction, but also discuss criteria for evaluating biblical texts for proclamation and use historical imagination to "re-vision" biblical texts and their worlds. Students explore the methodological approaches of the discipline as ways of asking critical questions rather than as just a cadre of technical skills. They discover modes of critical analysis for articulating their own interpretation rather than simply accepting and repeating the exegetical results of the masters in the field.

In short, I argue that theology, and theological education itself, is to be constructed as a transformative discursive practice which must position itself within the public space created by the logic of democracy. Biblical education must conceive of its discourses in terms of "a public health inspection." It must critically reflect on the concrete historical-political configurations and theological practices of Christian communities—both in the past and in the present—which have engendered the exclusion and dehumanization of "the Other" of freeborn, educated, and propertied men in Western society. At the same time it must seek to articulate alternative communal visions and democratic values. Such a conception of theology entails first and foremost a critical reflection on the sociocultural-political practices in which religious communities have been and are embedded and to which they contribute. Theological education for critical consciousness and transformative re-visioning of public sociopolitical and religious-ecclesial practices would be of interest not only to future ministers and theological educators but also to Christians who seek to shape public opinion and policy. The Bible has often legitimated (and still does today) the dehumanizing ideas and oppressive structures of Euro-American societies and cultures. Nevertheless, it has also transmitted theological visions and values of human dignity, community, and well-being that have fueled movements for freedom and justice throughout Christian history. It is this double legacy that compels us to work to transform biblical-theological education into an education for critical consciousness and commitment to justice.

Such a critical democratic model of theological education has difficulty taking root within the patriarchal discourses of the academy or in those of church institutions. At present, this model is developed in educational institutions and settings in the interstices between these two master-discourses. Openness to a democratic model of theological education is found most often within institutions oriented toward adult theological education and practiced at conferences and workshops on continuing education for ministry. It flourishes in base communities and feminist bible study groups. Such a positioning "in between" allows a democratic model of biblical education for liberation to challenge both the scientific-positivist as well as the religious-dogmatist paradigm of biblical-theological education.

Yet a critical refashioning of biblical studies in a democratic key is doomed to fail if it does not acknowledge the particular social location and perspective of women and other nonpersons who have been excluded from patriarchal democracy. The questions and problems that arise when women seek to become subjects of biblical interpretation and theology are not only engendered by the contradictory location of biblical studies in church and academy.[25] They also arise because of the contradiction inherent in being a feminist biblical teacher or student in a setting that traditionally has not only left out but actively excluded women and other nonpersons from becoming subjects of theology and biblical interpretation.

III.
WOMEN'S PROFESSIONAL THEOLOGICAL
EDUCATION: PATRIARCHAL SOCIALIZATION

Women and other theologically muted groups entering the theological professions have to change not only from a "lay" to a professional *persona* but also from a feminine supportive, marginal, silent, private *persona* to a masculine assertive, central, speaking, public one. Women entering the discipline enter into an immanent discourse between masters and students, fathers and sons, and opposing male schools of interpretations. They have to confront not only masculine doctrinal authority but also public authority in the university and church which for centuries was held by Western elite men. According to traditional scriptural (cf. 1 Tim. 2:12) and cultural norms, women are not to speak in public or to wield authority over men. Rule-making and speaking with authority in matters of religious or social importance is properly the domain of men. Women may contribute to knowledge in various secondary roles but the final authoritative word belongs to men. This ancient norm has been enforced through the centuries by the promulgation of scorn for women who challenge the norm and of praise for those who uphold it.[26]

To become speaking theological subjects, women students must "master" the clerical and academic discourses of the fathers which have been fashioned to exclude women. For, in Kuhn's terms,[27] to become a member of the community of scholars, students have to internalize the entire constellation of beliefs, values, techniques, shared worldviews, and systems of knowledge as maps or guidelines for thinking and speaking in a "scholarly" way. In the course of this socialization process, women students experience systemic contradictions which they often internalize as personal failure. If they "master" these conflicts by subordinating their own social or religious experiences to the ethos of their discipline they will finally speak and think in the professional idiom.

The process of acquiring the "insider's" language and public persona can be likened to the process of socialization into an alien culture. This process of becoming a Harvard, Princeton, or Yale "Man" is even more alienating for those women students and faculty who do not share at all the racial, social, cultural, or religious background of the elite white men who have shaped the academic disciplines and still do so. Black students, for instance, encounter much less of a fit between their own cultural languages and experiences and those of the theological disciplines.[28] Students of a different class background also experience acute self-alienation:

> My parents were immigrants and I retain to this day the immigrant's faith in education. But when I went to school, I travelled a greater distance from my home than anyone knew. I felt myself moving between two languages in each of which my other life was secret. In the public codes of the school I entered the secrets of literature and art and music. In the private codes of home I kept the secrets of my family's difference from the middle-class teachers and kids I spent the day with. . . . I struggled with the discomfort of those who feel out of place in the places they have taken. And things were no more comfortable at home. I had secrets and these were the secrets of my own inferiority, my own pretence of being a native speaker anywhere. . . . This is the hidden injury of class. . . . It is also the hidden injury of sex. For an educated woman speaker/reader travels far from her body. . . . The secret of femaleness is the secret of her inferiority. And yet, I still believe it better to speak than to be silent.[29]

Realizing that the educational process of theological professionalization amounts to socialization into an elite male Eurocentric *persona* makes it even more pressing to ask: How can theological education and its intellectual discourses be transformed in such a way that women and others who have been excluded from scholarly discourse and theological education can become speaking subjects and agents for its systemic change? Given the long history of patriarchal silencing of women in church and academy, it remains very difficult even for feminists to understand ourselves as speaking, theory-producing subjects in theological schools and to occupy resistant subject-positions in the dominant discourses of the discipline.

Women who enter theological schools for professional education have to decide between three options: The *first* is to embrace the discourses, traditions, or worldviews of the "male" academy and clergy, which have silenced and objectified us *as women*. Women who wish to be accepted as "honorary men" in biblical scholarship often do not want to question but rather to "master" theological discourses even better than men do. Their "theological masters" and professional guides are the "great men" in the field, and they often resent women faculty and students who question the patriarchal academic system on feminist terms. These students, among them white middle-class women especially, are often too happy to become "good daughters" of their theological or spiritual "fathers" in order to participate in the scholarly discourses of "the fathers." They conform to traditional norms of being a "good girl" or "good wife" who must not be too aggressive and self-assertive but must provide emotional and intellectual support by silently doing "shadow work" for the "great men" in their lives.[30]

Women adopting traditional patriarchal intellectual discourses and a scholarly masculine public *persona* tend to become positivist scientists when it comes to biblical scholarship or to function as ministerial deputies of ecclesiastical authority upholding biblical orthodoxy. By becoming honorary academic or clergymen, by speaking the language of our academic or spiritual Fathers without a foreign accent, women students and faculty tend to fall victim to the "marriage" or "romance plot,"[31] which limits their sense of what they as women can be and prohibits them from acquiring a "new identity," an identity which could transcend the limitations set by the old norms of femininity. They thereby risk not finding their own "diction" and muting their theological voices and religious creativity. Such a "melting pot" approach also forecloses any possibility of changing the kyriocentric knowledge and androcentric "optic" produced by academic and ecclesiastical discourses.

The *second* option for feminist students and faculty is to reject or disdain intellectual work, academic scholarship, and biblical religions because they represent elite white male discourses that undermine women's self-affirmation and self-determination. But to indict disciplined research, abstract theory, or intellectual exploration as "male/masculine" means to reinscribe the cultural stereotypes of men as rational thinkers and women as emotional and intuitive relaters. To claim, for instance, that a book with detailed bibliographic notes is "masculine" employs feminist rhetoric to invalidate and genderize research procedures which document that intellectual work is neither done in a vacuum nor simply the result of individual brilliance.

Rather than completely rejecting all academic discourses, some may simply express disdain for professional education as being caught up with the acquisition of external credentials. In this view, one who is dedicated to the "life of the mind" must remain oblivious to the politics of knowledge within the discipline, uninterested in shaping a career in a chosen field, or impervious to fighting for one's professional advancement. Being dedicated to the "life of the mind" often engenders a distaste for selecting courses or dissertation topics pragmatically. This is the case because women intellectuals tend to conceptualize the discovery of the "life of the mind" in terms of the cultural "romantic plot."

The very process which draws women into the realm of ideas is often construed as "falling in love" with one's chosen area and subject matter, as work pursued out of love; a book may be seen as a "love child," and written work understood as a virtual extension of the self. Critical evaluation and feedback on one's work is therefore often taken as a personal rejection and as a threat to one's self-esteem. The lure of teaching for women is the desire to achieve individual satisfaction rather than to bring about sociopolitical change in academic or ministerial institutions. Many women faculty are uneasy, for instance, with the authoritative lecture style because they are not so much interested in communicating a body of knowledge as in achieving personal interaction.[32]

This second option, whether it expresses itself in the total rejection of patriarchal academic institutions or in the refusal of women "to play the professional game," deprives feminists not only of the possibility of speaking differently in academy and church but also of the opportunity to acquire the intellectual tools, practical skills, and institutional standing that would allow us to produce a "different" knowledge of the world, to make our own theological voices heard, and to change the institutions of religious studies and theology in the interest of women and all other nonpersons. For, to variegate Audre Lorde's dictum, the master's tools will dismantle the master's house if we use them skillfully to analyze its architectonic frame and to build our own house, instead of executing the master's blueprints.

A *third* option therefore strives for intellectual bilingualism which speaks with a "foreign accent." If elite European-American women have been the cultural and religious channels that have mediated discourses of Western patriarchal domination, then we must resist "the race for theory"—to borrow a warning of Barbara Christian's[33]—that seeks to prove that we are the "real daughters" of our "theoretical fathers." This is necessary because an uncritical reproduction of our "father's tongue" places us in competition with our feminist academic sisters and does not allow us to respect the intellectual work and tradition of our feminist "theological mothers."[34] In order to enable a practice of resistance and "disloyalty" to patriarchal authority, feminist theory and theology must always remain a second-order reflection on feminist struggles for liberation as well as remain accountable to them.

Feminist biblical interpretation risks partial "collaboration" with the patriarchal academy and biblical religions in order to change and transform them. The strategic adoption of literalist biblical arguments and appeals to scriptural authority, for instance, are sometimes necessary to persuade a fundamentalist theological audience. Similarly, women's studies in religion are often forced to engage in a calculated compromise in order to establish their discourses as academic discourses, since academic standards of excellence have been formulated by elite Euro-American men. Such a partial collusion is often necessary not only for academic women to be heard but also to survive professionally. In a similar fashion, ordained women may sometimes have to engage in ecclesiastical patriarchal forms of discourse during their ministry.

However, one must remain acutely aware that such partial collusion is a pragmatic strategy for survival if it is not to lead to an unproblematic co-optation and willing collaboration with patriarchal ecclesiastical or academic communities of interpretation that have silenced, marginalized, and excluded women from their public discourses—and often still do. Such a practice of partial collusion must therefore be ethically justified as a strategy either to survive or to subvert patriarchal knowledge-systems. Without such practices of resistance and strategic collaboration, gender, feminist, or women's studies in religion simply reproduce knowledge about woman within the patriarchal discursive frame of either academy or church.

This third option of intellectual bilingualism compels us to explore the contradictory subject-position of the feminist scholar in religion. As women marked by race, class, and culture we belong to an exploited, marginalized, and silenced group, though as religious scholars we share in the educational privileges of the white male academic elite. This contradictory subject-position of feminist liberation scholars[35] in religion, however, provides not just occasions for co-optation but also a rich source of inspiration, energy, and creativity for doing our theological work.

If the major problem in theological education is not the tension between acquiring academic content and acquiring professional skills but the theological-intellectual and spiritual-professional colonization of women, then theological education can not be re-visioned by emphasizing preparation for pastoral church leadership. Rather, the development of a feminist biblical pedagogy must focus on women as speaking subjects and agents of theological education and acknowledge the public-social functions of such positioning.

Although critical feminist liberation theologians speak from within the disciplinary discourses of academy and church, we do so as the socio-political location of *resident aliens*, as both insider and outsider: insider by virtue of residence or patriarchal affiliation to a male citizen or institution; outsider in terms of language, experience, culture, and history. I propose therefore that the metaphor of resident alien is an apt figure also for a feminist movement and politics of liberation within the academy and church. Like the Syro-Phoenician, feminists enter the house of biblical scholarship or ministry as theological, cultural, and religious aliens. Those of us who have made biblical scholarship and ministry our place of residence must not forget that we are strangers in a land whose language, constitution, history, religion, and culture we did not create.

The metaphor of resident alien is fitting for the socio-political position from which a critical feminist theological education for liberation can speak. If the "White Lady" has been the civilizing channel and feminine "glue" in Western patriarchal domination, then white women as fairly recent "immigrants" in academy and ministry must resist the pressures to function as prized tokens who are "loyal to civilization." We must refuse to produce or teach biblical-theological knowledge that legitimates intellectual and religious discourses which vilify women.

If theological education is not to perpetuate women's religious self-alienation and theological silencing in biblical religions and Western culture, it must find pedagogical approaches that enable women to critically analyze and explore their own experience and social location. Feminist theological education therefore must be first of all a process of "conscientization," or education to critical consciousness. The skills of critical historical or literary analysis learned in biblical studies can also be used to engender critical reflection on experience and a systemic analysis of it.

Many women in theological schools seek to bring to the theological or exegetical discourses their own experiences and problems. An increasing number of women students and faculty insist on asking their own questions in terms of a hermeneutics of suspicion, on articulating their own historical and systematic reconstructions, and on claiming their own experiential, theological, and ecclesial authority. If they are not heard and their questions are not addressed as legitimate theological or interpretational problems, many students become alienated. Such alienation and frustration engenders anti-intellectual sentiment among many women in theological schools and deprives them of knowledge and intellectual power for change. If, however, women have become conscientized and are introduced to biblical theological studies as a critical process of reflection and reconstruction, they are apt to read biblical texts in a new way. They are able to re-vision biblical history as their own story and to theologically assess biblical texts and interpretations in terms of their oppressive or emancipatory functions in the past, present, and future.

IV.
A FEMINIST PEDAGOGY FOR THE *EKKLĒSIA*: RESISTANCES AND POSSIBILITIES

Feminists entering theological schools encounter various patriarchal structures that obstruct our quest for an educational environment in which our questions and values would be taken seriously. Such institutional resistances to the feminist transformation of theological education are many. I would like to single out for discussion here first the prevalent pedagogical approaches, then the procedures of validation, and, finally, the styles of reasoning that seek to maintain the dominant structures of patriarchal socialization. These pedagogical approaches, styles of reasoning, and validation procedures are determined by notions of authority as power that works from the top down and requires compliance. They are also determined by procedures for producing and validating knowledge which have been formulated by the Eurocentric Man of Reason.

PREVALENT PEDAGOGICAL APPROACHES

As far as I can see, the following four pedagogical models of theological education can be distinguished: The *first* model represents the traditional sermonic "deposit" approach of the patriarchal university, which Paulo Freire has termed the "banking" model of education. In this model the teacher "deposits" a body of knowledge for which students are passive receptacles. The teacher is the authority who "owns" the knowledge that students receive and "store" in their memory. The basic means of communication is the uninterrupted lecture. Students are successful in examinations when they can repeat the knowledge handed down by the professor. Fixed curricula or required reading lists ensure that students acquire all the knowledge deemed necessary for a competent professional in the discipline.

The *second* approach in theological education is the Socratic master-disciple, or the expert-apprentice model. In this educational model the teacher is the "master," who still knows all the answers to questions and controls the exegetical methods for solving interpretive problems. This model is more oriented to personal interaction between professor and students in specialized seminars, but it is the teacher who sets the terms of the interaction. The goal is not so much to communicate a body of knowledge as to establish "schools of interpretation," to train students in a certain way of reasoning and in reproducing the methods and skills deemed necessary to become an expert in the field.

The *third* pedagogical approach could be labeled the consumer or "smorgasbord" model of theological education. Because of the realization that it is impossible to communicate the body of encyclopedic theological knowledge in the short time that students can afford financially to enroll in theological schools, this model has almost completely replaced the curricular goals of the first model. In this model, students are seen as "consumers" who begin the school year with "a shopping period" for interesting courses and end it with a "consumer evaluation" of the product, i.e., course they purchased. In this model the teacher is construed as a "salesperson" and the students as consumers buying whatever catches their fancy. Although this model ascribes decisive agency to graduate-level students, it construes them as "consumers," in contrast to the first and second models which construe them as apprentices and future experts. This approach works in close cooperation with the *fourth* model in theological schools, which adopts a therapeutic-individualistic approach to education. Through a personalized "advising" system this pedagogical model seeks to help student-"consumers" find the right courses in the disturbing array of offerings and to "make them feel good" about their choices. Like the third model it also construes theological education in terms of individual satisfaction, individualist spirituality and personal edification. Like religion, theological education has become a "private" affair.

Whereas the first two "professional" educational approaches emphasize the agency of faculty to the detriment of that of students, the last two seem to accord students participatory agency but do so by construing them as individual buyers who purchase religious knowledge for their private consumption. At the same time, they obfuscate the fact that students have no share in the active production of knowledge. All four models function within a patriarchal-capitalist paradigm of theological education that codes the first two approaches as culturally "masculine" and the last two as resembling culturally "feminine" strategies. It seems therefore hardly accidental that the last two pedagogical models have gained considerable ground as women and other nonpersons have entered theological education in significant numbers.

Feminist studies have therefore sought to develop a different pedagogical model, one that does not reinforce the kyriarchal patterns of knowledge but seeks a democratic mode of constructing and communicating knowledge. Such a democratic feminist paradigm might develop a model of theological education that is problem-oriented, critical, constructive, collaborative, and dialogical. It uses available forms of communication such as lectures, group work, skills training, or discussion; forms of assessment such as grading, individual feedback, or interactive evaluation, and requirements such as papers, projects, exams, and journals for the sake of fostering critical consciousness and an alternative imagination.

Such a radical democratic feminist paradigm seeks to enable students and faculty to find their own theological voices by developing discourses of critique, empowerment, and possibility. It seeks to engage "in the complex process of redefining knowledge by making women's experience a primary subject for knowledge, conceptualizing women as active agents in the creation of knowledge, including women's perspective on knowledge, looking at gender [race, class, imperialism] as fundamental to the articulation of knowledge in Western thought and seeing women's and men's experience in relation [not only to the] sex/gender system"[36] but also to the complex multiplicative system of patriarchal dominations.

Most important, in order to speak with a different accent and inflection, feminist theological education must reimagine the "habits of thought" and argument that structure knowledge and imagination. It can only do so, however, if it can unmask and debunk the errors that are basic to the dominant tradition. According to Elizabeth Kamarck Minnich such errors are:

1. Faulty universalization or generalization, in which a particular select group or kind of people, such as elite Euro-American white propertied men, is deemed significant and taken to represent and set the standard of what it means to be human or to be scientific for all. All "Others" are made invisible, excluded, or subordinated.

2. Circular reasoning takes standards formulated by a particular group and declares them to be universal, so that all other groups have to conform to them. For instance, elite white male scholarship is declared as scholarship par excellence and therefore scholarship that does not follow the standards of this particular definition of scholarship is declared invalid.

3. Mystified concepts result in part from the first two errors. Such concepts are so deeply embedded in the cultural consciousness that they are rarely questioned although they have been formulated in the interest of a particular ruling group. For instance, academic excellence articulated by a certain group of men is taken as an objective, universal, disinterested standard and used to exclude others who do not serve the interests of a particular group.

4. Partial knowledge results from "posing and resolving questions within a tradition in which thinking is persistently shaped and expressed by the first three errors."[37]

PROCEDURES OF VALIDATION

Such a different feminist pedagogical model conflicts with the dominant professional model of theological education by which students become credentialed as professional academicians or ministers. In order to be acknowledged either as professional theologians or ministers, feminists must undergo a credentializing process attesting that they have acquired theological knowledge and exegetical or pastoral expertise. Experientially based pedagogical practices, as well as feminist claims to a different theological knowledge and process of biblical interpretation, must subject themselves to malestream validation procedures. As Patricia Hill Collins observes:

> Institutions, paradigms, and other elements of the knowledge validation procedure controlled by elite white men constitute the Eurocentric masculinist knowledge validation process. The purpose of this process is to represent a white male standpoint. Although it reflects powerful white male interest, various dimensions of the process are not necessarily managed by white men themselves.[38]

Although feminist scholars can produce knowledge claims that contest those of dominant biblical scholarship, malestream scholarship does not accept these competing theological knowledge claims, which are based on a different procedure of validation. Rather, the malestream academy declares them marginal, anomalous, or ideological and insists that women students as well as faculty be measured by the prevailing standards of excellence. Women seeking ordination face the same dilemma with respect to religious-pastoral knowledge claims. Students being tested on their knowledge of biblical interpretation, for instance, will be certified if they know the "whitemale" Euro-American tradition of biblical interpretation. Their knowledge of African-American or feminist biblical interpretation does not count. Conversely, students who have no knowledge of either African-American, Hispanic, or feminist biblical interpretation will be certified as competent. In a similar fashion, the scholarly work of feminist faculty will not be accorded the same professional acclaim as that of faculty that remains within the malestream Eurocentric tradition. Pioneering work of black feminists will be put down as "unscientific," whereas mediocre research that fine-tunes established interpretive approaches will be acclaimed and receive prestigious awards.

As long as only knowledge articulated from an elite white male Eurocentric standpoint is seen as scientific, universal, and objective, theological knowledge, like knowledge in other fields, will serve to maintain the dominant kyriarchal power relations in society and church. As long as academic discourse does not explicitly identify hegemonic biblical scholarship as "elite white male" and only qualifies alternative scholarship with "feminist, womanist, Asian, or African," it holds up elite white Eurocentric male knowledge as scholarship per se. Other knowledges in turn are "relegated to subcategories, or if brought into the 'mainstream' category, are improperly judged because they are placed against standards, closed within contexts and discourses, that not only did not include them in the first place but were founded by people who thought they ought to be excluded."[39]

STYLES OF REASONING

Feminists seeking to change biblical studies and theological education must not only problematize and challenge malestream standards of scientific and professional validation as partial, biased, and formulated in the interests of one particular group; they also must question dominant modes of reasoning and knowledge production in the Eurocentric malestream paradigm of knowledge that separates reason from the emotions to produce detached impartial knowledge. The more a scholar keeps a distance from her subject matter, remaining detached from the issues it raises, the more her knowledge is said to be objective and scientific.

The classic articulation of this ethos stems from Max Weber, who has decisively influenced the scientific posture of value neutrality. In a famous speech before students in 1909, Weber argued that university professors must restrict themselves to imparting objective and scientific information. Empirical statements must be distinguished from value judgments, since both rely on different forms of methodological validation. Empirical scientific knowledge relies on conditional judgments—if one does this one will achieve this goal. *Why* one would want to achieve this goal, in the second place, is a question of value judgments that cohere with a certain ethical system. In Weber's view, professors should only teach knowledge of the first kind in order not to proselytize by virtue of their authority for a certain value system.[40]

According to this value-free scientific ethos of the Man of Reason, whose particular perspective has been taken to be universal, value judgments are locked into a scale of descending worth or belong to a private, individualistic, religious, and totally relative area of reasoning. Consequently, students are taught that the values they hold are either totally right or totally wrong. Since students have not been taught how to reflect together and deliberate with each other about the values they consider most important, they tend to retreat either into doctrinal absolutism or liberal relativism. Yet, as Elizabeth Kamarck Minnich points out, "both absolutism and radical relativism make it possible, even necessary, to avoid serious engagement with differences understood from the beginning as being in transactional relation to each other."[41]

Whereas the ethos of value-free scientific pedagogy is articulated within the value system of patriarchal authority and students must silently absorb the materials on which the professor lectures, feminist pedagogical theory seeks to fashion an ethos of learning that does not undermine democratic thinking. Instead, it seeks to support and strengthen democratic modes of reasoning by recognizing the importance of experience, plural voices, emotions, and values in education. In a fascinating article on "The Education of Women as Philosophers," Elizabeth Young-Bruehl has argued that for women to become intellectuals they need to question both "the mental monism of the Enlightenment and the mental pluralism of the Enlightenment with its monistic evolutionary bias" in order to replace them with a conversational construct of mental processes; "We are not solitary, when we think. We are full of voices."[42] Since mental monism and the legitimation of patriarchal domination have mutually reinforced each other, it is important to conceptualize the notion of mental conversation and contestation in sociopolitical terms as a radically democratic and antiauthoritarian process. Young-Bruehl states, "The image of our minds as conversations is, I think, crucial to progressivism in political theory: it implies that mental and political democracies can be mutually supporting, in accord with the traditional constructing technique but not in accord with the traditional constructions."[43]

However, Page duBois has warned that the traditional modes of inquiry, for instance in seminar discussions or academic conferences, share in the kyriarchal mode of reasoning, which is competitive and combative. Its preferred mode of ascertaining truth is adversarial debate and the honing of arguments that can withstand the most acerbic assault. Hence, this form of reasoning and argument can be likened to forensic interrogation, to methods of arrest and discipline, to an understanding of logic and dialectic as police arts, to "a dividing, a splitting, a fracturing of the logical body, a process that resembles torture."[44] According to her, the Platonic dialogue locates truth in the mind of the master who controls the questions and answers. The search for truth requires hard labor; it must be hunted down, or coerced through persistent questioning.

Speaking from the subject-position of the resident alien, feminist teachers and students must confront this ethos, as well as its dominant modes of theological argument and pedagogy. As long as women and other nonpersons are forced to acquire theological knowledge and methodological skills within the kyriarchal framework of theological education in order to become "bona fide" residents in theology and religious studies, one of the major tasks of a feminist pedagogy is to make the mechanisms and implications of this mode of knowledge production explicit. Women and other theologically muted persons must learn to demystify the dominant structures of knowledge in order to find their own theological voices and to achieve intellectual satisfaction in their work.

Yet they will only be able to achieve these educational goals if they engage in the transformation of the present kyriarchal paradigm of knowledge into a *different* co-intentional,[45] radical democratic[46] paradigm of theological education that allows faculty and students to collaborate in creating as well as communicating the contents and methods of knowledge. In such a political paradigm of theological education, situated in the *ekklē-sia* of women, both teachers and students acknowledge that knowledge is power. They construe power, however, not in patriarchal terms, as control over, but in democratic terms, as energy that empowers and invigorates life. Whereas feminist pedagogy was long plagued by the ideal of collective "leaderless" educational interaction, it has moved to recognize enabling authority and to articulate a democratic understanding of power and alternating leadership.[47]

An Italian feminist group in Milan, for instance, has articulated the concept of the "symbolic mother," a concept which recognizes that power differentials exist between women on grounds of experience, expertise, age, etc. They argue that feminist freedom is not to be construed in libertarian terms as freedom from all constraint, but that it entails a personal and social debt. Whereas women owe nothing to men, women owe their freedom to other women. Each woman's symbolic debt to other women is figured in the concept of the "symbolic mother." This concept, as Teresa de Lauretis writes, extends the mother-daughter relationship "beyond the confines of the 'natural' and the 'domestic' to enable an alliance, a social contract between them. Without that social contract and the structure of symbolic mediation that supports it, no freedom or self-determination exists for women."[48] Yet, rather than place this articulation of the "symbolic mother" into the gender-framework of an originary female difference, I suggest it should be positioned within the struggles of women and other marginalized people for freedom and autonomy.

Following Paula Gunn Allen I would therefore prefer to situate such a symbolic mediation within the democratic tradition of the "symbolic women of wisdom and of valor," which she characterizes as the "grandmother's tradition."

> The root of oppression is loss of memory. . . . The vision that impels
> feminists to action is the vision of the Grandmothers' society, the
> society that was captured in the words of the sixteenth-century ex-
> plorer Peter Martyr nearly five hundred years ago. It is the same
> vision repeated over and over by radical thinkers of Europe and
> America. . . . That vision, as Martyr told it, is of a country where
> there are "no soldiers, no gendarmes or police, no nobles, kings, re-
> gents, prefects, or judges, no prisons, no lawsuits. . . . All are equal
> and free . . . "[49]

Within such a democratic "tradition of the grandmothers," students can
engage biblical texts within the framework of a dialogic-democratic model
of biblical education. Such a model can integrate experience and imagination, reason and emotion, thinking and feeling, valuation and vision, as
well as critical inquiry, scientific accuracy, intellectual clarity, and responsible persuasion in the process of interpretation. In the following critical
reflection Diana Scholl displays such a different style of engagement as she
reflects on her attempt to reimagine Elizabeth, whose story is told in Luke
1:5–80:

> This was an immensely powerful experience of writing for me. In
> writing I found what I wanted to say was only the beginning of what
> needed saying. . . . I had spent many hours working with the text,
> researching its historical context and retracing the theological interests
> of Luke. Not to mention those of modern commentators. I applied all
> my critical, analytical skills to try to liberate Elizabeth who was so
> deeply embedded and ensnared in the text. I spent time feeling angry
> and frustrated and depressed. Here was yet another biblical woman so
> (hopelessly?) absorbed by the androcentric and patriarchal structures
> of her society, religion and history that I could not be sure that she
> could be "remembered."
>
> This was my greatest learning in this exercise: to re-tell the story
> as *Elizabeth's* story meant liberating her from the text. The only story
> I *knew* was not-her story. Did she exist at all outside of this story?
> Can any woman exist outside of male discourse? When you are Other
> than the story, do you even have a story?
>
> . . . My first step in the re-telling was a rejection of the biblical
> agenda which dictates that we know Elizabeth by her failures, her lack
> of reproductive success. But that was not my starting point. I started
> with the assumption of her personal power and strength, with Eliza-
> beth on center stage. What is the purpose of Elizabeth telling her
> story? What does she have to give us? I began with the priority of
> "dangerous memory." This is what she wants to tell us. This is why
> it is necessary for her to tell her story. I see how this shifts the entire

agenda of the story: Elizabeth thinks theologically; she talks about her feelings and relationships; she listens to her heart and spirit; she finds her vocation in prophecy; she immerses herself in solidarity with other women. Her focus is not on Zechariah or Temple rituals or the blame/mercy pattern of the barrenness/pregnancy she experienced. To put herself at the center of the story changes the entire story.

. . . The story includes the painfulness of social prejudices against childless women as well as the extreme danger for an "older" woman to become pregnant. We see women of the first century as knowledgeable about the limits that patriarchal society sets on them. I think it is verging on elitism to assume that 20th century women see what no historical woman was sophisticated enough to know. We also see biblical women as uneducated, illiterate, and effectively separated from the power of words. And their struggle against that oppression. In the relationship between Elizabeth and Mary we see the tremendous healing and joy and unity that can be experienced between two women different in age, status, and resources.

The most thought provoking difference I found between my story and Luke's is how God's relationship to men and women is portrayed. For my story it is quite direct for both Elizabeth and Mary. Zechariah is in the background, as is John. In Luke's story, because of his determination to assert the supremacy of the male experience of God, either Zechariah or John are continually inserted between Elizabeth and God. This is clearest when Elizabeth is most prophetic at the visitation of Mary. Luke focuses twice on the leaping of the fetus who is the *true* prophet and who must, sadly enough, depend on this woman to give voice to what *he* recognizes. The frustration of the male forced to work through a woman is amply illustrated. Perhaps this is the male fear—swallowed by the Spirit-filled woman, always once removed from God, caught forever in the womb dependent, out of control, powerless.

But must women bear the crushing results of men's defensive assertion of *their* power and authority and control over women by being silenced or subordinated or exploited? My own interpretative perspective in this story works against the inevitability of this pattern by giving Elizabeth a voice to cry out. My goal was to remember the dangerous memories as contributing to the collective memory of women which empowers us for the struggle for liberation. I think that this story of Elizabeth did that for me.

I too have felt the constraints of patriarchal religion and society. I have felt silenced and judged. I have felt the thrill of prophetic words spoken with my sisters. I have known them to be rejected by men. I have found solidarity and strength and hope in community with women. I find myself in a patriarchal church with little hope of acceptance. I need Elizabeth to be part of me so that I might persevere.

And now that I have heard her story, HER story, maybe I can.[50]

7

SHEBA –
THE POWER OF WISDOM

Still I Rise

You may write me down in history
With your bitter, twisted lies,
You may trod me in the very dirt
But still, like dust, I'll rise.
. . . .

Out of the huts of history's shame
I rise
Up from a past that's rooted in pain
I rise

I'm a black ocean, leaping and wide,
Welling and swelling I bear in the tide.
Leaving behind nights of terror and fear
I rise
Into a daybreak that's wondrously clear
I rise

Bringing the gifts that my ancestors gave,
I am the dream and the hope of the slave,
I rise
I rise
I rise.[1]

She Stood Upright

Luke 13:10–17

Naming is an act of creation, knowledge a source of vision. To quote Audre Lorde: "When I speak of knowledge . . . , I am speaking of that dark and true depth which understanding serves, waits upon, and makes accessible through language to ourselves and others. It is this depth within each of us that nurtures vision."[2] Since the powerlessness of women is reflected by their namelessness, feminist discourses have centered on women's power to name themselves and the world. Claiming this power, I have given the nameless woman of Luke 13:10–17 a proper name: Sheba, the black queen of wisdom who in the Hebrew Bible is described as having visited King Solomon "with camels, bearing spices, and very much gold, and precious stones." The queen of the South had heard of Solomon's fame and came "to test him with hard questions." (1 Kings 10:1–13; 2 Chron. 9:1–12). For more than three thousand years, her story has not only fascinated the imagination of Jews, Christians, and Muslims, but also left its traces in at least a dozen different cultural traditions.[3]

I have invited Sheba to preside over the last chapter of this book because her figuration embodies a critical feminist biblical interpretation that puts "hard questions" to the reigning epistemology of biblical criticism. It does so in order to open up "the rich dark depth" of submerged religious knowledges that inspire visions for a different future of the *ekklēsia* of women. Sheba presiding over this last chapter does not end the "dance of interpretation" that Miriam began. Rather, she recalls and gathers some of the key concepts and practices of a critical feminist biblical interpretation which have been theorized in previous chapters. In short, my main goal in this chapter is to demonstrate how a feminist process of interpretation for liberation engages in the critical reading of a particular biblical text.

Like the story of the Syro-Phoenician which has accompanied us through these chapters, the story of the stooped woman also can be read as an ideo-story, which according to Mieke Bal is a story whose "characters are strongly opposed so that dichotomies can be established" and whose "representational makeup promotes concreteness and visualization."[4]

Since its narrative is not closed but open, it allows readers to elaborate the protagonists of the story in an imaginative and typological fashion. But whereas cultural readings take such stories out of their original context, scientific exegesis tends to "drown" them either in their literary or historical contexts.

Annette Kolodny has pointed out that readers do not engage texts in "themselves," but that insofar as readers have been taught *how* to read they activate reading paradigms.[5] In addition, feminist theorists have stressed that both professional and nonprofessional readers draw on the "frame of meaning,"[6] or contextualization, provided by shared symbolic constructions of social worlds. In light of this theory, a critical feminist biblical interpretation must explicate its own reading paradigm or reading formation[7] in relation to the hegemonic symbolic world constructions which they engage.

According to Kolodny, reading paradigms or reading formations organize the practice of reading by relating texts, readers, and contexts to one another in specific ways. For instance, whereas a dogmatic reading paradigm relates texts, readers, and contexts in terms of Church doctrine, a historical reading seeks the text's "original" meaning, and a narrative analysis traces the text's androcentric symbolic world constructions. In short, biblical texts, readers, and contexts are not fixed once and for all in their relations to each other but function differently within different reading formations. If reading paradigms establish different relations between texts, readers, and contexts, then such different rhetorical readings cannot be adjudicated in terms of "the true meaning of the text itself"; rather, they can only be assessed politically in terms of their implications and consequences for the struggle to transform patriarchal relations of oppression.

However, such an evaluative positioning stands in tension with the hegemonic reading paradigms in biblical studies. If the literary canonization of texts in general places works beyond the reach of critical scrutiny, the canonization of sacred scriptures in particular engenders even more uncritical acceptance. Readers of biblical texts learn to valorize and validate them rather than to critically interrogate and assess scriptural worlds along with their visions, values, and prescriptions. Canonization compels readers to offer increasingly more ingenious interpretations, not only in order to establish "the truth of the text itself" or "a single sense" meaning of the text, but also to sustain the acceptance and affirmation of biblical texts either as sacred Scripture or as cultural classic.

Therefore, a "canonical reading" stands in tension with a critical feminist biblical interpretation that cannot presuppose the merits or liberating truth of the androcentric canonical text. Rather, by taking the experience and analysis articulated in feminist struggles to transform patriarchy[8] as its point of departure, feminist biblical interpretation seeks to develop methods for contesting the patriarchal values encoded in Scripture. By engaging in critical strategies that interrupt, disconnect, and disrupt the prevailing paradigms of interpretation, it seeks to empower women to read androcentric biblical texts differently.

Such an interpretive procedure is both critical and reconstructive. It understands the Bible as prototype, as a formative root-model of Christian identity that, rather than possessing timeless normativity and universal validity, requires critical discussion and evaluation. In short, a critical feminist reading for transformation attends first to the ways in which patriarchal power is encoded in biblical texts; secondly to the consequences of these androcentric inscriptions for women as biblical characters, readers, or critics; and thirdly to the implications of unmasking these inscriptions, not just for a feminist reconstruction of the past, but also for the transformation of the present.[9]

In seeking to empower women to become reading subjects and critical agents of interpretation, able to claim the authority of struggle for evaluating biblical texts and discourses, a critical feminist reading paradigm must pay attention to the "frame of meaning" determining its readings. By making the dominant symbolic "frame of meaning" conscious it can empower women to participate as reading subjects in the construction of meaning while at the same time becoming aware of such a process of construction. Having explored a critical feminist paradigm of interpretation for liberation in the preceding chapters, in this chapter I seek to map the interface between the practice of reading biblical texts and the dominant symbolic "frame of meaning."

I have argued that the Western cultural "frame of meaning" is not just androcentric but that it is *kyriocentric* (master-centered). The gender asymmetry of grammatically androcentric Western languages obfuscates or mystifies the kyriocentric and patriarchal character of their social world constructions insofar as such asymmetry does not allow for "naming" persons doubly marked by gender and race or class if they are not male. This comes to the fore in the common parlance that speaks for instance of "women, blacks, Asians, and the poor," as though women are not also black, Asian, or poor. Advertisements that refer to women and minorities also suggest that women do not belong to so-called minority groups. The Western androcentric linguistic system further obfuscates its kyriocentricity by organizing language and the world in terms of opposing or complementary binary dualisms.

In the following pages I will approach a biblical text utilizing this feminist analytic model of kyriocentrism and patriarchy. Luke 13:10–17, the story of the woman bent double who was freed from her infirmity, has become a paradigm for the oppression and liberation which Christian women experience in biblical religion. The miracle story about the woman who was freed from her bondage[10] can be read independently from the ensuing "controversy dialogue." Although Luke has integrated this miracle story into the narrative in such a way that it is difficult to isolate a source on stylistic grounds, it is nevertheless possible to read the miracle story as an independent story.[11]

"There was a woman afflicted by a spirit of infirmity[12] for eighteen years, bent over and unable to straighten up. Jesus saw her, called her, and said to her: 'Woman you are freed of your infirmity.' And Jesus laid hands on her and immediately she was made straight and she praised G-d."

The story is simple. The woman was bent double, she has suffered from a "spirit of infirmity" for eighteen long years.[13] She hears the call, experiences the laying on of hands, stands upright and praises G-d, who has freed her from her bondage. The woman has moved from margin to center, from invisibility to presence, from silence to the praise of G-d.[14] In the miracle story, Jesus points to the life-giving, liberating power of G-d that places the woman at center stage.[15] The healing is announced by Jesus in the passive voice as something already accomplished before his own intervention: "You have been freed" emphasizes completion prior to present reality. Moreover, the effect of the healing, "she was straightened up," is described in another divine passive. Therefore, the woman responds appropriately by praising G-d, not by expressing gratitude to Jesus.

Luke interprets the healing story as a story about demonic possession and liberation. Luke describes Jesus' public ministry by saying that "he was going about doing good and healing all who were oppressed by the devil" (Acts 10:38). The summary description of healings at Capernaum (4:40) stresses that Jesus healed all of them through the laying on of hands, and demons went out of people. Healing/delivery in the ministry of Jesus and his disciples is equated with the victory over the reign of demonic powers in the end time.[16] It makes the liberating power of G-d experientially available.

I.
FRAME OF MEANING: GENDER

Reader-oriented criticism[17] has made us conscious that we always read a text from our own perspective and fill in the gaps and silences of the text on the basis of our own experience.[18] Read in an androcentric way that privileges the healing power of Jesus as male gendered—a reading that inserts itself into the subject-position of the woman bent double—the miracle story of the woman freed from her infirmity both reinscribes female religious dependency and self-alienation and augments male self-affirmation and importance.

Readers who do not problematize the naturalness and givenness of gender ascribe the power of healing and liberation to the Man Jesus who is understood in contrast to the woman victim. Whereas Christians almost never substitute "Jew" when we read "Jesus" or "Christ," because "Jew" is often a negatively defined term in Christian discourse, we almost always read the Man Jesus and thereby contextualize[19] our reading in terms of cultural gender dualism. A reading of the Gospels in terms of such biological gender positivism,[20] however, cannot but reinforce the power of the androcentric, grammatically masculine text insofar as it does not distinguish between exclusive gender-specific patriarchal texts on the one hand, and conventional, collective, grammatically masculine generic language on the other.[21] Even feminist interpretations cannot but help reinscribing a cultural-patriarchal "politics of Otherness" when they insist on the maleness of Jesus, and in romance fashion read the Gospel text as elaborating his masculine gender position.

Feminist reader-response criticism analyzes the complex process of reading androcentric texts as a cultural or theological praxis. By elucidating how gender determines the reading process, it underlines the importance of the reader's particular sociocultural location.[22] Reading and thinking in an androcentric symbol-system requires identifying with a cultural patriarchal system whose values engender self-alienation and are often misogynist.

The androcentric text derives its seductive "power" from its generic aspirations that play on women's authentic desires and liberatory interests in order to harness them for the process of "immasculation."[23] Thus, focusing on Jesus as a masculine figure theologically establishes Christian identity as male identity in a cultural masculine-feminine contextualization. Concentrating on the maleness of Jesus when reading the Gospels thus "doubles" women's self-alienation. Not only is our experience not articulated, but women also suffer "the powerlessness which results from the endless division of self against self."[24] To be male means to be universal, means to be divine, means to be *not female*.

Yet, reading androcentric biblical texts, I propose, does not necessarily lead to the reader's male identification. Since androcentric language claims to be generic, we can consciously deactivate masculine/feminine gender contextualization in favor of an abstract, degenderized reading. However, empirical studies have shown that men and women read so-called generic masculine language ("man," "he") differently. Reading experiments[25] have found that men report a higher incidence of male imagery when completing neutral sentences with generic pronouns. To change masculine

200

theological language into gender-neutral language, e.g., father into parent, is therefore not enough, since men tend to continue to read such so-called generic language as male language. It is usually argued that masculine religious language needs to be changed because it is offensive to women, yet these studies show that androcentric language must be changed because it sustains the presumption of male superiority.

Women, on the other hand, associate virtually no images with generic masculine pronouns according to the results of these experiments. This may be because when reading androcentric texts we unconsciously suppress their literal meaning, choosing instead to understand ourselves as included in the generic meaning of such texts. Christian women have read, and often still read, androcentric biblical texts as generic-inclusive texts without attending to the fact of Jesus' maleness or the masculinity of G-d language. As Virginia Fabella points out, in an interpretation that does not focus on gender but on class and colonialism, women tend to read androcentric language generically: "In the Asian Women's Consultation in Manila, the fact that Jesus was male was not an issue, for he was never seen as having used his maleness to oppress or dominate women."[26]

Catherine Belsey explains why women can sustain such a contradictory ideological position when reading unmarked generic male texts: "We [women readers] participate in the liberal-Humanist discourse of freedom, self-determination and rationality and at the same time in the specifically feminine discourse offered by society of submission, relative inadequacy, and irrational intuition."[27] It is precisely this contradictory position that has allowed women readers to resist the *kyriarchal identification* engendered by the androcentric, racist, classist, or colonialist text. For, once we have become conscious of the oppressive rhetorical functions of kyriocentric language, women readers can no longer tolerate this contradiction. Yet, this contradictory subject-position can easily be exchanged not for the forbidden ungendered position but for the complementary quasi-bigendered subject-position of reading. However, if this complementary position is not problematized in an anti-patriarchal reading, the contradictory position of women readers cannot be exploited for change but leads to further self-alienation.

Such a change becomes possible when women become conscious of the dynamics of the generic male text: An explicitly feminist anti-patriarchal "contextualization" demystifies the naturalized binary gendered subject-positions that misrepresent the complex patriarchal relations of domination and generate "the languages of oppression." Feminist biblical interpretation can only interrupt its readings of the Gospel in terms of male/female romance when it problematizes the androcentric "frame of meaning" which determines how the Gospel is read. If in a patriarchal symbolic order scholars as well as lay readers "naturally" read the Man Jesus, thereby ascribing theological significance to the phallic representation of Jesus, a feminist critical reading must make conscious that such a gendered representation is a cultural construction. It can do so if it abandons a gendered reading and instead shifts its attention away from the Man Jesus to the oppression of the woman, who is the repressed opposite in androcentric texts.

The controversy story of the woman who was freed to stand upright presents her illness as a bondage caused by Satan. Early Christian "apocalyptic" theology sees the world and human beings in it as caught up in the struggle between the life-destroying powers of evil and the life-giving power of G-d. While in the last analysis these evil powers cannot frustrate the life-giving purpose of G-d, their power is still real and has its effects in the present world.[28] Their hostility against life and human wholeness is expressed in their attempt to enslave human beings and, ultimately, in their crucifixion of the Christ. Apocalyptic early Christian theology explains the execution of Jesus as having been caused by these cosmic and political powers but not as willed by G-d.[29] A critical feminist interpretation for liberation does not seek to "demythologize" this apocalyptic language of mythic powers in order to existentialize and depoliticize it.[30] Rather, it reads such apocalyptic power representations as sociopolitical language, and it has named the life-destroying power of Western society and religions *patriarchy*,[31] a system which produces ideological gender-dualism but is not identical with it.

As I have argued in chapter 4, patriarchy must not be understood solely as male supremacy and phallocratic sexism, but as the multiplicative interstructuring of racism, sexism, class exploitation, militarist colonialism, and dehumanizing exclusion, be it religious or cultural. The Western understanding of patriarchy as a complex pyramidal system of structures of prejudice and oppression was first theorized in Aristotelian political philosophy as a gradated, political, male status and power system of domination and subordination, authority and obedience, ruler and subject in household and state. Since the democratic ideal invites the participation of all citizens, classical (and modern bourgeois) philosophy had to legitimize the exclusion of freeborn women and Greek-born slave women and men from democratic government. Their "nature" is defined in terms of their subordinate status and social function in order to argue that their "nature" makes them unfit to rule.[32] This basic contradiction between the democratic claim to the full equality of all human beings and their subordinate position in the patriarchal structures of household and state, a characteristic of classical democracy, has defined Western Euro-American notions of democracy and continues to structure the modern bourgeois symbolic order.

202

Western patriarchy did not originate in biblical religions but was mediated and perpetuated through Christianity, the dominant Western religion for almost two thousand years. Insofar as the Bible has mediated the ancient pattern of patriarchal submission and has proclaimed G-d and Christ in patriarchal terms, this patriarchal pattern has defined Christian self-understanding and community throughout the centuries. Through the work of influential theologians such as Augustine and Thomas Aquinas, this Aristotelian-biblical construct of the inferior human "natures" of slaves and freeborn women has been woven into Christian theology's basic fabric.

Reproducing societal patriarchy, Christian religious patriarchy has defined not only women but all subjugated peoples and races as "the Other," as "nature" to be exploited and dominated by powerful men. Obedience, economic dependence, and sexual control are still the sustaining forces of societal and ecclesiastical patriarchy. Such patriarchal Christian theology has legitimated racism, colonialism, classism, and hetero/sexism in society and church. It has encouraged not only the sacrifice of people to authoritarian systems but also the exploitation of the earth and its resources. Its posture of divine domination and absolute *power over* has licensed imperialism and militarism that have brought us to the brink of atomic annihilation.

Many stories of women held in bondage by the powers of patriarchy and unable to stand upright could be told today. The story of the young woman who had to give up her child for adoption because the Catholic college did not teach effective birth control and had no housing and day care facilities for single mothers; of the two-year-old who was raped and beaten by her father; of the woman on welfare who lives with ten children in one room; of the theology professor who was told by white students that she had no authority as a black woman teacher; of the church administrator who lost her job because she loved a woman and not a man; of the wife who was counseled to suffer the beatings of her husband for Christ's sake; of the little girl who comes home from church/synagogue and asks, Mummy, does G-d have only sons and no daughters? The artist Mary Lou Sleevi tells their stories by re-telling that of the woman bent double in a different way:

A Stooped Woman

Healing is in process.
She is empowered
to stand straight and free.
A small, bony woman

203

bent over double with her eyes to the ground,
had shuffled around
the house of worship for years. . . .

When he saw the double outcast,
Jesus called her to him.
That was her first Surprise,
She had the backbone to come
as fast as she could. . . .

A question mark—?—
is the shape of sexism
on the back of society today. The answer,
an exclamation point—!—
is making its way. . . .

Both are body signs of church
called to repentance and healing
even on Sunday.

Ever since Jesus,
woman has been backbone of church.
Shortly thereafter,
she was returned to the background.

She has always been where church is,
her head bowed not only in prayer.
Schooled in retreat,
she was put on a pedestal
where movement is strictly limited. . . .

Out of experience and prayer,
she is talking back and walking
ahead.
She is beyond the reach
of a pat on the head.
It deprives her; circumscribes her.
Exclusion disables, inclusion enables.
Behind the screen of golden rhetoric,
who knows better? It is *her* back!

She's a Crossing Point,
a shunned world
the church fears to touch
for fear it will touch back.
It will.

Raised by Jesus
to a lonely vantage point
in an obscure house of worship

in an unnamed town
an anonymous woman
is a sign of Good News!

Here is a very little story,
seldom told on Sunday.

We are witnessing a new miracle
of empowering one another
We glorify God
in stretching our backs![33]

In the healing story, Jesus, who was born with the privileges of a Jewish male, focuses attention on the woman bent double and insists that she must be healed. So must Christian men do today. They must recognize that if they insert themselves by virtue of their gender into the phallic subject—position, they uphold the "Law of the Father" and facilitate the exploitation and oppression of women in society and church. Therefore, it is not enough for men to reject as patriarchal ideologies all symbolic theological constructions of the subordination or complementarity of "women's special nature and place"; they must also relinquish their patriarchal privileges and join women in the struggle to overcome the infirmity and bondage imposed by patriarchy.

Recognizing ourselves in the subject-position of the woman bent double, women can break the power of "immasculation" by rejecting the prescribed feminine subject-position as the non-male and by consciously recognizing ourselves *as women* deformed and exploited by societal and ecclesiastical patriarchy. Those of us who are privileged in terms of race, class, culture, and education must reject the temptation to insert ourselves as quasi-equals into the complementary position *vis-à-vis* the elite, white, propertied, Euro-American "given" phallic subject-position. We must become conscious that until every woman is free, no woman is truly able to overcome patriarchal infirmity and bondage.

Just as the woman bent double did not ask for healing from the Man Jesus but came to the synagogue to praise G-d, so Christian women must realize that our liberation will not come from the men in the churches. As long as we who are privileged in terms of race and class identify with the men who hold positions of power in society and church rather than with our sisters living on the bottom of the patriarchal pyramid, we will not be able to see that we suffer from the same patriarchal bondage. Only when we recognize the women bent double in our midst will we be able to articulate theologically a vision of G-d's salvation and community that allows all women to become free from patriarchal dehumanization. Mutuality between women and women, as well as between women and men, is

205

only possible when, in a feminist conversion, we reject the structural evil of patriarchy and our personal collaboration in it. The preferential option for the poor must be spelled out as a commitment to the liberation struggle of women, not only because the majority of the poor are women and children dependent on women, but also because the female subjectivity burdened by multiplicative oppressions "is complementary with ungendered subjectivity: the forbidden and unarticulated possibility of a way of differentiating individuals and signification *otherwise* than by the phallus."[34] Placing the woman bent double in the center of our attention allows for an antipatriarchal reading. By taking the subject-position of the woman bent by multiplicative patriarchal oppressions, such a reading goes against the grain of the logic of patriarchy. It can be mapped as follows:

PRESCRIBED
Patriarchy
Kyriocentrism

FORBIDDEN
Basileia
Domination free

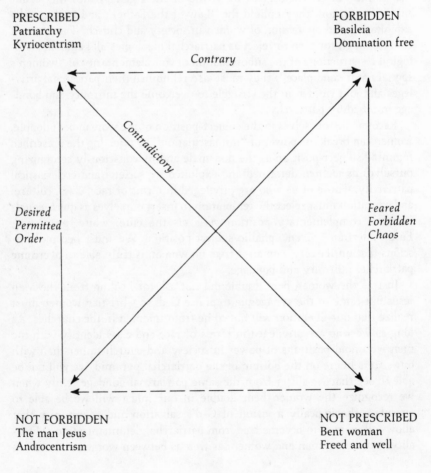

Contrary

Contradictory

Desired
Permitted
Order

Feared
Forbidden
Chaos

NOT FORBIDDEN
The man Jesus
Androcentrism

NOT PRESCRIBED
Bent woman
Freed and well

Taking the subject-position of the woman who was enabled to stand upright in turn requires that readers refuse to take the subject-position offered by patriarchy and resist reading the story in terms of kyriocentrism. Simultaneously, such a reading presupposes a democratic vision of society free of domination. Such an antipatriarchal reading is, however, not possible if one does not disrupt Luke's rhetorical contextualization and frame of meaning.

II.
FRAME OF MEANING:
LUKE'S ANTI-JEWISH RHETORIC

In Luke's Gospel[35] the miracle story is expanded into a so-called controversy dialogue or pronouncement story so that the text now represents a "hybrid" form.[36] This Lukan controversy about Jesus' healing on the Sabbath is preceded by the allegory of the barren fig tree (13:6–9), which is set in a political context (13:1–5). In the Hebrew Bible the fig tree often stands for Judah or Israel. The gardener then acts as an advocate, pleading the cause for the unproductive tree. Just as a final chance to bear fruit is given to the tree, so too a final opportunity for repentance is granted to Israel. D. L. Tiede writes, "The possibility of repentance appears to be more remote than the threat of destruction. Nevertheless, the time of Jesus' ministry is an extended, prolonged campaign to save Israel."[37] Still, the reader knows that ultimately Jesus' call to repentance meets with rejection.

The public character of Jesus' prophetic ministry[38] is also stressed in the hybrid form of this miracle-story/controversy dialogue in 13:10–17. The introduction, "Jesus was teaching in one of the synagogues," seems typically Lukan. It alludes to the inauguration of Jesus' public ministry in 4:16–30 and recalls 6:1–11, where Jesus is called in verse 5 "the kyrios [= Lord] of the Sabbath." Jesus' announcement of his mission of salvation in the synagogue of Nazareth in 4:14–30, as well as the Sabbath confrontation in 6:1–11, lead to controversy and conflict with his own people, provoking them to want to kill him. Moreover, 13:10–17 is at the center of the editorial unit 12:49 to 13:35, which focuses on Jesus' painful mission whose rejection brings judgment.[39]

The leader of the synagogue correctly objects that in order to heal the woman it was not necessary for Jesus to transgress against the Sabbath prescriptions of the Torah. The Lukan Jesus does not argue in response that it was necessary to heal the woman because her illness was fatal. Rather, Jesus healed her in order to set her free from her infirmity. The point of comparison is this: Just as one is permitted to care for household animals on the Sabbath, so also can one act for the welfare of a daughter of Abraham.[40] This response characterizes the woman by the "name of the Father" as a member of the people of G-d. What seems puzzling is that the response of the Lukan Jesus does not take notice of the objection made by the synagogue official, whose precise point it is that there are six days on which acts of healing are permitted. He does not argue that the woman should not have been healed, but asks: "If the woman was disabled for eighteen long years, why couldn't Jesus wait one more day?" And why indeed not?

By placing Jesus and his offensive action in the center of the controversy, the dialogue not only ascribes the miracle to Jesus rather than to G-d, but also makes the woman the focus of discursive struggle. Although she has become occasion and object of male debate, she no longer inhabits a subject-position in the text. The Lukan text has transformed the whole story from a woman-focused to a male-centered sacred text by merging a Sabbath controversy with the healing story. Whereas in the healing story the woman had moved from margin to center, in the present text she has become the object of men's religious conflict and has remained so for centuries. Not the well-being of people, but rather the "Law of the Father," has remained central to theological debate.

It is the authority of the Bible, the teachings about the Sabbath, and Jesus' offense against it, that have taken center stage. Thus, in the controversy story the woman has become invisible again. At the end of the story the crowd takes her place praising G-d. Clearly this story calls for a hermeneutics of suspicion. By turning the miracle story into a controversy dialogue, Luke or one of his predecessors has transformed the healing story into a debate with the leadership of the synagogue which reflects the tensions between the early Christian community and its Jewish mother-community in the last quarter of the first century.[41]

The story of the bent woman has become a site for the struggle between Christian and Jewish men over the religious authority to interpret the "Law of the Father." If Jervell[42] is correct that Luke has coined the title "daughter of Abraham" and that in his double-work Luke includes women not because they are women but because they are *Jewish* women or women attracted to Judaism, then the rhetoric and the structure of Luke 13:10–17 indicate that a major object of this debate was the position of Jewish women. Christian women readers who insert themselves uncritically into the Christian subject-position structured by the text become implicated in its anti-Jewish rhetoric and identity-formation without realizing that what is at stake is their own participation as actors in the Christian story.

In Luke's Gospel the story of the woman bent double concludes the first part of the travel-narrative and builds the bridge to the second part.[43] Jesus' journey to Jerusalem leads to his suffering and death, which is brought about by the conspiracy of the Jerusalem leaders against him. The Jerusalem leaders, and not the Romans, are responsible for Jesus' execution according to Luke.[44] This wider context for the bent woman's story is consistent with Luke's polemical reinterpretation in 13:10–17, which uses the healing of the woman to make a point. It is Jesus, not the leader of the synagogue, who gives the right interpretation of the Sabbath Torah. The religious controversy over the observance of the Sabbath law, instead of the liberation of the woman bent double, now captures readers' attention. This Lukan emphasis opens the door for the anti-Jewish reading that has prevailed in the history of interpretation.

Usually, when reading early Christian Scriptures, Christians identify with Jesus, although many share the theological understanding of biblical authority that is expressed by the leader of the synagogue. Christians can do so because in the process of reading we obliterate the tension between the authority of Jesus and the authority of the biblical text which exists in the controversy dialogue. Claiming for ourselves the biblical authority of Jesus, Christians read these passages in an anti-Jewish way, get angry with the leader of the synagogue, and feel religiously and morally superior to Judaism.[45]

If Christian readers would instead insert themselves into the subject-position of the official who is insisting on the authority of the Bible, then many would applaud his statement, "There are six days when one has to work; come on one of them to be healed," for this would seem a very reasonable theological argument. Biblical law and authority must not be jeopardized just because a woman cannot wait a day longer to be made healthy and whole. Today, conservative churchmen and theologians insist that patriarchal biblical texts must be upheld as G-d's word in the face of so-called secular humanism and radical feminism which, according to them, promote freedom of speech, breakdown of marriage, the rights of homosexuals, and the rights of women to terminate pregnancy. In reading the controversy dialogue it never occurs to them that Jesus might have been a secular humanist!

Christian feminists who want to claim the revelatory authority of this text as liberating for women also highlight the tension between the action of Jesus and the argument of the synagogue leader. However, they too tend to neglect to question the anti-Jewish tendencies inscribed in the controversy dialogue. Rather, they perpetuate these anti-Jewish tendencies which place the Jewish official and the crowd in opposition to Jesus and the "daughter of Abraham," proclaiming Jesus as the feminist, in contrast to patriarchal Judaism. They thereby recuperate traditional interpretations which contrast the barren fig tree, the symbol of the synagogue, with the cured woman, who symbolizes the church. Such a feminist apologetic reading thus continues the tradition of dualistic anti-Jewish interpretation, not with reference to the church and Israel but to Jesus and Judaism.[46] Such a Christian feminist apologetic fails to explore why the Lukan controversy dialogue not only uses the story of Luke 13:10–17 for controversial, anti-Jewish purposes, but also why it allows the woman to become eclipsed.

A critical feminist theological hermeneutics[47] for transformation also must avoid separating the miracle story as the authoritative essential word of G-d from the Lukan redaction in order to explain away the androcentric tendencies of the Lukan redaction or to judge them as time-conditioned. While it is important for a hermeneutics of remembrance to trace the development of biblical texts and their traditions, the earliest layer cannot become the canonical criterion for theological evaluation. Finally, reducing this androcentric story to an abstract prophetic or eschatological critical principle to claim a feminist liberating dynamics for it prevents us from exposing and holding up for critical reflection the text's anti-Jewish features.

A cursory review of the commentaries on this text indicates that by elaborating on the skillful redaction of Luke they also embellish its anti-Jewish theological perspective.[48] By stressing the anti-Jewish rhetoric of the Lukan controversy, scholars also reinforce its androcentric tendencies. Following Luke, they focus on the controversy between Jesus and the synagogue president and overlook the story of the woman who was enabled to walk upright. A *critical feminist interpretation for liberation* must therefore lay open for theological reflection and critical evaluation both the anti-Jewish and androcentric tendencies of contemporary interpretations, and those of the Lukan text itself which has generated them. It cannot just read the Lukan texts about "women." Rather, without losing its focus on women, a critical feminist interpretation for liberation must analyze the whole narrative of Luke's Gospel, studying the rhetorical strategies which inscribe patriarchal structures privileging elite, propertied, powerful men.[49]

III.
FRAME OF MEANING:
POLITICAL-RHETORICAL STRUGGLE

The interpretation of Luke-Acts is very controversial in biblical studies. Many scholars argue that Luke is the "Gospel of liberation" because it presents Jesus as a prophet preaching "good news" to the poor and lowly, as a friend of women, and as an advocate of social justice or nonviolent resistance. Others contend that Luke-Acts, as a call to repentance addressed to Christians of wealth and repute, deals with questions of well-to-do members who sought an accommodation with the dominant structures of the Roman empire. Hence the Lukan work, they argue, characterizes women as subordinate members of the Christian community and presents Christian movement and mission as being in line both with the ancestral traditions of Judaism and with Greco-Roman religions. It was a lawful religious cult well integrated in Greco-Roman society. For apologetic reasons, so this theory goes, Luke attempts to mute the "radical" traditions of the Jesus movement that ascribe to women, the poor, and the outcast a significant role. While I agree with the latter reading in terms of Greco-Roman religious apologetic and "propaganda" (i.e., public discourse), I would suggest that we read Luke's work in terms of both the liberationist and the adaptationist argument. Such a reading recognizes the submerged traditions which are inscribed in the text as competing rhetorical strategies. In the public debate of the *ekklesia*, these strategies are engendered by the diverse struggles over the symbolic order which Luke's rhetoric seeks to shape.

Since the "rhetorical situation" of a text is best detected in its opening and closure, one needs to read the middle section of the gospel in light of its beginning and end. According to the preface, Luke 1:1–4, the author explicitly intends to write an orderly, historical account of Christian beginnings for an elite male audience whose domain is history. Luke therefore sets out to "contain" Jesus and his movement by insinuating in the first two chapters that Jesus, on the one hand, through Joseph, belongs to the royal house of David and, on the other, that the priestly ruling class has legitimized his person and mission. As Mosala writes: "Mary, probably a single mother from the ghettos of colonized Galilee, needed the moral clearing of the priestly sector of the ruling class,—those who were targets of Luke's Gospel."[50]

Women, such as Elizabeth and Mary, have a prominent place in the beginning of the Gospel as speaking subjects proclaiming the good news of salvation. With the men and the angels, they announce that Jesus is Israel's savior, who dethrones the powerful, uplifts the lowly, and fills the hungry with good things. Jesus' birth is "good news"; it means peace and salvation. Therefore, readings from the vantage point of Latin American and other liberation theologies often claim the *Magnificat* and the whole infancy narrative, as well as Jesus' inaugural sermon in Nazareth, as liberating texts for the poor and oppressed. Yet, such readings tend to neglect the Gospel's political and religious identity construction. A careful analysis of Luke's rhetorical strategies shows how the preaching of the "good news" and its fulfillment in the praxis of the prophet Jesus meets resistance and rejection by his own people and leadership. Moreover, in the infancy narra-

211

tive one can already detect tendencies to play down Jewish political hopes in favor of imperial Roman theology. Like the divine emperor, the newborn child is the savior who restores the social order and brings peace.[51]

If one reads the beginning of the Gospel in light of the end, one realizes that Luke inscribes these Jewish political and Roman universalist tendencies in order to subvert them. He does so by emphasizing that the execution of Jesus as "king of the Jews" was a failure of Roman justice under pressure from the Jewish leadership. Pilate declares Jesus innocent three times and gives him over to the Jews for crucifixion. The oracle addressed to the daughters of Jerusalem,[52] and the references to women at the crucifixion, burial, and empty tomb, implicate the women characters in this anti-Jewish drama.[53]

Such anti-Jewish rhetorical strategies in Luke are combined with spiritualizing tendencies which insist that Jesus' and Caesar's empire (*basileia*) belong to different domains. Jesus brings "peace in heaven" (19:38) and reigns sovereign in paradise (23:43). Thus the text works hard to subvert the earthly messianic hopes of the infancy narratives proclaimed by Jewish women and men. It articulates instead Christian identity as grounded in Luke's depoliticization of "the good news for the poor" and in the assertion that the Jewish people and their leaders have rejected Jesus and caused his death. Therefore, the text must be deconstructed in a feminist critical reading before Luke's Gospel can be reclaimed in terms of a global praxis for liberation.

The rhetoric of the passion narrative also underlines Luke's patriarchal tendency to characterize women's discipleship and apostolic witness in "feminine" terms. Luke corrects Mark's reference to the women disciples who witness Jesus' death (15:40–41) by adding "and all his acquaintances" (23:49). As we have seen, Luke refers to the women disciples at the beginning of Jesus' ministry (8:1–3), but his summary account no longer states that they were followers (*akoluthein*) of Jesus. Instead, he emphasizes that the women around Jesus were healed from many infirmities and that the well-to-do supported Jesus and his male apostles with their possessions.

This tendency to eclipse women's discipleship becomes especially obvious when one analyzes Luke's account of the passion and resurrection. Luke follows Mark in characterizing the women, and especially Mary of Magdala, as the witnesses of Jesus' death, burial, and resurrection: the primary facts of the Christian proclamation. That the women are mentioned three times suggests that the tradition already understood this repetition as providing a "chain of witness."[54] However, Luke corrects the Markan account, maintaining that the women were not the only or even the primary witnesses of Jesus' crucifixion (23:47). Luke, in distinction to Mark 16:8, knows that the women told the message of Easter to the eleven and to the rest of the disciples (24:9), but he stresses that the male disciples did not believe them: "These words seemed to them an idle tale" (24:11). The women are characterized as true believers, because they remembered his words (24:8ff), whereas the two Emmaus-disciples needed to receive lengthy instruction and the sign of the breaking of bread (24:25–31) before they believed. Nevertheless, Luke does not include in his narrative a story about Jesus' appearance to Mary Magdalene or any other woman disciple, but emphasizes that it is Peter who verifies what the women report (24:12). He and not Mary of Magdala is the first to whom Jesus appears after the resurrection. The statement "The Lord has risen indeed and has appeared to Simon" (24:34) is a "confessional formula" similar to that of the tradition preserved in 1 Corinthians 15:4ff.

These Lukan rhetorical strategies must be situated within the early Christian debate about whether Mary of Magdala or Peter is the primary witness of the resurrection. Luke clearly exhibits apologetic tendencies when he maintains that not just the women but all of Jesus' acquaintances stood under the cross. Luke 24:24 limits the women's message to the information about the empty tomb by stressing "that some of those who were with us [according to v. 12 it was Peter] went to the tomb, and found it just as the woman had said, but him they did not see." The women are therefore credited as trustworthy, but their witness is confined to the discovery of the empty tomb. The true witness of Jesus' resurrection is Peter (24:34). This Lukan rhetorical strategy of playing down the role of the women disciples probably serves apologetic interests in defending against Jewish and pagan attacks that accuse Christians of basing their faith upon the witness of untrustworthy women.[55]

The opening of Acts confirms this reading of Luke's rhetorical strategy as seeking to eclipse women's leadership. In Acts 1:14 the apostolic women, whom readers recognize from the Gospel, represent the nascent community together with Mary, the mother of Jesus and the twelve. Yet 1:16 addresses the congregation as "men and brethren" (*andres, adelphoi*). Moreover, because of their gender, the apostolic women are disqualified from being elected to the circle of the twelve (1:21–22) and from replacing Judas in *diakonia* and apostleship (1:15.25), although they do fulfill the stated requirements of having been with Jesus on the way from Galilee to Jerusalem and of having witnessed his resurrection (see Luke 8:1–3; 10:38–42; 24:1ff). In short, although Luke never vilifies women and nowhere openly argues against them, his subtle politics of signification removes them from apostolic leadership and relegates them to the ranks of community membership.

In a comprehensive narratological analysis of Luke's Gospel, J. M. Dawsey has pointed to the difference between the voice of Jesus and that of

213

the narrator. The Lukan Jesus speaks the simple language of the people, and his popular style is consonant with his inaugural sermon in 4:16ff. Jesus' ministry consists of bringing the dispossessed and marginal into the *basileia*—the empire of G-d which is already present but hidden. The narrator, on the other hand, "is part and in some sense leader of the worshipping community who calls Jesus Lord, remembers his miraculous power, speaks a special language . . . but does not understand the humiliation of Jesus."[56] The narrator who sees the story of Jesus as that of the exalted Lord speaks the language of the educated and addresses the questions of the elite members of the community.[57]

Dawsey argues that the author called Luke sides with the voice of Jesus and not with that of the narrator. He suggests that "the purpose of the irony at play in the views of the narrator and of Jesus would likewise be to chafe the audience into a change of perspective."[58] However, such a reading in terms of irony falters if one focuses attention on the narrative voice of Jesus with respect to the speech of women characters. In 2:48–49 Jesus' mother speaks and is silenced; in 10:38–42 Martha, who speaks, is silenced; in 11:27–28 the voice of the woman from the crowd is silenced; and in 23:27–30 the "daughters of Jerusalem" are told not to bemoan Jesus' fate but their own.

Rather than assume with Dawsey that the author sides with the voice of Jesus, one has to keep in mind that it is the author who articulates both voices, the voice of the narrator as well as that of Jesus, as rhetorical strategies. Both voices eclipse women's apostolic leadership, deradicalize the notion of discipleship, and are deeply implicated in the author's anti-Jewish polemics. The narrative association of Jesus with popular speech and with concern for the outcast serves to point readers to the radical beginnings of Christianity, while at the same time co-opting them into reading these beginnings from the perspective of the well-to-do, elite men of the community. Such a rhetorical strategy of containment has long been recognized as part and parcel of the religious propaganda and apologetic rhetoric enacted in the public arenas of Greco-Roman antiquity.

IV.
FRAME OF MEANING:
LIBERATING THEOPOLITICAL VISION

A feminist critical interpretation committed to the liberation of women and other oppressed peoples from patriarchal dehumanization must not explain away the patriarchal character of Luke's rhetoric and perspective by claiming that its anti-Jewish bias, its subtle eclipsing of women's apostolic leadership, and its elite male interests are due to the author's use of irony. Rather, a critical feminist reading must resist the rhetorical strategies of Luke-Acts and critically assess their symbolic representations since at once they reinscribe and silence the alternative voices which the text works hard to suppress. A critical feminist reading can do so by reading Luke's rhetoric against its ideological grain and by construing it as an active participant in an ongoing early Christian debate. The hegemonic rhetoric of Luke seeks to silence or co-opt for patriarchal ends.

Such a reading "against the grain," I submit, must critically unmask the androcentric and kyriocentric strategies of the text, dislodging the story from its anti-Jewish rhetorical contextualization in Luke's Gospel in order to recontextualize it, undermining its oppressive dynamics. Such a recontextualization, which stresses a different theological framework, is possible when one reads the story about the woman bent double as a performative sign of the *basileia* (empire)—of G-d's envisioned world.[59]

The two parables that follow the healing story liken the *basileia*, which signifies G-d's intended world, to the mustard seed (13:18–19), which a man sowed, and to the leaven (13:20–21), which a woman mixed into or hid away in a sizable amount of flour. The parable of the mustard seed is not a contrast, but a growth parable stressing that Jesus' ministry makes the *basileia* initially present, as the small beginning of the future. Thus the parable of the leaven likens the *basileia* to leaven which a woman took. It stresses the leaven's power to affect the whole. The parable images G-d as a woman baking bread. It does not specify the woman's social status, but ancient sources about bread production suggest that she was a domestic worker—either a poor freeborn woman, a village woman, a freedwoman, or a slave, since in the cities bread was produced commercially by men.[60] Thus the parable images G-d not simply as a woman but as a poor working or slave woman!

The (possibly pre-Lukan) rhetorical unit Luke 13:10–13.18–21 that connects the story of the bent woman who was healed with the *basileia* stories that follow stresses through parable and miracle story that Jesus' ministry seeks the wholeness and well-being of everyone in Israel. All three stories can thus be read as stories about the *basileia*. The woman bent double who is freed from her bondage makes experientially available the caring presence and power of *Baker-Woman-G-d* at work in the words and praxis of the Jesus movement. Despite opposition from the religious leadership, the common people recognize the wonderful things[61] that have happened in their midst.

The salvation of G-d's *basileia*, of G-d's intended world, becomes experientially available whenever Jesus and his followers, both women and men, cast out demons, heal the sick and ritually unclean, and tell stories about the lost who are found, about the uninvited who are invited, or about the least who will be first. The power of G-d's restored creation is realized in their table community with the poor, the sinners, the tax collectors, the prostitutes—with all those who do not belong because they are religiously deficient in the eyes of the pious and righteous. The *basileia* does not spell patriarchal power but human well-being. It is like the dough that has been leavened but has not yet been transformed into bread. The *basileia* is like the fetus in the womb not yet transformed in birth to a child.

Although the salvation and happiness of G-d's intended world can already be experienced through healings, parables, and inclusive discipleship community, Jesus' first followers, women and men, nevertheless still hope for and expect the future in-breaking of G-d's *basileia* when death, suffering, and injustice will finally be no more. The praxis and vision of the *basileia* are the mediation of G-d's future in the midst of the oppressive structures and life-destroying powers of the present. This future is available to all members of the people of G-d. Everyone is invited. In sum, the well-being and happiness of everyone is the central vision of the *basileia* movement.

The healing of the woman bent double tells about the caring presence and power of G-d at work in the words and praxis of this movement. We do not know whether the woman who was freed from her bondage to a spirit of infirmity joined this movement. Her story is cut off and forever lost in historical silence. We know of her at all only because she has become the occasion for theological debate. Like so many other women, she remains nameless, faceless, and forgotten. A critical interpretation for transformation therefore needs not just a hermeneutics of suspicion, reconstruction, and critical evaluation but also a hermeneutics of creative imagination, actualization, and ritualization that can give voice to the voiceless, names to the nameless, and remembrance to the forgotten. Therefore, we must look again at the woman bent double, who was freed from her bondage and empowered to stand upright, seeing her as the following poem by Alice Walker has glimpsed her: in her imagination the woman becomes a paradigm of both patriarchal oppression and of the *basileia*, a sign of courage and hope for today and the future.

Remember?

Remember me?
I am the girl
With the dark skin
whose shoes are thin
I am the girl

with rotted teeth
I am the dark
rotten-toothed girl
with the wounded eye
and the melted ear.

I am the girl
holding their babies
cooking their meals
sweeping their yards
washing their clothes
Dark and rotting
and wounded, wounded.

I would give
to the human race
only hope.

I am the woman
with the blessed dark skin
I am the woman
with the teeth repaired
I am the woman
with the healing eye
the ear that hears

I am the woman: Dark
repaired, healed
Listening to you.

I would give
to the human race
only hope.

I am the woman
offering two flowers
whose roots are twin

Justice and Hope

Let us begin.[62]

NOTES

INTRODUCTION

1. Audre Lorde, *The Black Unicorn: Poems* (New York: Norton, 1978), 94.

2. Margaret Atwood, *The Handmaid's Tale* (New York: Ballantine Books, 1987), 241.

3. Ibid., 112–113.

4. For this expression, see G. Gutiérrez, *The Power of the Poor in History* (Maryknoll: Orbis Press, 1983), 93.

5. See Jonathan Culler, *On Deconstruction* (Ithaca: Cornell University Press, 1982), 43–64.

6. See Adrienne Munich, "Notorious Signs, Feminist Criticism and Literary Tradition," in *Making A Difference: Feminist Literary Criticism*, ed. Gayle Green and Kopelia Kahn (New York: Methuen, 1985), 238–260.

7. Elisabeth Schüssler Fiorenza, *Bread Not Stone: The Challenge of Feminist Biblical Interpretation* (Boston: Beacon Press, 1984).

8. See, for instance, Rosemary Radford Ruether's review in *Journal of the American Academy of Religion* 49 (1986), which states that "for [Schüssler] Fiorenza women-church is the authoritative norm of correct hermeneutics" and that I "define women-church as the authentic expression of the primitive Christian discipleship of equals." She argues that I do not "prove that even the discipleship of equals was women-identified rather than male-identified." Such a misreading of my text, which appropriates the key notions of "prototype" and "women-church" for itself and overlooks carefully argued distinctions is puzzling, to say the least. Marie E. Isaacs in *Theology*, November 1987, on the other hand, correctly "is left with the impression that a hermeneutics of suspicion rather than a hermeneutics of remembrance predominates." She misses the point, however, when she asserts that such a hermeneutics "has the effect of leaving us with large parts of the Bible as unusable" and goes on to suggest that such a hermeneutics evokes the danger "of not being obliged to wrestle with those parts of Scripture which are uncongenial to me personally and/or to the contemporary situation."

9. Rebecca S. Chopp, "Feminism's Theological Pragmatics: A Social Naturalism of Women's Experience," *The Journal of Religion* 67 (1987): 239–256 has perceptively contextualized my proposal of a feminist critical interpretation of the Bible within the North American pragmatic tradition.

10. Such a writing of G-d is meant to indicate that G-d is "in a religious sense unnameable" and belongs to the "realm of the ineffable." G-d is not G-d's "proper name." See Rebecca S. Chopp, *The Power to Speak: Feminism, Language, God* (New York: Crossroad, 1989), 32.

11. See also Sharon Welch, *Communities of Resistance and Solidarity* (Maryknoll: Orbis Press, 1985), 7: "the referent of the phrase 'liberating God' is not primarily God but liberation. That is, the language here is true not because it corresponds with something in the divine nature but because it leads to actual liberation in history. The truth of God language and of all theological claims is measured . . . by the fulfillment of its claims in history."

12. See the review by Amy-Jill Levine in *Signs* (Fall 1986), 185.

13. See Sheila Greeve Davaney's review essay, "Reclaiming God's Power in the Struggle for Liberation," *Books & Religion* 13(6) (1985).

14. Caroline Ramazanoglu, *Feminism and the Contradictions of Oppression* (London: Routledge, 1989), has pointed to the tendency in feminist discourse to set up the agnostic or atheist Western feminist as "superior knower." Against such a stance she argues: "New-wave feminists have tended to have little interest in religion. Yet religion can be the dominant factor in the personal identity and cultural location of millions of women around the world. If religion is one of the most important and immediate factors which enable a woman to know who she is, and to give meaning to her life, an international feminist movement cannot afford to ignore religion" (151).

15. See Tikva Frymer-Kensky's review in *Biblical Review* (Summer 1987).

16. For the concept of "relations of ruling" see Dorothy Smith, *The Everyday World as Problematic: A Feminist Sociology* (Boston: Northeastern University Press, 1987): "The ruling apparatus is that familiar complex of management, government, administration, professions, and intelligentsia, as well as the textually mediated discourses that coordinate and interpenetrate it. Its special capacity is the organization of particular places, persons, and events into generalized and abstract modes vested in categorical systems, rules, laws, and conceptual practices. The former thereby become subject to an abstracted and universalized system of ruling mediated by texts" (108).

17. See, e.g., Barbara Smith, ed., *Home Girls: A Black Feminist Anthology* (New York: Kitchen Table: Women of Color Press, 1983), and bell hooks, *Feminist Theory: From Margin to Center* (Boston: South End Press, 1984).

18. Cheryl Johnson-Odim, "Common Themes, Different Contexts: Third World Women and Feminism," in *Third World Women and the Politics of Feminism*, ed. C. T. Mohanty, A. Russo, and L. Torres (Bloomington: Indiana University Press, 1991), 316.

19. Marge Piercy, *Circles on the Water: Selected Poems* (New York: Knopf, 1982), xii.

20. Claudia V. Camp, "Female Voice, Written Word: Women and Authority in Hebrew Scripture," in *Embodied Love: Sensuality and Relationship as Feminist Values*, ed. P. M. Cooey, S. A. Farmer, and M. E. Ross (San Francisco: Harper & Row, 1987), 97–114.

21. See also Maria Harris, *Teaching Religious Imagination* (San Francisco: Harper & Row, 1987).

22. See especially Nancy K. Miller, "Arachnalogies: The Woman, the Text, and the Critic," in *The Poetics of Gender*, ed. Nancy K. Miller (New York: Columbia University Press, 1986), 270–295.

23. This name is not found in the canonical text either of Mark 7:24–30 or Matthew 15:21–28, but only in the extracanonical Pseudo-Clementine Homilies. For the Greek text see Bernhard Rehm and J. Irmscher, eds., *Die Pseudoklementinen* (Berlin: Akademie-Verlag, 1953), 42–43 and 196–197.

24. See my article "Auf den Spuren der Weisheit—Weisheitstheologisches Urgestein," in *Auf den Spuren der Weisheit: Sophia—Wegweiserin für ein neues Gottesbild*, ed. Verena Wodtke (Freiburg: Herder, 1991), 24–40, and S. Cady, M. Ronan, and H. Taussig, *Wisdom's Feast: Sophia in Study and Celebration* (San Francisco: Harper & Row, 1989).

25. The collage entitled She-ba (English *she* and Hebrew *ba* = to come), which the black artist Romare Bearden created in 1970, depicts her as a powerful liberation queen and majestic contradictory figure of black consciousness. See C. Greene, *Romare Bearden: The Prevalence of Ritual* (New York: Museum of Modern Art, 1970); Myron Schwartzman, *Romare Bearden: His Life and Art* (New York: H. N. Abrams, 1990). See also L. Williams and C. S. Finch, "The Great Queens of Ethiopia," in *Black Women in Antiquity*, ed. Ivan Van Sertima (New Brunswick: Transaction Books, 1985), 12–35, esp. 16–20.

26. James B. Pritchard, ed., *Solomon and Sheba* (London: Phaidon, 1974); Rolf A. Beyer, *Die Königin von Saba: Engel und Dämon: Der Mythos einer Frau* (Bergisch Gladbach: G. Lübbe Verlag, 1987).

27. *The Oxford Classical Dictionary*, 502–503.

28. This is the title of Carol Gilligan's widely influential book, *In a Different Voice: Psychological Theory and Women's Development* (Cambridge, Mass.: Harvard University Press, 1982). However, such a "different voice" must be constructed not in terms of the Western logic of identity, but in terms of the logic of *ekklēsia*.

29. The word "yes" (*nai*) is not found anywhere else in the Gospel and is missing from important manuscripts, such as Papyrus 45. See T. A. Burkill, *New Light on the Earliest Gospel* (Ithaca: Cornell University Press, 1972), 72 n. 3.

30. See, for instance, Herman C. Waetjen, *A Reordering of Power: A Socio-Political Reading of Mark's Gospel* (Minneapolis: Augsburg Fortress Press, 1989), 135, who explains Jesus' ethnocentric refusal as "Jesus' passionate dedication to the fulfillment of Jewish need." Although Waetjen notes the weak manuscript attestation of "yes," he bases his interpretation on it: "She affirms the validity of his proverb by acknowledging Jewish priority. She does not want to deprive the children of their bread."

31. For a feminist reading see Monika Fander, *Die Stellung der Frau im Markusevangelium: Unter besonderer Berücksichtigung kultur- und religionsgeschichtlicher Hintergründe* (Altenberge: Telos Verlag, 1989), 75, who argues that the "but" (*de*) in verse 28 places the response of the woman in the center of

attention. Moreover, the doubling of the verb (*apekrithei kai legei*) places additional emphasis on her speech act.

32. See H. M. Humphrey's suggestive article "Jesus as Wisdom in Mark," *Biblical Theology Bulletin* 19 (1989): 48–53.

33. This text is inspired by Proverbs 9:1–5 and Cady, Ronan, and Taussig, *Wisdom's Feast,* 182.

1. MIRIAM – LEADING THE DANCE

1. Frances E. W. Harper, "Learning to Read," in Frances E. W. Harper, *Sketches of Southern Life* (Philadelphia: Merrihew, 1872).

2. Margaret Fell, *Women's Speaking Justified, Proved and Allowed by the Scriptures* (London 1666; reprint Amherst: Mosher Book & Tract Committee, New England Yearly Meeting of Friends, 1980).

3. Antoinette L. Brown, "Exegesis of I Corinthians XIV, 34, 35 and I Tim II, 11,12," *Oberlin Quarterly Review* 3 (1849): 358–373. Brown wrote this article as a student at Oberlin, where, in 1850, she was the first woman to complete the historical course, although the school would not grant her a degree.

4. Christine de Pizan, *Letter of Othea to Hector*, trans. Jane Chance (Newburyport: Focus Library of Medieval Women, 1990).

5. Katherine C. Bushnell, *God's Word to Women: One Hundred Bible Studies on Women's Place in the Divine Economy* (Probably privately published by the author in 1923; reissued by R. B. Munson, North Carolina).

6. See my forthcoming article on "Feminist Hermeneutics" in the *Abingdon Dictionary of the Bible*.

7. To my knowledge, this expression was first used in the work of the feminist sociologist Dorothy Smith.

8. Adrienne Rich, *The Dream of A Common Language: Poems 1974–1977* (New York: Norton, 1978), 3.

9. For different taxonomies, see, e.g., M. A. Tolbert, "Defining the Problem: The Bible and Feminist Hermeneutics," *Semeia* 28 (1983): 113–126; C. Osiek, "The Feminist and the Bible: Hermeneutical Alternatives," in *Feminist Perspectives on Biblical Scholarship*, ed. A. Yarbro Collins (Atlanta: Scholars Press, 1985), 93–106; G. Gerber Koontz and W. Swartley, eds., *Perspectives on Feminist Hermeneutics* (Elkhart: Institute of Mennonite Studies, 1987); K. Doob Sackenfeld, "Feminist Perspectives on Bible and Theology," *Interpretation* 42(1) (1988): 5–18; and the special issue of *Daughters of Sarah* (May/June 1989), "A Closer Look: Feminist Biblical Interpretation."

10. For a critique of a dichotomizing taxonomy that sees the Bible either as totally sexist or seeks to exonerate it, see also Mieke Bal, *Death and Dissymmetry: The Politics of Coherence in the Book of Judges* (Chicago: University of Chicago Press, 1988), 34.

11. Marie Therese Winter, *WomanWord: A Feminist Lectionary and Psalter: Women of the New Testament* (New York: Crossroad, 1990), xii.

12. See Marjorie Proctor-Smith's article, "Images of Women in the Lectionary," in *Women—Invisible in Church and Theology*, ed. E. Schüssler Fiorenza and M. Collins (Concilium 182; Edinburgh: T. & T. Clark, 1985), 51–62.

13. Such a complementary approach is indicated in the titles of Phyllis Trible's two major works, *God and the Rhetoric of Sexuality* (Philadelphia: Fortress Press, 1978) and *Texts of Terror: Literary Feminist Readings of Biblical Narratives* (Philadelphia: Fortress Press, 1984).

14. See, for instance, L. Swidler, *Biblical Affirmations of Women* (Philadelphia: Westminster Press, 1979).

15. See, for instance, the critique of Swidler's work by B. Brooten, "Early Christian Women and Their Cultural Contexts," in Collins, ed., *Feminist Perspectives*, 65–92, and her "Jewish Women's History in the Roman Period: A Task for Christian Theology," *Harvard Theological Review* 79 (1986): 22–30.

16. Antoinette L. Brown, "Exegesis of I Corinthians XIV., 34, 35; And I Timothy, II., 11.12," *Oberlin Quarterly Review* 5(1849):372.

17. See, e.g., the essays written from an Evangelical perspective in A. Mikelsen, ed., *Women, Authority and the Bible* (Downers Grove, Ill.: Intervarsity Press, 1986).

18. Aileen S. Kraditor, ed., *Up from the Pedestal: Landmark Writings in the American Women's Struggle for Equality* (Chicago: Quadrangle Books, 1968), 54.

19. Kraditor, *Up from the Pedestal*, 109.

20. E. Cady Stanton, ed., *The Original Feminist Attack on the Bible: The Woman's Bible*, vol. 2, facsimile ed. (New York: Arno Press, 1974), 200.

21. See the special section, "Feminist Translation of the New Testament" in *Journal of Feminist Studies in Religion* 6(2) (1990) with contributions by Elizabeth Castelli, "Les belles infideles/Fidelity or Feminism? The Meaning of Feminist Biblical Translation," 25–40; Clarice Martin, "Womanist Interpretation of the New Testament: The Quest for Holistic and Inclusive Translation and Interpretation," 41–62; and the response by Joanna Dewey, Peggy Hutaff, and Jane Schaberg, 63–86.

22. See Eduard Lohse, *Colossians and Philemon* (Hermeneia; Philadelphia: Fortress Press, 1971), 174 n. 44.

23. See especially Deborah Cameron, *Feminism and Linguistic Theory* (London: Macmillan, 1985), who argues for a serious feminist re-examination of how gender and sex affect the use of language: "the repeated assertion that these gender phenomena are just part of the language, open only to a technical and apolitical explanation, simply serves to obscure the ideological and prescriptive nature of what grammarians do" (70).

24. Ibid., 63.

25. For extensive discussion see my article "The 'Quilting' of Women's History: Phoebe of Cenchreae," in *Embodied Love: Sensuality and Relationship as Feminist Values*, ed. P. M. Cooey, S. A. Farmer, and M. E. Ross (San Francisco: Harper & Row, 1987), 35–50.

26. See the excellent book by Marjorie Procter-Smith, *In Her Own Rite* (Nashville: Abingdon Press, 1990).

27. See, for instance, B. A. Withers, ed., *Language and the Church* (New York: National Council of Churches, 1984); P. D. Miller, Jr., "The Inclusive Language Lectionary," *Theology Today* 41 (1984): 26–33; Sharon Ringe, "Standing Toward the Text," *Theology Today* 43 (1987): 552–557.

28. See the excellent book by B. Wren, *What Language Shall I Borrow? God-Talk in Worship: A Male Response to Feminist Theology* (New York: Crossroad, 1989).

29. African-American feminists have derived the expression *womanist* from Alice Walker's work. See Katie G. Cannon, *Black Womanist Ethics* (Atlanta: Scholars Press, 1988) and the roundtable discussion with Renita Weems, et al., "Christian Ethics and Theology in Womanist Perspective," *Journal of Feminist Studies in Religion* 5(2) (1989): 83–112. To my knowledge the expression *mujerista theology* was first used by Ada Maria Isazi-Diaz. See her article "The Bible and Mujerista Theology," in Susan Brooks Thistlethwaite and Mary Potter Engel, eds., *Lift Every Voice: Constructing Christian Theologies From the Underside* (San Francisco: Harper & Row, 1990), 261–269, and the forthcoming roundtable discussion on mujerista theology in *Journal of Feminist Studies in Religion* 8(1) (1992).

30. See, e.g., Winter, *WomanWord;* Martha A. Kirk, CCVI, *Celebrations of Biblical Women's Stories: Tears, Milk and Honey* (Kansas: Sheed & Ward, 1987).

31. For early attempts, see the two books by Rachel C. Wahlberg, *Jesus According to A Woman*, rev. ed. (New York: Paulist Press, 1986) and *Jesus and the Freed Woman* (New York: Paulist Press, 1978).

32. See Judith Plaskow, *Standing Again at Sinai* (San Francisco: Harper & Row, 1990), 52–60.

33. Vincent Wimbush, "The Bible and African Americans: An Outline of an Interpretive History," in *Stony the Road We Trod,* ed. Cain Hope Felder (Minneapolis: Augsburg Fortress Press, 1991), 81–97. See also Cheryl Townsend Gilkes, " 'Mother to the Motherless, Father to the Fatherless': Power, Gender and Community in Afrocentric Biblical Tradition," in *Interpretation for Liberation,* ed. K. G. Cannon and E. Schüssler Fiorenza (Semeia 47; Atlanta: Scholars Press, 1989), 57–86.

34. See for instance the classic by Edith Deen, *All the Women of the Bible* (1955; San Francisco: Harper & Row, 1988).

35. Hazel V. Carby, "On the Threshold of Woman's Era: Lynching, Empire and Sexuality," in *Race, Writing and Difference,* ed. Henry Louis Gates, Jr. (Chicago: University of Chicago Press, 1986), 301–328, and Kwok Pui Lan, "The Image of the 'White Lady': Gender and Race in Christian Mission," in *A Special Nature of Women?,* ed. A. Carr and E. Schüssler Fiorenza (Concilium; London: SCM Press, 1991), 19–27.

36. Renita Weems, *Just a Sister Away: A Womanist Vision of Women's Relationships in the Bible* (San Diego: Lura Media, 1988).

37. For the increase in illiteracy among women in the past twenty years see the United Nations report, *Women of the World 1970–1990: Trends and Statistics* (New York: The United Nations Publications, 1991).

38. P. Scharper and S. Scharper, eds., *The Gospel in Art by the Peasants of Solentiname* (Maryknoll: Orbis Press, 1984).

39. See especially the work of Elisabeth Moltmann-Wendel, *The Women Around Jesus* (New York: Crossroad, 1982).

40. See especially the work of Margaret Miles, *Carnal Knowing: Female Nakedness and Religious Meaning in the Christian West* (Boston: Beacon Press, 1989) and her earlier book, *Image as Insight* (Boston: Beacon Press, 1985).

41. See, e.g., S. Cady, M. Ronan, and H. Taussig, *Wisdom's Feast: Sophia in Study and Celebration* (San Francisco: Harper & Row, 1989); and Verena Wodtke, ed., *Auf den Spuren der Weisheit* (Freiburg: Herder, 1991).

42. See, for instance, Jane Dillenberger, "The Magdalen: Reflections on the Image of the Saint and Sinner in Christian Art," in *Women, Religion and Social Change*, ed. Y. Yazbeck Haddad and E. Banks Findley (Albany: State University of New York Press, 1985), 115–145; and C. Kinstler, *The Moon Under Her Feet: The Story of Mary Magdalene in the Service of the Great Mother* (San Francisco: Harper & Row, 1989), an imaginative retelling of the birth, life, and death of Christ by Mary Magdalene from a matriarchal perspective.

43. Meinrad Craighead, *The Mother's Song: Images of God the Mother* (New York: Paulist Press, 1986).

44. Mary Lou Sleevi, *Women of the Word* (Notre Dame: Ave Maria Press, 1989).

45. Dina Cormick, letter of July 21, 1991.

46. See, e.g., P. Wilson-Kastner et al., eds., *A Lost Tradition: Women Writers of the Early Church* (Washington: University Press of America, 1981); E. A. Clark and D. F. Hatch, *The Golden Bough: The Oaken Cross: The Virgilian Cento of Faltonia Betitia Proba*, Texts and Translations Series/AAR 5 (Chico, Calif.: Scholars Press, 1981) and Elizabeth A. Clark, *The Life of Melania, the Younger: Introduction, Translation and Commentary*, Studies in Women and Religion 14 (Lewiston, N.Y.: Edwin Mellen Press, 1984).

47. A. von Harnack, "Probabilia über die Addresse und den Verfasser des Hebräerbriefes," *Zeitschrift für die Neutestamentliche Wissenschaft* (1900): 16–41; see also the popular account by Ruth Hoppin, *Priscilla: Author of the Epistle to the Hebrews* (New York: Exposition Press, 1969).

48. See the discussion of female authorship by Mary Lefkowitz, "Did Ancient Women Write Novels?," and Ross S. Kraemer, "Women's Authorship of Jewish and Christian Literature in the Greco-Roman Period," in Amy-Jill Levine, ed., *"Women Like This": New Perspectives on Jewish Women in the Greco-Roman World* (Atlanta: Scholars Press, 1991), 199–219 and 221–242.

49. Elizabeth A. Clark, *Ascetic Piety and Women's Faith: Essays on Late Ancient Christianity*, Studies in Women and Religion 20 (Lewiston, N.Y.: Edwin Mellen Press, 1986), 135.

50. Ibid., 143.

51. See, for instance, the observations on Proba in Clark, *Ascetic Piety*, 124–174.

52. William H. Myers, "The Hermeneutical Dilemma of the African American Biblical Student," in Felder, ed., *Stony the Road*, 40–56.

53. See the critique of white feminist scholarship by Jaqueline Grant, *White Women's Christ and Black Women's Jesus* (Atlanta: Scholars Press, 1989) and Barbara Hilkert Andolsen, *Daughters of Jefferson, Daughters of Bootblacks: Racism and American Feminism* (Macon: Mercer University Press, 1986).

54. Dale Spender, *Women of Ideas (And What Men Have Done To Them)* (Boston: Routledge & Kegan, 1982), 19f.

55. See, for instance, Mary F. Lefkowitz and Mary Fant, *Women in Greece and Rome* (Toronto: Samuel-Stevens, 1977) and especially the important work of Ross Kraemer, ed., *Maenads, Martyrs, Matrons, Monastics: A Sourcebook on Women's Religion in the Greco-Roman World* (Philadelphia: Fortress Press, 1988) for documentation and literature.

56. Joan Kelly, *Women, History and Theory* (Chicago: University of Chicago Press, 1984), xii–xiii; J. Wallach Scott, "Gender: A Useful Category of Historical Analysis," in *Coming to Terms: Feminism, Theory, Politics* (New York: Routledge & Kegan, 1989), 81–100.

57. See Jane McIntosh Snyder, *The Woman and the Lyre: Women Writers in Classical Greece and Rome* (Carbondale: Southern Illinois University Press, 1989).

58. See, for instance, L. Portefaix, *Sisters Rejoice: Paul's Letter to the Philippians and Luke-Acts as Received by First Century Philippian Women*, Coniectana Biblica NT Series 20 (Stockholm: Almqvist & Wiksell International, 1988).

59. Carol Meyers, *Discovering Eve: Ancient Israelite Women in Context* (New York: Oxford University Press, 1988) and especially Peggy L. Day, ed., *Gender and Difference in Ancient Israel* (Minneapolis: Augsburg Fortress Press, 1989).

60. See B. Brooten, *Women Leaders in the Ancient Synagogue* (Chico, Calif.: Scholars Press, 1982); G. Mayer, *Die jüdische Frau in der hellenistisch-römischen Antike* (Stuttgart: Verlag Kohlhammer, 1987).

61. See, for instance, Antoinette Clark Wire, *The Corinthian Women Prophets: A Reconstruction through Paul's Rhetoric* (Minneapolis: Augsburg Fortress Press, 1990); B. Bowman Thurston, *The Widows: A Woman's Ministry in the Early Church* (Minneapolis: Augsburg Fortress Press, 1989); Virginia Burrus, *Chastity as Autonomy: Women in the Stories of the Apocryphal Acts* (Lewiston, N.Y.: Edwin Mellen Press, 1987).

62. David L. Balch, *"Let Wives Be Submissive." The Domestic Code in 1 Peter*, SBLMS 26 (Chico, Calif.: Scholars Press, 1981); "Hellenization/Acculturation in 1 Peter," in Charles H. Talbert, ed., *Perspectives on 1 Peter* (Macon: Mercer University Press, 1986), 79–101; "Household Codes," in David Aune, ed., *The New Testament and Greco Roman Literature* (Atlanta: Scholars Press, 1987).

63. See especially the work of Luise Schottroff, *Befreiungserfahrungen: Studien zur Sozialgeschichte des Neuen Testaments* (München: Kaiser Verlag, 1990).

64. Cf. H. Aram Veeser, ed., *The New Historicism* (New York: Routledge, 1989); Dominick LaCapra, *Rethinking Intellectual History: Texts, Contexts, Language* (Ithaca: Cornell University Press, 1983); Theda Skocpol, ed., *Vision and*

Method in Historical Sociology (New York: Cambridge University Press, 1984); and *Poetics Today*, 9(2) (1988), "The Rhetoric of Interpretation and the Interpretation of Rhetoric," ed. Paul Hernadi.

65. Susan Ackermann, " 'And the Women Knead Dough': The Worship of the Queen of Heaven in Sixth-Century Judah," in Day, ed., *Gender and Difference*, 110.

66. For the next section, see my book *In Memory of Her: A Feminist Historical Reconstruction of Christian Origins* (New York: Crossroad, 1983) and chapter 3 in this book.

67. For the discussion of this model, see Rowan Williams, "Does It Make Sense to Speak of Pre-Nicene Orthodoxy?" in *The Making of Orthodoxy*, ed. Rowan Williams (Cambridge: Cambridge University Press, 1989), 1–23. For a discussion of the information which was suppressed or marginalized by such a model, see Karen L. King, ed., *Images of the Feminine in Gnosticism: Studies in Antiquity and Christianity* (Philadelphia: Fortress Press, 1989), as well as the work of Elaine Pagels.

68. See especially the work of M. Bal, E. Fuchs, J. C. Exum, M. A. Tolbert, and G. O'Day.

69. See, for instance, the contributions of Janice Capel Anderson, "Matthew: Gender and Reading," and Elizabeth Struthers Melbon, "Women and Men in the Gospel of Mark," in *The Bible and Feminist Hermeneutics*, ed. Mary Ann Tolbert, (Chico, Calif.: Scholars Press, 1983), 3–28 and 28–48.

70. Portefaix, *Sisters Rejoice*, seeks to utilize reader-response criticism for the historical reconstruction of the audience of Paul.

71. See, for instance, the sophisticated model for narratological analysis developed by Bal, *Death and Dissymmetry*, 248–249 (Appendix 1).

72. Pamela J. Milne, "The Patriarchal Stamp of Scripture," *Journal of Feminist Studies in Religion* 5(1) (1989): 17–34, forcefully argues that the biblical text itself is structured as male mythology. Therefore feminist reformist or revisionist interpretations are unsuccessful in repressing that mythology.

73. Phyllis Trible's work has sought to trace such a "woman's point of view" in the Hebrew Bible but ignores the patriarchal determinants of this point of view. See the critique of Trible's work by Esther Fuchs and Pamela Milne.

74. See, for instance, K. M. Craig and M. A. Kristjansson, "Women Reading as Men/Women Reading as Women: A Structural Analysis for the Historical Project," in *Poststructural Criticism and the Bible: Text/History/Discourse*, ed. Gary A. Phillips, Semeia 51 (Atlanta: Scholars Press, 1990), 119–136.

75. See especially the work of Esther Fuchs: "The Literary Characterization of Mothers and Sexual Politics in the Hebrew Bible," and "Who is Hiding the Truth? Deceptive Women and Biblical Androcentrism," in Collins, ed., *Feminist Perspectives*, 117–136 and 137–144; "Structure and Patriarchal Functions in the Biblical Betrothal Type-Scene," *Journal of Feminist Studies in Religion* 3 (1987): 7–13; "Marginalization, Ambiguity, Silencing: The Story of Jephthah's Daughter," *Journal of Feminist Studies in Religion* 5(1) (1989): 35–46; " 'For I Have the Way of

Women': Deception, Gender, and Ideology in Biblical Narrative" in *Reasoning with the Foxes: Female Wit in a World of Male Power*, ed. J. Cheryl Exum and Johanna W. H. Bos, Semeia 42 (Atlanta: Scholars Press, 1988), 68–83.

76. For a critical analysis of the relationship of various literary critical methods to feminist analysis, see also the responses of Kathleen M. Ashley, "Interrogating Biblical Deception and Trickster Theories: Narratives of Patriarchy or Possibility?," and Mieke Bal, "Tricky Thematics," to the other articles in Exum and Bos, eds., *Reasoning With the Foxes*, 103–116 and 133–155.

77. For instance, Lone Fatum, "Women, Symbolic Universe and Structures of Silence: Challenges and Possibilities in Androcentric Texts," *Studia Theologica* 43 (1989): 61–80, criticizes the project of a feminist reconstruction in terms of a positivist understanding of androcentric language.

78. For literature pertinent to this section see the bibliographical references in chapter 7.

79. See Virginia Fabella, "A Common Methodology for Diverse Christologies," in *With Passion and Compassion: Third World Women Doing Theology*, ed. V. Fabella and M. Oduyoye (Maryknoll: Orbis Press, 1988), 116.

80. See the last chapter of this book, which utilizes rhetorical reader-response criticism to analyze a biblical text.

81. Chung Hyun Kyung, *Struggle To Be the Sun Again: Introducing Asian Women's Theology* (Maryknoll: Orbis Press, 1991), 122, n. 7.

82. See, e.g., *Voices from the Margins: Interpreting the Bible in the Third World*, ed. R. S. Sugirtharajah (Maryknoll: Orbis Press, 1991) and *Lift Every Voice: Constructing Christian Theologies from the Underside*, ed. Susan Brooks Thistlethwaite and Mary Potter Engel (San Francisco: Harper & Row, 1990).

83. See, e.g., Katie Geneva Cannon, "Slave Ideology and Biblical Interpretation," in Cannon and Schüssler Fiorenza, eds., *Interpretation for Liberation*, 9–24.

84. See especially the contributions in the Asian feminist theological journal *In God's Image* and the contributions of Kwok Pui Lan, "God Weeps With Our Pain," *East Asian Journal of Theology* 22 (1984): 228–232 and "Discovering the Bible in the Non-Biblical World," in Cannon and Schüssler Fiorenza, eds., *Interpretation For Liberation*, 25–42.

85. Sr. Vandana, "Water—God's Extravaganza: John 2.1–11," in Sugirtharajah, ed., *Voices From the Margin*, 117–128.

86. See Elsa Tamez, ed., *Through Her Eyes: Women's Theology from Latin America* (Maryknoll: Orbis Press, 1989).

87. Elsa Tamez, "Women's Rereading of the Bible," in Fabella and Oduyoye, eds., *With Passion and Compassion* (Maryknoll: Orbis Press, 1988), 179.

88. June Jordan, "Strong Beyond All Definition . . . ," *The Women's Review of Books* IV (July–August 1987): 1, 20.

89. For such a proposal see, e.g., my Society of Biblical Literature presidential address, "The Ethics of Biblical Interpretation: Decentering Biblical Scholarship," *Journal of Biblical Literature* 107(1) (1988): 3–17.

90. Day, *Gender and Difference*, 1–2. However, such a distinction can only be maintained if feminist liberation theological interpretations are caricatured.

91. Elaine Showalter, "Women's Time, Women's Space: Writing the History of Feminist Criticism," in *Feminist Issues in Literary Scholarship*, ed. Shari Benstock (Bloomington: Indiana University Press, 1987), 42; see also Nina Baym, "The Madwoman and Her Languages: Why I Don't Do Feminist Literary Theory," ibid., 45–61.

92. For a discussion of such a critical theory of language see Cameron, *Feminism and Linguistic Theory*.

93. See the special section, "Feminist Translation of the New Testament," in *Journal of Feminist Studies in Religion* 6(2) (1990): 25–86.

94. Cf. for instance the analysis of T. Drorah Setel, "Prophets and Pornography: Female Sexual Imagery in Hosea," in *Feminist Interpretation of the Bible*, ed. L. Russell, 86–95; and R. Weems, "Gomer: Victim of Violence or Victim of Metaphor," in Cannon and Schüssler Fiorenza, eds., *Interpretation for Liberation*, 87–104.

95. The Sri Lankan theologian Aloysius Pieris, in *An Asian Theology of Liberation* (Maryknoll: Orbis Press, 1988), 87, suggests that the term Third World not be used just as a geographical term but that "it is a theological neologism for God's own people. It stands for the starving sons and daughters of Jacob—of all places and all times—who go in search of bread to a rich country, only to become its slaves. In other words, the Third World is not merely the story of the South in relation to the North or of the East in relation to the West. It is something that happens wherever and whenever socioeconomic dependence in terms of race, class, or sex generates political and cultural slavery, fermenting thereby a new peoplehood." The reality of oppression which Pieris names "Third World," I have identified as the system of patriarchal domination and subordination, exploitation and poverty.

96. For these characterizations of bourgeois biblical readings, see Johannes Thiele, "Bibelauslegung im gesellschaftlich-politischen Kontext," in *Handbuch der Bibelarbeit*, ed. W. Langer (München: Kösel Verlag, 1987), 106–114.

97. Jürgen Habermas, *The Theory of Communicative Action* (Boston: Beacon Press, 1987).

98. For a concise review of the theological discussion on biblical interpretation and reception, see Francis Schüssler Fiorenza, "The Crisis of Scriptural Authority: Interpretation and Reception," *Interpretation* 44(4) (1990): 353–368, and D. Jodock, "The Reciprocity Between Scripture and Theology," ibid., 369–382.

99. See also Wilhelm Wuellner, "Hermeneutics and Rhetorics: From 'Truth and Method' to 'Truth and Power'," *Scriptura* S 3 (1989): 1–54; and Burton L. Mack, *Rhetoric and the New Testament* (Minneapolis: Augsburg Fortress Press, 1990); W. Brueggemann, "At the Mercy of Babylon: A Subversive Rereading of the Empire," *Journal of Biblical Literature* 110(1) (1991): 3–22.

100. For a feminist elaboration of the hermeneutical paradigm, see Sandra M. Schneiders, *Beyond Patching: Faith and Feminism in the Catholic Church* (New York: Paulist Press, 1991), 57–91.

101. For the role of imagination in proclamation, see T. G. Long, "The Use of Scripture in Contemporary Preaching," *Interpretation* 44(4) (1990): 341–352.

102. Maureen Mara, a student at Boston College, audited my course "Gospel Stories of Women" in the Spring of 1990 and wrote the following paper in the context of a group project on Herodias.

2. ARACHNE – WEAVING THE WORD

This chapter is a greatly expanded and revised version of an article which has appeared in two quite different versions: "A Feminist Critical Interpretation for Liberation: Martha and Mary (Lk 10:38–42)," *Religion and Intellectual Life* 3 (1986): 16–36 and "Theological Criteria and Historical Reconstruction: Martha and Mary (Lk 10:38–42)," in *Protocol of the Fifty-Third Colloquy: 10 April 1986*, ed. Herman Waetjen (Berkeley: Center for Hermeneutical Studies in Hellenistic and Modern Culture, 1987), 1–12, 41–63.

1. Adrienne Rich, *A Wild Patience Has Taken Me This Far: Poems (1978–1981)* New York: Norton, 1981), 14.

2. Nancy K. Miller, "Arachnalogies: The Woman, The Text, and the Critic," in *The Poetics of Gender*, ed. Nancy K. Miller (New York: Columbia University Press, 1986), 271ff.

3. Roland Barthes, *The Pleasure of the Text* (New York: Hill and Wang, 1975), 64.

4. Miller, "Arachnalogies," 272.

5. Such a critical feminist model of text and interpretation has affinities with the understanding of midrash developed by Gerald L. Bruns, "The Hermeneutics of Midrash," in *The Book and the Text: The Bible and Literary Theory*, ed. Regina Schwartz (Oxford: Basil Blackwell, 1990), 189–213.

6. See Paolo Freire, *Pedagogy of the Oppressed* (New York: Seabury Press, 1973).

7. Cf. Beverly Wildung Harrison, *Making the Connections: Essays in Feminist Social Ethics* (Boston: Beacon Press, 1985), 235–263.

8. See Christine Schaumberger, "Subversive Bekehrung," in *Schuld und Macht: Studien zu einer feministischen Befreiungstheologie*, ed. C. Schaumberger and L. Schottroff (München: Kaiser Verlag, 1988), 153–282, 202–216, for a discussion of the difficulties in moving women's groups from the sharing of experience to a critical political analysis.

9. For such a deliberate misreading, see George W. Stroup, "Between Echo and Narcissus: The Role of the Bible in Feminist Theology," *Interpretation* 42(1) (1988): 25.

10. Jean Wyatt, *Reconstructing Desire: The Role of the Unconscious in Women's Reading and Writing* (Chapel Hill: University of North Carolina Press, 1990), 215f; see also Linda K. Christian-Smith, *Becoming a Woman Through Romance* (New York: Routledge, 1990): "Popular fiction, a literary fantasy in which one can dream about an identity and pleasures often beyond what is socially possible or acceptable . . . encourages reflection on problems from everyday life and on various alternatives in the imagination" (9).

11. Lynn Gottlieb, "The Secret Jew: An Oral Tradition of Women," in *On Being A Jewish Feminist: A Reader*, ed. Susannah Heschel (New York: Schocken Books, 1983), 273.

12. Eugene LaVerdiere, "The One Thing Required," *Emmanuel* (September 1983): 398–399.

13. For literature and discussion of this text, see Joseph Fitzmyer, *The Gospel According to Luke X–XXIV* (Garden City: Doubleday, 1985), 891–895; for more popular commentaries, see Frederick W. Danker, *Jesus and the New Age: A Commentary on St. Luke's Gospel*, rev. ed. (Philadelphia: Fortress Press, 1988), 224–226; David L. Tiede, *Luke*, Augsburg Commentary Series (Minneapolis: Augsburg Publishing House, 1988), 210f.

14. It is usually shocking but potentially liberating to students who have internalized in one form or another a doctrine of the Bible as verbal inspiration to come to realize that scholars not only interpret but also establish the original text of the Bible. For a critical discussion of these textual variants, see Jutta Brutscheck, *Die Maria-Martha-Erzählung: Eine redaktionsgeschichtliche Untersuchung zu Lk 10,38–42*, BBB 64 (Frankfurt-Bonn: Verlag Peter Hanstein, 1986), 4–29; M. Zerwick, "Optima Pars (Lc 10,38–42)," *Verbum Domini* 27 (1929): 294–298; M. Augsten, "Lukanische Miszelle," *New Testament Studies* 14 (1967/68): 581–583; A. Baker, "One Thing Necessary," *Catholic Biblical Quarterly* 27 (1965): 127–135; Gordon D. Fee, "One Thing Needful? Luke 10:42," in *New Testament Criticism*, ed. E. J. Epp and G. D. Fee (Cambridge: Cambridge University Press, 1981), 61–76.

15. See Daniel A. Scanyi, "Optima Pars. Die Auslegungsgeschichte von Lk 10, 38–42 bei den Kirchenvätern der ersten vier Jahrhunderte," *Studia Monastica* 2 (1960): 5–78; A Kemmer, "Maria und Martha: Zur Deutungsgeschichte von Lk 10,38ff im alten Mönchtum," *Erbe und Auftrag* 40 (1964): 355–367; J. B. Lotz, "Martha und Maria," *Geist und Leben* 32 (1959): 161–165.

16. Ben Witherington III, *Women in the Ministry of Jesus*, SNTSM 51 (Cambridge: Cambridge University Press, 1984), 101.

17. See W. H. Wuellner and R. C. Leslie, *The Surprising Gospel: Intriguing Psychological Insights from the New Testament* (Nashville: Abingdon Press, 1984), 110; see also Wuellner's response to my interpretation of the text in E. Schüssler Fiorenza, "Theological Criteria and Historical Reconstruction."

18. R. Conrad Wahlberg, *Jesus According to a Woman* (New York: Paulist Press, 1976), 79.

19. However, please note that I do not analyze John 11 and 12 here in terms of a hermeneutics of suspicion but only in terms of a hermeneutics of reconstruction. If I were to focus here on the Fourth Gospel, such a hermeneutics of suspicion and critical evaluation would be absolutely necessary for a critical feminist interpretation for liberation.

20. Rudolph Bultmann, *History of the Synoptic Tradition* (New York: Harper & Row, 1968), 33.

21. See Jutta Brutscheck, *Maria-Martha-Erzählung*, 30–49.

22. To explain away this dynamic of the story with reference to notions of the

Eastern world is to miss the point. "The immediate reaction of most of us in the Western world is to ask why Martha didn't go directly to Mary. Why was it necessary to go to Jesus at all? But the ways of the Eastern world follow precisely the route that Martha took. Instead of open and direct confrontation, the Eastern world characteristically works through a third person to avoid any loss of face on anyone's part. Martha's approach to Jesus was thoroughly consistent with the culture in which she lived" (Wuellner and Leslie, *The Surprising Gospel*, 111). It is obvious, however, that Luke did not plot the story in such a way because he wanted Martha to save face. The opposite seems to be the case. The narrative discredits Martha.

23. Mary Rose D'Angelo, "Women Partners in the New Testament," *Journal of Feminist Studies in Religion* 6(1) (1990): 65–86, suggests that *adelphē*, sister, should be read as a missionary title and Martha and Mary understood as a missionary pair. Such a contextualization in the practices of the early Christian missionary movement as I have developed them in *In Memory of Her*, 160–184, is likely and supports my interpretation here. However, her further conclusion that both are a paradigm for lesbian couples who shared "their lives in the Christian mission in relationships that were parallel to those of husband and wife missioners" cannot be substantiated since we do not know whether female-male teams, such as Prisca and Aquila, were married couples.

24. Unfortunately the article of Adele Reinhartz, "From Narrative to History: The Resurrection of Mary and Martha," in Amy-Jill Levine, ed., "*Women Like This*," 161–184 was not yet available when I revised this chapter. However, her argument against my interpretation overlooks that the rhetoric of kyriocentric texts functions differently with respect to women and men.

25. For elaboration and documentation of such a hermeneutics, see my *In Memory of Her: A Feminist Theological Reconstruction of Christian Origins* (New York: Crossroad, 1983).

26. For the patriarchal shaping of the household and the householder motifs in Luke-Acts that "mollifies the revolutionary eschatological language of the Q-tradition" and in Acts "portrays conversion of households from the top down," see L. Michael White, "Scaling the Strongman's 'Court'," *Forum* 3(3) (1987): 18.

27. Gerd Theissen, *Sociology of Early Palestinian Christianity* (Philadelphia: Fortress Press, 1978) and the critical review by W. Stegemann, "Vagabond Radicalism in Early Christianity? A Historical and Theological Discussion of a Thesis Proposed by Gerd Theissen," in *The God of the Lowly: Socio-Historical Interpretations of the Bible*, ed. W. Schottroff and W. Stegemann (Maryknoll: Orbis Press, 1984), 148–168.

28. For further discussion and literature, see my *In Memory of Her*, 139f. For a more positive evaluation of Luke's remark in 8:1–3 see Witherington, *Women in the Ministry of Jesus*, 117. Yet by construing Luke's historical context as rabbinic Judaism, he succumbs to an anti-Jewish reading.

29. See F. W. Danker, *Benefactor, Epigraphic Study of a Graeco-Roman and New Testament Semantic Field* (St. Louis: Clayton Press, 1982); David Lull, "The

Servant-Benefactor As a Model of Greatness (Lk 22:24–30)," *Novum Testamentum* 28 (1986): 289–305.

30. H. Moxnes, *The Economy of the Kingdom: Social Conflict and Economic Relations in Luke's Gospel* (Philadelphia: Fortress Press, 1988), 133f.

31. See especially E. Laland, "Die Martha-Maria-Perikope Lukas 10, 38–42," *Studia Theologica* 13 (1959): 70–85.

32. Such parallel stories are: Zachariah and Mary (1:1–2:26–38); Simon and Anna (2:25–38); the healings of the demoniac and of Simon's mother-in-law (4:31–39); centurion's slave and the son of the widow of Nain (7:1–17); the good Samaritan and the sisters at Bethany (10:29–42); the Sabbath healing of the woman bent double and of the man with dropsy (13:10–17; 14:1–6); the parables of mustard seed and leaven (13:18–21) and of the lost sheep and lost coin (15:4–10); the stories of the widow and tax-collector (18:1–14); of Simon and Cyrene and the women of Jerusalem (23:26–31); the healings of Aeneas and Dorcas (Acts 9:32–42); the vision of the Macedonian and the conversion of the Lydian (Acts 16:9–15); the conversions of Dionysus and Damaris (Acts 17:34).

33. Constance F. Parvey, "The Theology and Leadership of Women in the New Testament," in *Religion and Sexism*, ed. Rosemary Radford Ruether (New York: Simon & Schuster, 1974), 139.

34. Acts 8:3; 9:1f; 17:11f; 22:5f.

35. Acts 1:16; 2:29.37; 13:15.26.38; 15:7.13; 23:1.6; 28:17.

36. Compare, e.g., Hermann-Josef Venetz, "Die Suche nach dem 'einen Notwendigen'," *Orientierung* 54 (1990): 185–189; see also W. S. Anderson and the minutes of the overall discussion found in Waetjen, ed., *Protocol of the Fifty-Third Colloquy: 10 April 1986*, 17–20, 41–63.

37. See now also Steven Davies, "Women in the Third Gospel and the New Testament Apocrypha," in Amy-Jill Levine, ed., *"Women Like This,"* 185–198. In this article Davies has abandoned his positive reading of the Lukan double-work and therefore no longer believes that it was authored by a woman.

38. Robert W. Wall, "Martha and Mary (Luke 10,38–42) in the Context of a Christian Deuteronomy," *Journal for the Study of the New Testament* 35 (1989): 19–35, connects all three pericopes in terms of the deuteronomic Shema.

39. I am following here the analysis of Jutta Brutscheck, *Maria-Martha-Erzählung*, 50–64.

40. See the analysis of the dualisms structuring this passage and its Lukan context by Kerry M. Craig and M. A. Kristjansson, "Women Reading as Men/Women Reading as Women: A Structural Analysis for the Historical Project," in *Poststructural Criticism and the Bible: Text/History/Discourse*, ed. Gary Phillips, *Semeia* 51 (Atlanta: Scholars Press, 1990): 119–136. However, their structural analysis reinscribes cultural gender dualism insofar as they assume without question that one reads either *as a man* or *as a woman*.

41. At stake for theologians in such an interpretation that privileges the listening Mary is their own "masculine" authority to speak which requires a "feminine" audience to listen. See for a similar discussion but with a somewhat different

emphasis, Walter Magaß, "Maria und Martha—Kirche und Haus: Thesen zu einer institutionellen Konkurrenz," *Linguistica Biblica* 27(28) (1973): 2–5.

42. The contrasting opposition between Mary and Judas corresponds to the anti-Jewish tendencies in the Fourth Gospel. Whereas the "sectarian" tendencies of the Fourth Gospel allow for women's leadership, the apologetic interests of Luke's gospel vis-à-vis the Roman patriarchal order leads to the downplaying of women's leadership roles. A clue to this editorial tendency is found in Acts 16:21, where Paul is accused of advocating "customs which it is not lawful for Romans to practice."

43. For a similar interpretation see Frances Beydon, "A temps nouveau, nouvelles questions: Luc 10,38–42," *Foi & Vie: Cahier Biblique* 28 88(5) (1989): 25–32. However, she does not refer to my work.

44. Since such an exploration generally does not belong to the task of professional exegesis, it is also not very well developed in feminist biblical studies. See, however, Susan Brooks Thistlethwaite, "Every Two Minutes: Battered Women and Feminist Interpretation," in *Feminist Interpretation of the Bible*, ed. Letty M. Russell (Philadelphia: Westminster Press, 1985), 96–110; Renita J. Weems, *Just a Sister Away: A Womanist Vision of Women's Relationships in the Bible* (San Diego: Lura Media, 1988); and the feminist collections of sermons by Annie Lally Milhaven, ed., *Sermons Seldom Heard* (New York: Crossroad, 1991).

45. Janice Radway, *Reading the Romance: Women, Patriarchy and Popular Literature* (Chapel Hill: University of North Carolina Press, 1984), 209–222.

46. Ben Witherington III, *Women in the Ministry of Jesus*, SNTSM 51 (Cambridge: Cambridge University Press, 1984), 118.

47. Letty M. Russell, "Women and Ministry," in A. L. Hageman, *Sexist Religion and Women in the Church* (New York: Association Press, 1974), 55ff.

48. All quotes are taken from R. Richardson Smith, "Liberating the Servant," *The Christian Century* 98 (1981): 13–14; see also R. Propst, "Servanthood Redefined: Coping Mechanism for Women Within Protestant Christianity," *Journal of Pastoral Counseling* 17 (1982): 14–18.

49. Rosemary Radford Ruether, *Sexism and God-Talk: Toward a Feminist Theology* (Boston: Beacon Press, 1983), 207; see also the various contributions of Letty M. Russell.

50. Examples of such a hermeneutics of imagination are, e.g., Martha Ann Kirk, CCVI, *Celebrations of Biblical Women's Stories: Tears, Milk and Honey* (Kansas: Sheed & Ward, 1987), and Miriam Therese Winter, *WomanWord: A Feminist Lectionary and Psalter: Women of the New Testament* (New York: Crossroad, 1990).

51. See, for instance, Heidemarie Langer and Herta Leistner, "Mary and Martha," in *Women's Prayer Services*, ed. Iben Gjerding and Katherine Kinnamon (Mystic: Twenty-Third Publications, 1987), 71–73, and the interpretation of the Ecumenical Women's Group Aarhus, "Mary and Martha," ibid., 55.

52. Quoted from a paper by Jean Young, written after a workshop in the Feminist Spirituality Program of Immaculate Heart College in Los Angeles, August 1984.

53. Revised and quoted from a paper by Gena Marie Stinnett, who participated in the same workshop.

3. MARY OF MAGDALA – RE-MEMBERING THE PAST

This chapter draws on materials of my article "Text and Reality—Reality as Text: The Problem of a Feminist Historical and Social Reconstruction Based on Texts," *Studia Theologica* 43 (1989), 19–34. I want to thank not only Professors Halvor Moxnes and Turid Karlsen Seim for inviting me to the University of Oslo, but also the seminar participants from other Nordic countries for their warm reception, insights, and questions.

1. I have revised "A Wandering Aramaean . . ." by Mother Thunder Mission, in Gjerding and Kinnamon, eds., *Women's Prayer Series,* 41.

2. Michelle Cliff, "A Journey into Speech," in *The Graywolf Annual Five: Multicultural Literacy,* ed. R. Simonson and S. Walker (Saint Paul: Graywolf Press, 1988), 59.

3. For the following discussion, see my book *Bread Not Stone: The Challenge of Feminist Biblical Interpretation* (Boston: Beacon Press, 1984).

4. Anne Merideth, Integration Paper for Course on New Testament Theology, November 1989.

5. See Renato Rosaldo, *Culture and Truth: The Remaking of Social Analysis* (Boston: Beacon Press, 1989).

6. See Sandra Harding, *The Science Question in Feminism* (Ithaca: Cornell University Press, 1986); Terry R. Kendal, *The Woman Question in Classical Sociological Theory* (Miami: Florida University Press, 1988); Mary Lyndon Shanley and Carole Pateman, eds., *Feminist Interpretations and Political Theory* (University Park: Pennsylvania State University Press, 1991); Christine Farnham, ed., *The Impact of Feminist Research in the Academy* (Bloomington: Indiana University Press, 1987).

7. Itumeleng J. Mosala, *Biblical Hermeneutics of Black Theology in South Africa* (Grand Rapids: Eerdmans, 1989), 55.

8. See the critique of the work of Hans Frei and George Lindbeck by M. A. Tolbert, *Sowing the Gospel: Mark's World in Literary-Historical Perspective* (Minneapolis: Augsburg Fortress Press, 1989), 25 n. 8, and the critical review of her book by V. K. Robbins, "Text and Context in Recent Studies of the Gospel of Mark," *Religious Studies Review* 17 (1991): 16–23: "Indeed the principles of formalism and New Criticism finally dominate in such a manner that the interpretation significantly suppresses the intertextuality of the narrative and virtually drives its intertextuality out of sight by the time the interpretation reaches its conclusion" (18).

9. Janice Capel Anderson, "Matthew: Gender and Reading," *Semeia* 28 (1983): 26.

10. Elizabeth Struthers Melbon, "Fallible Followers: Women and Men in the Gospel of Mark," *Semeia* 28 (1983): 47.

11. See Jürgen Becker, ed., *Die Anfänge des Christentums: Alte Welt und Neue Hoffnung* (Stuttgart: Kohlhammer, 1987); Howard C. Kee, "Sociology of the New Testament," in *Harper's Bible Dictionary*, ed. P. J. Achtemeier (San Francisco: Harper & Row, 1985), 961–968, lists along with his own work that of Judge, Meeks, and Theissen.

12. Linda Hutcheon, *The Politics of Postmodernism* (London: Routledge, 1989), 168.

13. See, e.g., the contributions of Elizabeth Meese, *Crossing the Double Cross: The Practice of Feminist Criticism* (Chapel Hill: University of North Carolina Press, 1986); S. Benhabib and D. Cornell, eds., *Feminism as Critique* (Minneapolis: University of Minnesota Press, 1987); Teresa de Lauretis, ed., *Feminist Studies/ Critical Studies* (Bloomington: Indiana University Press, 1986); G. Greene and C. Kahn, eds., *Making a Difference: Feminist Literary Criticism* (New York: Methuen, 1983); J. Newton and D. Rosenfelt, eds., *Feminist Criticism and Social Change: Sex, Class and Race in Literature and Culture* (New York: Methuen, 1983); M. Pryse and Hortense J. Spillers, eds., *Conjuring: Black Women, Fiction and Literary Tradition* (Bloomington: University of Indiana Press, 1985).

14. Linda Alcoff, "Justifying Feminist Social Science," *Hypatia* 2 (1987): 116ff.

15. Judith Newton, "History as Usual?: Feminism and the New Historicism," *Cultural Critique* 9 (1988): 87–121.

16. Joan Kelly, *Women, History, and Theory* (Chicago: University of Chicago Press, 1984), xii, xiii.

17. Sandra Harding, "The Method Question," *Hypatia* 3 (1987): 30; Nancy Hartsock, "Rethinking Modernism: Minority vs. Majority Theories," *Cultural Critique* 7 (1987): 205f. See also Karen Dugger, "Social Location and Gender-Role Attitudes: A Comparison of Black and White Women," *Gender & Society* 2 (1988): 425–448.

18. Newton, "History as Usual?," 98.

19. See Richard Harvey Brown, *Society as Text: Essays on Rhetoric, Reason, and Reality* (Chicago: University of Chicago Press, 1987), 97–112.

20. Feminist historians therefore question accepted schemes of periodization. See, e.g., Kelly, *Women, History, and Theory*, 19–50.

21. Hayden White, *Tropics of Discourse: Essays in Cultural Criticism* (Baltimore: Johns Hopkins University Press, 1978), 98.

22. Hutcheon, *Politics of Postmodernism*, 81.

23. Chris Weedon, *Feminist Practice and Poststructuralist Theory* (Oxford: Blackwell, 1987).

24. B. Creed, "From Here to Modernity: Feminism and Postmodernism," *Screen* 28(2) (1987): 47–67.

25. Harding, *The Science Question*, 191. For a different emphasis, see Nancy C. M. Hartsock, *Money, Sex and Power: Toward a Feminist Historical Materialism* (New York: Longman, 1983).

26. Kelly, *Women, History, and Theory*, 51–64.

27. Compare, e.g., Nancy M. Hartsock, "The Feminist Standpoint: Developing the Ground for a Specifically Feminist Historical Materialism," and Sandra M. Harding, "Why Has the Sex/Gender System Become Visible Only Now?" in *Dis-*

covering Reality: Feminist Perspectives on Epistemology, Metaphysics, Methodology, and Philosophy of Science, ed. S. Harding and M. B. Hintikka (Dordrecht: D. Reidel, 1983), 283–310 and 310–324. Also see Terry Winant, "The Feminist Standpoint: A Matter of Language," *Hypatia* 2 (1987): 142.

28. See also T. Modlesky, "Feminism and the Power of Interpretation: Some Critical Readings," in *Feminist Studies/Critical Studies,* ed. Teresa de Lauretis (Bloomington: Indiana University Press, 1986), 121–138.

29. For the redefinition of "humanist" in terms of Afro-American women's tradition, see Patricia Hill Collins, *Black Feminist Thought: Knowledge, Consciousness and the Politics of Empowerment* (Boston: Unwin Hyman, 1990).

30. See especially the first three chapters in my *In Memory of Her.* Judith Plaskow, "Standing Again at Sinai: Jewish Memory from a Feminist Perspective," *Tikkun* 1 (1987): 28–34, has adapted this model for a feminist reconstruction of Jewish history; Carol P. Christ, *Laughter of Aphrodite: Reflections on a Journey to the Goddess* (San Francisco: Harper & Row, 1987), has used it to reclaim Goddess history.

31. Adrienne Munich, "Notorious Signs, Feminist Criticism, and Literary Tradition," in Greene and Kahn, eds., *Making A Difference,* 256.

32. See the revised version of my article, "A Feminist Critical Interpretation for Liberation: Martha and Mary (Lk 10:38–42)," *Religion & Intellectual Life* 3 (1986): 21–36 in chapter 3 which takes the discussion in Waetjen, ed., *Protocol of the Fifty-Third Colloquy* into account.

33. See also my article, "Die Anfänge von Kirche, Amt, und Priestertum in feministisch-theologischer Sicht," in *Priesterkirche,* ed. P. Hoffmann (Düsseldorf: Patmos, 1987), 62–95.

34. See Susan Moller Okin, *Women in Western Political Thought* (Princeton: Princeton University Press, 1979), 15–98; Elizabeth V. Spelman, *Inessential Woman: Problems of Exclusion in Feminist Thought* (Boston: Beacon Press, 1988), 19–56.

35. Page duBois, *Centaurs & Amazons: Women and the Pre-History of the Great Chain of Being* (Ann Arbor: University of Michigan Press, 1982).

36. The plight of slave women is not addressed in Natalie Harris Bluestone's interpretation, *Women and the Ideal Society: Plato's Republic and Modern Myths of Gender* (Amherst: University of Massachusetts Press, 1987).

37. DuBois, *Centaurs & Amazons,* 133ff.

38. See Schüssler Fiorenza, *In Memory of Her,* 254–260; duBois, *Centaurs & Amazons,* 141–146.

39. Sharon Ringe, "A Gentile Woman's Story," in *Feminist Interpretation of the Bible,* ed. L. Russell (Philadelphia: Westminster Press, 1985), 68.

40. Gail R. O'Day, "Surprised by Faith: Jesus and the Canaanite Woman," *Listening: Journal of Religion and Culture* 24 (1989): 299.

41. E. M. Wainwright, *Towards a Feminist Critical Reading of the Gospel According to Matthew,* BZNW 60 (Berlin: de Gruyter, 1991).

42. H. Koester, *Introduction to the New Testament,* vol. 2 (Philadelphia: Fortress Press, 1982), 205f.

43. Alfred Schutz, *Collected Papers II: Studies in Social Theory* (The Hague:

M. Nijhoff, 1964): "The context of meaning in which a predecessor's experience was located differs radically from the context in which the 'same' experience would appear for a contemporary. Consequently, the experience cannot be the 'same.' I can say, however, that my predecessor's experience was human experience: I can interpret it in the context of my knowledge of the structure of human experience as meaningful experience in general" (60). However, note the idealistic, universalizing tenor of this statement, which does not indicate its particular sociopolitical location! For a feminist assessment of Schutz, see Louise Levesque-Lopman, *Claiming Reality: Phenomenology and Women's Experience* (Totowa: Rowman & Littlefield, 1988).

4. JUSTA – CONSTRUCTING COMMON GROUND

1. Margaret Goss Burroughs, "Everybody But Me," in *The Forerunners*, ed. Woodie King, Jr. (Cambridge: Harvard University Press, 1975).

2. Christine Schaumberger and Luise Schottroff, *Schuld und Macht. Studien zu einer feministischen Befreiungstheologie* (München: Chr. Kaiser Verlag, 1988), 202–216.

3. For a discussion and definition of the term, see Maggie Humm, *The Dictionary of Feminist Theory* (Columbus: Ohio State University Press, 1990), 159–161; Gerda Lerner, *The Creation of Patriarchy* (New York: Oxford University Press, 1986), 231–243. In contrast to Lerner, I am not interested in the origins of patriarchal domination but in its delineation as a heuristic historical category.

4. For a problematization and discussion of the essentialist/constructivist opposition, see Diana Fuss, *Essentially Speaking: Feminism, Nature & Difference* (New York: Routledge, 1989).

5. Adriana Cavarero, "L'elaborazione filosofica della differenza sessuale," in *La ricerca delle donne. Studi femministi in Italia*, ed. Maria Cristina Marcuzzo and Anna Rossi-Doria (Turin: Rosenberg, 1987), 173–187. See also her "Die Perspektive der Geschlechterdifferenz," in *Differenz und Gleichheit: Menschenrechte haben [k]ein Geschlecht*, ed. Ute Gerhard et al. (Frankfurt: Ulrike Helmer Verlag, 1990), 95–111.

6. Teresa de Lauretis, "The Essence of the Triangle or, Taking the Risk of Essentialism Seriously: Feminist Theory in Italy, the U.S., and Britain," *Difference* 1(2) (1989): 32.

7. In the United States see especially Anne Ulanov's work, and in Germany the work of Christa Mulack and the discussion of her work by Cornelia Giese, *Gleichheit und Differenz: Vom dualistischen Denken zur polaren Weltsicht* (München: Verlag Frauenoffensive, 1990).

8. See Mary Daly, *GynEcology: The Metaethics of Radical Feminism* (Boston: Beacon Press, 1978) and *Pure Lust: Elemental Feminist Philosophy* (Boston: Beacon Press, 1984). For a critical assessment of Daly's work, see Hester Eisenstein, *Contemporary Feminist Thought* (Boston: G. K. Hall, 1983), esp. 107–115; Ruth

Großmaß, "Von der Verführungskraft der Bilder: Mary Daly's Elemental-Feministische Philosophie," in *Feministischer Kompaß, patriarchales Gepäck: Kritik konservativer Anteile in neueren feministischen Theorien,* ed. R. Großmaß and C. Schmerl (Frankfurt: Campus Verlag, 1989), 56–116.

9. For a critical discussion, see Domna Stanton, "Language and Revolution: The Franco-American Dis-Connection," in *The Future of Difference,* ed. H. Eisenstein and A. Jardine (Boston: G. K. Hall, 1980), 73–87; Gayatri Chakravorty Spivak, "French Feminism in an International Frame," in *In Other Worlds: Essays in Cultural Politics* (New York: Methuen, 1987), 134–153; Alexandra Busch, "Der metaphorische Schleier des ewig Weiblichen—Zu Luce Irigaray's Ethik der sexuellen Differenz," in Großmaß and Schmerl, eds., *Feministischer Kompaß,* 117–171.

10. Sara Ruddick, "Maternal Thinking," *Feminist Studies* 6 (1980): 342–367 and her book *Maternal Thinking. Toward a Politics of Peace* (Boston: Beacon Press, 1989); for a critical discussion, see Lorraine Code, *What Can She Know? Feminist Theory and the Construction of Knowledge* (Ithaca: Cornell University Press, 1991), 87–97; A. Carr and E. Schüssler Fiorenza, eds., *Motherhood: Experience, Institution, Theology,* Concilium 206 (Edinburgh: T. & T. Clark, 1989); U. Pasero und U. Pfäfflin (HgbInnen) *Neue Mütterlichkeit. Ortsbestimmungen,* GTB Siebenstern 577 (Gütersloh: Mohn, 1986).

11. Domna C. Stanton, "Difference on Trial: A Critique of the Maternal Metaphor in Cixous, Irigaray, and Kristeva," in *The Poetics of Gender,* ed. Nancy K. Miller (New York: Columbia University Press, 1986), 176.

12. E. A. Grosz, "The In(ter)vention of Feminist Knowledges," in *Crossing Boundaries: Feminisms and the Critique of Knowledges,* ed. Barbara Caine, E. A. Grosz, and Marie de Lepervanche (Sydney: Allen & Unwin, 1988), 97–103.

13. Compare, e.g., bell hooks, *Feminist Theory: From Margin to Center* (Boston: South End Press, 1984), *Talking Back: Thinking Feminist/Thinking Black* (Boston: South End Press, 1989) and *Yearning: Race, Gender, and Cultural Politics* (Boston: South End Press, 1990); Paula Giddings, *When and Where I Enter: The Impact of Black Women on Race and Sex in America* (New York: William Morrow, 1984); Cheryl A. Wall, ed., *Changing Our Own Words: Essays on Criticism, Theory, and Writing by Black Women* (New Brunswick: Rutgers University Press, 1989); Henry Louis Gates, Jr., ed., *Reading Black: Reading Feminist* (New York: Meridian, 1990); Patricia Hill Collins, *Black Feminist Thought: Knowledge, Consciousness and the Politics of Empowerment* (Boston: Unwin Hyman, 1990); Joanne M. Braxton and Andrèe Nicola McLaughlin, eds., *Wild Women in the Whirlwind: Afro-American Culture and the Contemporary Literary Renaissance* (New Brunswick: Rutgers University Press, 1990).

14. Laura Kipnis, "Feminism: The Political Consciousness of Postmodernism?," in *Universal Abandon? The Politics of Postmodernism,* ed. A. Ross (Minneapolis: University of Minnesota Press, 1988), 162.

15. See Abdul R. JanMohamed, "The Economy of Manichean Allegory: The Function of Racial Difference in Colonialist Literature," in *Race, Writing and Difference,* ed. Henry Louis Gates, Jr. (Chicago: University of Chicago Press, 1986), 78–106.

16. Chris Weedon, *Feminist Practice and Poststructuralist Theory* (New York: Basil Blackwell, 1987), 41.

17. Tamsin E. Lorraine, *Gender, Identity, and the Production of Meaning* (Boulder: Westview Press, 1990).

18. Ibid., 181.

19. Teresa L. Ebert, "The Romance of Patriarchy: Ideology, Subjectivity, and Postmodern Feminist Cultural Theory," *Cultural Critique* 10 (1988): 19.

20. The discussions of Lacan, Foucault, and Althusser in feminist theory are numerous. For a good introduction to this complex field of reasoning, see Weedon, *Feminist Practice and Poststructuralist Theory*.

21. Ebert, "The Romance of Patriarchy," 30.

22. Ibid., 25.

23. Ibid., 33.

24. Whereas the self-designation feminist seems to be more and more rejected in Third World women's theological discourse, Third World theorists refuse to give up the term feminism for three reasons: Firstly, because the term evokes a long tradition of political struggles; secondly, because they are concerned that Third World feminists participate in setting the agenda and shaping the practices of global feminism; and, thirdly, because they insist on constructing a model of feminist theorizing that is inclusive, widens their options, and enhances their understanding. See, for instance, bell hooks, *Talking Back*, 181f; and Cheryl Johnson-Odim, "Common Themes, Different Contexts: Third World Women and Feminism," in *Third World Women and The Politics of Feminism*, ed. Chandra Talpade Mohanti, Ann Russo, Lourdes Torres (Bloomington: Indiana University Press, 1991), 314–327; see also Hill Collins, *Black Feminist Thought*.

25. See the contributions on "Rassismus, Antisemitismus, Fremdenhass: Geteilter Feminismus," in *Beiträge zur feministischen Theorie und Praxis* 13(27) (1990).

26. Elizabeth Gross, "Conclusion: What is Feminist Theory?", in *Feminist Challenges: Social and Political Theory*, ed. Carol Pateman and Elizabeth Gross (Boston: Northeastern University Press, 1986), 195.

27. Iris Marion Young, *Throwing Like a Girl and Other Essays in Feminist Philosophy and Social Theory* (Bloomington: Indiana University Press, 1990), 21–35.

28. Hill Collins, *Black Feminist Thought*, 225–230, speaks of race, class, and gender as three distinctive but interlocking systems of oppression that are part of one overarching structure of domination. What I have named "patriarchy" she calls "matrix of domination." A better expression for either "patriarchy" or "matrix of domination" might be "patrix of domination."

29. Deborah K. King, "Multiple Jeopardy, Multiple Consciousness: The Context of Black Feminist Ideology," *Signs* 14(1) (1988): 42–72, reprinted in *Black Women in America: Social Science Perspectives*, ed. Micheline R. Malson et al. (Chicago: University of Chicago Press, 1990), 270.

30. Caroline Ramazanoglu, *Feminism and the Contradictions of Oppression* (New York: Routledge, 1989), 128.

31. Sylvia Walby, *Patriarchy at Work: Patriarchal and Capitalist Relations in Employment* (Minneapolis: University of Minnesota Press, 1986), 5–69, also understands patriarchy as a complex system of interrelated social structures. These different sets of patriarchal relations shift historically and produce different constellations of patriarchy in different times and cultures.

32. For such a discussion see Hannelore Schroeder, "Feministische Gesellschaftstheorie," in *Feminismus: Inspektion der Herrenkultur,* ed. Luise F. Pusch, edition Suhrkamp NF 192 (Frankfurt: Suhrkamp Verlag, 1983), 449–476, esp. 463–466 and 470.

33. The classical expression of this dualism is a saying ascribed to Thales. Similar statements are found in variations in other classical texts which state that men should give thanks to the Gods that they were not created uneducated, or as women. The saying was known in Jewish tradition and is probably rejected in the baptismal tradition of Gal. 3:28.

34. Page duBois, *Torture and Truth: The New Ancient World* (New York: Routledge, 1991), 123.

35. Cynthia Farrer, *The Origins of Democratic Thinking: The Invention of Politics in Classical Athens* (Cambridge: Cambridge University Press, 1988), 170. Strangely enough, Farrer does not problematize the exclusion of women from Athenian democracy.

36. Susan Moller Okin, *Women in Western Political Thought* (Princeton: Princeton University Press, 1979); Page duBois, *Centaurs & Amazons: Women and the Pre-History of the Great Chain of Being* (Ann Arbor: University of Michigan Press, 1982); duBois, *Torture and Truth;* M. E. Hawkesworth, *Beyond Oppression: Feminist Theory and Political Strategy* (New York: Continuum, 1990); E. C. Keuls, *The Reign of the Phallus: Sexual Politics in Ancient Athens* (New York: Harper & Row, 1985); A. Rouselle, *Porneia: On Desire and the Body in Antiquity* (New York: Basil Blackwell, 1988).

37. By the term kyriocentric I mean to indicate that not all men dominate and exploit all women but that elite Western educated propertied Euro-American men have articulated and benefited from women's and other "nonpersons'" exploitation. See my article, "The Politics of Otherness: Biblical Interpretation as a Critical Praxis for Liberation," in *The Future of Liberation Theology: Essays in Honor of Gustavo Gutierrez,* ed. M. H. Ellis and O. Maduro (Maryknoll: Orbis Press, 1989), 311–325.

38. Elizabeth V. Spelman, *Inessential Woman: Problems of Exclusion in Feminist Thought* (Boston: Beacon Press, 1988), 19–56.

39. See Christine Faure, *Democracy Without Women* (Bloomington: Indiana University Press, 1991).

40. J. McGowan, *Postmodernism and Its Critics* (Ithaca: Cornell University Press, 1991), 10–20.

41. For a feminist discussion of different models of democracy see Carol C. Gould, *Rethinking Democracy: Freedom and Social Cooperation in Politics* (Cambridge: Cambridge University Press, 1988), and especially also Anne Phillips, *En-*

gendering Democracy (University Park: The Pennsylvania State University Press, 1991).

42. See my discussion of the Haustafel or household code tradition as patriarchal codes of submission in *Bread Not Stone* and in *In Memory of Her*.

43. For this expression, see Genevieve Lloyd, *The Man of Reason: "Male" and "Female" in Western Philosophy* (Minneapolis: University of Minnesota Press, 1984); Robin May Schott, *Cognition and Eros: A Critique of the Kantian Paradigm* (Boston: Beacon Press, 1988); Linda J. Nicholson, *Feminism/Postmodernism* (New York: Routledge, 1990).

44. In addition to the work of Chakravorty Spivak, see also Trin T. Minh-ha, *Woman, Native, Other: Writing Postcoloniality and Feminism* (Bloomington: Indiana University Press, 1989).

45. Joan Cocks, *The Oppositional Imagination: Feminism, Critique and Political Theory* (New York: Routledge, 1989), 212f.

46. bell hooks, *Talking Back*, 175.

47. In her book *Sexism and God-Talk: Toward a Feminist Theology* (Boston: Beacon Press, 1983), R. Radford Ruether speaks of the Church as "liberation community" and of "the creation of autonomous feminist base communities as the vehicle for developing a community of liberation from sexism" whose relationship to the institutional Church becomes a "creative dialectic rather than a schismatic impasse" (205–206). However she does not yet use the term "women-church."

48. See Letty Russell's attempt to rescue this image in *Household of Freedom* (Philadelphia: Westminster, 1987) in feminist liberation theological terms.

49. Erin White's critique misapprehends this attempt to articulate a "political" concept that could mediate between the understandings of church as home space and exodus from the patriarchal church into a liberated zone or into women's home space. When she argues that I construe two movements, one involved in a struggle against patriarchal institutions and one moving away from them, she—not I—construes such "totalizing either-or strategies." Such a misapprehension occurs because she continues to conceptualize women-church in anthropological terms as female-centered mythology and as male-female mutuality rather than in terms of the conflict between patriarchy and *ekklēsia*. See also her response to my paper, "Daughters of Vision and Struggle," in Elaine Lindsay, ed., *Towards a Feminist Theology: Papers and Proceedings* (Helensburgh: The Conference Committee, 1990), 15–21 and 36–37, where she also construes my account of different articulations of women-church in oppositional terms.

50. For the Dutch situation, see Lieve Troch, "The Feminist Movement in and on the Edges of the Churches in the Netherlands: From Consciousness-Raising to Womenchurch," *Journal of Feminist Studies in Religion* 5(2) (1989): 113–128; for German-speaking countries, see Hedwig Meyer-Wilmes, *Rebellion auf der Grenze: Ortsbestimmung feministischer Theologie* (Freiburg: Herder, 1990), 20–41, and the journals *Schlangenbrut* and *Fama*; for Australia, see *Women Church: An Australian Journal of Feminist Studies in Religion* and Erin White and Mary Tulip, *Knowing Otherwise. Feminism, Women and Religion* (Melbourne: Lovell Publishing, 1991); for Asia, see the reports in the journal *In God's Image*. See also the

special section on "Asian and Asian American Women" in *Journal of Feminist Studies in Religion* 3(2) (1987): 103–134, edited and introduced by Rita Nakashima Brock, as well as Nakashima Brock's report with Naomi Southard, "The Other Half of the Basket: Asian American Women and the Search for a Theological Home," 135–149.

51. See Elga Sorge's announcement that she has founded an independent German women-church that performs weddings and other services for its members.

52. Rita Nakashima Brock, *Journeys by Heart: A Christology of Erotic Power* (New York: Crossroad, 1988), 66–70, replaces the notion of the *ekklēsia* of women with *Christa/Community* of erotic power in order to distinguish it from church. "Church is one, but not the only manifestation of *Christa/Community*" (114 n.8). However, this language lacks the political connotation of *ekklēsia*.

53. Mary Hunt, *Fierce Tenderness: A Feminist Theology of Friendship* (New York: Crossroad, 1991), 159f, speaks of women-church as the *ekklēsia of justice* but tends to identify it with a community of justice-seeking friends. However, such an identification is in danger of restricting the discourses of the *ekklēsia* to those who are alike or in sympathy with each other.

54. Luce Irigaray, "Equal to Whom?," *Differences* 1 (1989): 69.

55. Ibid., 73.

56. Ibid., 74.

57. See Morny Joy's very perceptive discussion of Irigaray's critique: "Equality or Divinity—A False Dichotomy?," *Journal of Feminist Studies in Religion* 6(1) (1990): 9–24.

58. McGowan, *Postmodernism*, 220–280.

59. Chandra Talpade Mohanti, "Introduction: Cartographies of Struggle," in Mohanti, Russo, and Torres, eds., *Third World Women and the Politics of Feminism*, 1–47.

60. Nancy Fraser, *Unruly Practices: Power, Discourse and Gender in Contemporary Social Theory* (Minneapolis: University of Minnesota Press, 1989), 165.

61. E. Frances White, "Africa on My Mind: Gender, Counter Discourse and African-American Nationalism," *Journal of Women's History* 2(1) (1990): 87.

62. For the trenchant critique of postmodern theory and its sociopolitical implications from a sociotheological point of view, see Gregory Baum, "Theories of Post-Modernity," *The Ecumenist* 29(2) (1991): 4–11.

5. SOPHIA – DISCERNING THE SPIRIT

1. Della Burt, "Spirit Flowers," in *Black Sister: Poetry by Black Women (1746–1980)*, ed. Erlene Stetson (Bloomington: Indiana University Press, 1981), 161–162.

2. With postmodern theory I do not understand ideology as "false conception, distorted consciousness, or just a set of ideas," but as "the organization of material signifying practices that constitute subjectivities and produce the lived relations by which subjects are connected" to the dominant relations of power in a dominant

social formation. See Teresa L. Ebert, "The Romance of Patriarchy: Ideology, Subjectivity, and Postmodern Feminist Cultural Theory," *Cultural Critique* 10 (1988): 23.

3. Peggy L. Day, *Gender and Difference in Ancient Israel* (Minneapolis: Augsburg Fortress Press, 1989), 2.

4. See the assessment of my work by Rebecca Chopp, "Feminism's Theological Pragmatics: A Social Naturalism of Women's Experience," *The Journal of Religion* 67(2) (1987): 239–256, esp. 247–252.

5. See Sheila Greeve Davaney, "Problems With Feminist Theory: Historicity and the Search for Sure Foundations," in *Embodied Love: Sensuality and Relationship as Feminist Values,* ed. P. M. Cooey, S. A. Farmer, and M. A. Ross (San Francisco: Harper & Row, 1987), 79–95; for a different postmodern misreading, see also Mary McClintock Fulkerson, "Contesting Feminist Canons: Discourse and the Problem of Sexist Texts," *Journal of Feminist Studies in Religion* 7(2) (1991): 53–74.

6. Carol P. Christ, "Embodied Thinking: Reflections on Feminist Theological Method," *Journal of Feminist Studies in Religion* 5(1) (1989): 7–15.

7. See Hazel V. Carby, " 'On the Threshold of Woman's Era': Lynching, Empire and Sexuality," in *Race, Writing and Difference,* ed. Henry Louis Gates, Jr. (Chicago: University of Chicago Press, 1986), 301–328.

8. For this expression, see Houston A. Baker, Jr., "Caliban's Triple Play," in Gates, ed., *Race, Writing,* 381–395.

9. Mae Gwendolyn Henderson, "Speaking in Tongues," in *Changing Our Own Words: Essays on Criticism, Theory, and Writing by Black Women,* ed. Cheryl A. Wall (Rutgers: State University Press, 1989), 37.

10. See Harold Bloom, *The Anxiety of Influence: A Theory of Poetry* (New York: Oxford University Press, 1973).

11. Sandra M. Gilbert and Susan Gubar, *The Madwoman in the Attic: The Woman Writer and the Nineteenth-Century Literary Imagination* (New Haven: Yale University Press, 1979).

12. See Henning Graf Reventlow, *The Authority of the Bible and the Rise of the Modern World* (Philadelphia: Fortress Press, 1985), for extensive documentation and review of literature, esp. 3–6 and notes, 415–626.

13. Ibid., 413.

14. For the discussion of major works and issues, see Brice R. Wachterhauser, ed., *Hermeneutics and Modern Philosophy* (Albany: State University of New York Press, 1986) and Kurt Mueller-Vollmer, ed., *The Hermeneutics Reader: Texts of the German Tradition from the Enlightenment to the Present* (New York: Crossroad, 1988).

15. H. Y. Gamble, *The New Testament Canon: Its Making and Meaning* (Philadelphia: Fortress Press, 1985), 86.

16. Iris Marion Young, "Impartiality and the Civic Public: Some Implications of Feminist Critiques of Moral and Political Theory," in *Feminism as Critique: On the Politics of Gender,* ed. Seyla Benhabib and Drucilla Cornell (Minneapolis: University of Minnesota Press, 1987), 61.

17. For this expression see Genevieve Lloyd, *The Man of Reason: "Male" and*

"Female" in *Western Philosophy* (Minneapolis: University of Minnesota Press, 1984).

18. For the discussion of major proposals, see the literature in my *Bread Not Stone*. For more recent works and issues, see Donald K. McKim, ed., *A Guide to Contemporary Hermeneutics: Major Trends in Biblical Interpretation* (Grand Rapids: Eerdmans Publishing Co., 1986); Charles M. Wood, "Theological Hermeneutics," *Quarterly Review* 7(3) (1987): 91–100; J. Severino Croatto, *Biblical Hermeneutics: Toward a Theory of Reading Toward the Production of Meaning* (Maryknoll: Orbis Press, 1987), and K. Berger, *Hermeneutik des Neuen Testaments* (Gütersloh: Gerd Mohn, 1988).

19. See the review and discussion of research on the historical Jesus by Werner Georg Kümmel, "Jesusforschung seit 1981," *Theologische Rundschau NF* 53 (1988): 229–249, and 54 (1989): 1–53.

20. See also Jose Miguez Bonino, ed., *Faces of Jesus: Latin American Christologies* (Maryknoll: Orbis Press, 1984).

21. For Jesus in theological discussions see William M. Thompson, *The Jesus Debate: A Survey and Synthesis* (New York: Paulist Press, 1985).

22. See, for instance, the movement of the "New Quest" in the 1950s and 1960s, or the work of the "Jesus Seminar" in the 1980s. For the interconnections of this quest with the development of the bourgeois subject, see Dieter Georgi, "Leben-Jesu-Theologie/ Leben-Jesu-Forschung," *Theologische Real Enzyklopedie* 20 (1991): 566–575.

23. For an explication and critique of the method of correlation see Francis Schüssler Fiorenza, "The Crisis of Hermeneutics and Christian Theology," in *Theology at the End of Modernity*, ed. Sheila Greeve Davaney (Philadelphia: Trinity Press, 1991), 117–140.

24. Gamble, *The New Testament Canon*, 71.

25. See Francis Schüssler Fiorenza, "The Crisis of Scriptural Authority; Interpretation and Reception," *Interpretation* 44(4) (1990): 367, for documentation and discussion of these hermeneutical approaches.

26. Ibid., 362.

27. Compare, e.g., G. Lerner, *The Creation of Patriarchy* (New York: Oxford University Press, 1986), or M. French, *Beyond Power: On Women, Men and Morals* (New York: Ballantine, 1986).

28. Phyllis Trible has consistently developed such a hermeneutical approach in her work. See her biographical statement, "The Pilgrim Bible on a Feminist Journey," reprinted in *Daughters of Sarah* 15(3) (1989): 4–7.

29. See L. Russell, ed., *Feminist Interpretation of the Bible* (Philadelphia: Westminster Press, 1985).

30. R. Radford Ruether, in Russell, ed., *Feminist Biblical Interpretation*, 117.

31. Page duBois, *Torture and Truth: The New Ancient World* (New York: Routledge, 1991), 125.

32. Ibid., 124–125.

33. Pamela Dickey Young, *Feminist Theology/Christian Theology: In Search of Method* (Minneapolis: Augsburg Fortress Press, 1990), 80–93.

34. Mary Ann Tolbert, "Protestant Feminists and the Bible: On the Horns of

a Dilemma," *Union Seminary Quarterly Review* 43(1–4) (1989): 1–17. Except for her criticism of the notion of the *ekklēsia* of women, to which, in her experience, Protestant students have a difficult time relating, Tolbert's proposal is not very different from my own.

35. Matilda Joslyn Gage, *Women, Church & State: The Original Exposé of Male Collaboration Against the Female Sex* (1893, reprint Watertown: Persephone Press, 1980), xxix.

36. Vincent L. Wimbush, "The Bible and African Americans: An Outline of an Interpretative History," in *Stony the Road We Trod*, ed. Cain H. Felder (Minneapolis: Augsburg Fortress, 1991), 88.

37. Howard Thurman, *Jesus and the Disinherited* (Nashville: Abingdon, 1949), 31f.

38. K. G. Cannon, "Slave Ideology and Biblical Interpretation," *Semeia* 47 (1989): 9–24.

39. C. Townsend Gilkes, "Mother to the Motherless," *Semeia* 47 (1989): 65.

40. Kwok Pui Lan, "Discovering the Bible in the Non-Biblical World," *Semeia* 47 (1989): 25–42.

41. Chung Hyun Kyung, *Struggle To Be the Sun Again* (Maryknoll: Orbis Press, 1991), 111.

42. Ada Maria Isasi-Diaz, "The Bible and Mujerista Theology," in *Lift Every Voice: Constructing Christian Theologies from the Underside*, ed. Brooks Thistlethwaite and Potter Engel (San Francisco: Harper & Row, 1990), 268.

43. For this title see William L. Andrews, *Sisters of the Spirit* (Bloomington: Indiana University Press, 1986), a reprint of the spiritual autobiographies of Jarena Lee, Zilpha Elaw, and Julia A. J. Foote.

44. *Productions of Mrs. Maria W. Stewart*, published by Friends of Freedom and Virtue, Boston, 1835; reprinted in *Spiritual Narratives*, ed. Sue E. Houchins (New York: Oxford University Press, 1988), 77.

45. Andrews, *Sisters of the Spirit*, 20.

46. See Young, "Impartiality and the Civic Public," in Benhabib and Cornell, eds., *Feminism as Critique*, 73–76.

47. Graham Shaw, *The Cost of Authority. Manipulation and Freedom in the New Testament* (Philadelphia: Fortress Press, 1983), 12.

48. Barbara Newman, *Sister of Wisdom: St. Hildegard's Theology of the Feminine* (Berkeley: University of California Press, 1987), 64. (For Hildegard's original Latin, see App.B, p. 275.)

49. Henderson, "Speaking in Tongues," 17.

50. Ibid., 24, 37.

51. For the material in this section, see U. Luz, *Das Evangelium des Matthäus (2. Teilband: Mt 8–17)*, EKK I/2 (Einsiedeln: Benzinger Neukirchener Verlag, 1990), 431ff.

52. Schüssler Fiorenza, *In Memory of Her*, 138.

53. Laurel Schneider, paper for my seminar, "Synoptic Miracle Stories," Fall semester, 1988.

6. PRISCA – TEACHER OF WISDOM

I want to thank the Association of Theological Schools for supporting research on this chapter through a Theological Issues Research Award for the Spring semester, 1988.

1. E. M. Broner and Nomi Nimrod, "A Woman's Passover Haggadah," *Ms.*, April 1977, 53–56.

2. For this emphasis see also Ched Myers, *Binding the Strong Man: A Political Reading of Mark's Story of Jesus* (New York: Orbis Press, 1988), 168.

3. For such an argument see Schüssler Fiorenza, *In Memory of Her*, 175–184.

4. For discussion and literature see ibid., 178–189.

5. Ibid., 294–309.

6. See the entry on Hypatia in Jennifer S. Uglow and Frances Hinton, eds., *The International Dictionary of Women's Biography* (New York: Continuum, 1985), 234.

7. See for instance C. Bunch and S. Pollack, eds., *Learning Our Way: Essays in Feminist Education* (Trumansburg: The Crossing Press, 1988); G. Bowles and R. Duelli Klein, eds., *Theories of Women's Studies* (Boston: Routledge & Kegan, 1983); M. Culley and C. Portuges, eds., *Gendered Subjects: The Dynamics of Feminist Teaching* (Boston: Routledge & Kegan, 1985); C. M. Schrewsbury, "What is Feminist Pedagogy," *Women Studies Quarterly* 15(3–4) (1987): 6–14; K. Weiler, *Women Teaching For Change: Gender, Class and Power* (South Hadley: Bergin & Garvey Publishing, 1988); L. Weis, ed., *Class, Race, and Gender in American Education* (Albany: State University of New York Press, 1988); S. L. Gabriel and I. Smithson, eds., *Gender in the Classroom: Power and Pedagogy* (Urbana: University of Illinois Press, 1990).

8. The Cornwall Collective, *Your Daughters Shall Prophesy: Feminist Alternatives in Theological Education* (New York: Pilgrim Press, 1980).

9. Arlene Swidler and Walter E. Conn, eds., *Mainstreaming Feminist Research for Teaching Religious Studies* (Washington: University Press of America, 1979).

10. The Mud Flower Collective, *God's Fierce Whimsy: Christian Feminism and Theological Education* (New York: Pilgrim Press, 1985).

11. For such an exploration see Rebecca Chopp's and my own contribution in *The Education of the Practical Theologian: Responses to Joseph Hough and John Cobb's Christian Identity and Theological Education*, ed. Don S. Brown, David Polk, and Ian S. Evison (Atlanta: Scholars Press, 1989).

12. Gayatri Chakravorty Spivak, in *The Post-Colonial Critic: Interviews, Strategies, Dialogues*, ed. Sarah Harasym (New York: Routledge, 1990), 42f. See also her *In Other Worlds: Essays in Cultural Politics* (New York: Methuen, 1987).

13. For pre-1980 statistics see the Cornwall Collective, *Your Daughters Shall Prophesy*, 49–53. In the 1980s the number of women in liberal theological schools surpassed the 50 percent mark.

14. See Genevive Lloyd, *The Man of Reason: "Male" and "Female" in Western Philosophy* (Minneapolis: University of Minnesota Press, 1984): "Philosophers have at different periods been church men, men of letters, university professors.

But there is one thing they have had in common throughout the history of the activity. They have been predominantly male; and the absence of women from the philosophical tradition has meant that the conceptualization of Reason has been done exclusively by men" (108).

15. Although in the past year two women were appointed professors, the feminist theologian Dr. Silvia Schroer, director of the Swiss Catholic Bibelwerk in Zürich and first in line for a professorship in biblical introduction at the distinguished Roman Catholic theological faculty of the University of Tübingen, was denied appointment in August 1991 by the local bishop, because of her feminist biblical publications.

16. Stanley Fish, *Is There a Text in this Class? The Authority of Interpretive Communities* (Cambridge: Harvard University Press, 1980).

17. Florence Howe, *Myth of Coeducation: Selected Essays 1964–1983* (Bloomington: Indiana University Press, 1984), 221–230.

18. Adrienne Rich, "Toward a Woman Centered University," in *On Lies, Secrets and Silence: Selected Prose, 1966–1978* (New York: Norton, 1979), 134.

19. See the critical reflections on the Arizona project for curriculum integration by S. Hardy Aiken, K. Anderson, M. Dinnerstein, J. Nolte Lensinck, P. MacCorquodale, eds., *Changing Our Minds: Feminist Transformations of Knowledge* (Albany: State University of New York, 1988), 134–163.

20. Krister Stendahl, "Ancient Scripture in the Modern World," in *Scripture in the Jewish and Christian Traditions: Authority, Interpretation, Relevance,* ed. Frederick E. Greenspahn (Nashville; Abingdon Press, 1982), 202–214.

21. See J. L. Segundo, *The Liberation of Theology* (Maryknoll, N.Y.: Orbis Press, 1976); J. Severino Croatto, *Biblical Hermeneutics: Toward a Theory of Reading as the Production of Meaning* (Maryknoll, N.Y.: Orbis Press, 1987); and the application of liberation hermeneutics to biblical exegesis by C. Rowland and M. Corner, *Liberating Exegesis: The Challenge of Liberation Theology to Biblical Studies* (Louisville: Westminster/John Knox Press, 1989).

22. Elisabeth Schüssler Fiorenza, "The Ethics of Biblical Interpretation: Decentering Biblical Scholarship," *Journal of Biblical Literature* 107(1) (1988): 3–17.

23. Teresa de Lauretis, ed., *Feminist Studies/ Critical Studies* (Bloomington: Indiana University Press, 1986), 9.

24. On an experientially based education, see John H. Fish, "Liberating Education," in C. Amjad-Ali and W. Alwin Pitcher, eds., *Liberation and Ethics* (Chicago: Center for the Scientific Study of Religion, 1985), 15–29, esp. the chart on p. 27.

25. On this problem compare, e.g., J. C. Hough, Jr., and J. B. Cobb, Jr., *Christian Identity and Theological Education* (Chico, Calif.: Scholars Press, 1985).

26. N. Aisenberg and M. Harrington, *Women of Academe: Outsiders in the Sacred Grove* (Amherst: University of Massachusetts Press, 1988), 65.

27. Thomas Kuhn, *The Structure of Scientific Revolutions,* 2d ed. (Chicago: University of Chicago Press, 1962).

28. See especially bell hooks' reflections on a revolutionary feminist pedagogy, on graduate school, on being black at Yale, and on class and education in her book *Talking Back* (Boston: South End Press, 1989), 49–84.

29. Jo Anne Pagano, *Exiles and Communities: Teaching in the Patriarchal Wilderness* (Albany: State University of New York Press, 1990), 135f.

30. For documentation of such a "supportive" self-effacing role for women in theological work, see R. Köbler, *Schattenarbeit: Charlotte von Kirschbaum—Die Theologin an der Seite Karl Barth's* (Köln: Pahl-Rugenstein, 1987). Much research needs to be done to uncover such "support work," if the history of women's contribution to theological discourse is ever to be written.

31. For the "marriage/romance plot," which outlines the old feminine norms, and the quest plot, which articulates the values of public life and seeks to change consciousness, see Rachel Blau DuPlessis, *Writing Beyond the Ending: Narrative Strategies of Twentieth-Century Women Writers* (Bloomington: Indiana University Press, 1985).

32. For extensive documentation of women's experiences in educational institutions, see Aisenberg and Harrington, *Women of Academe*, 64–134.

33. Barbara Christian, "The Race for Theory," *Feminist Studies* 14 (1988): 67–79.

34. See, in place of many others, Mary McClintock Fulkerson, "Contesting Feminist Canons: Discourse and the Problem of Sexist Texts," *Journal of Feminist Studies in Religion* 7(2) (1991): 53–74.

35. See also Patricia Hill Collins, "Learning from the Outsider Within: The Sociological Significance of Black Feminist Thought," *Social Problems* 33 (1986): 14–32.

36. M. L. Andersen, "Changing the Curriculum in Higher Education," *Signs* 12(2) (1987): 222–254.

37. Elizabeth Kamarck Minnich, *Transforming Knowledge* (Philadelphia: Temple University Press, 1990), 51–175.

38. Patricia Hill Collins, *Black Feminist Thought: Knowledge, Consciousness and the Politics of Empowerment* (Boston: Unwyn Hyman, 1990), 203.

39. Kamarck Minnich, *Transforming Knowledge*, 43.

40. Max Weber, "Wissenschaft als Beruf," in. M. Weber, *Gesammelte Aufsätze zur Wissenschaftslehre* (Tübingen, 1922). See also Ija Lazari-Pawloska, "Das Problem der Wertfreiheit im Universitätsunterricht," in Halina Bendowski and Brigitte Weisshaupt (HgbInnen), *Was Philosophinnen denken* (Zürich: Amman Verlag, 1983), 30–36.

41. Kamarck Minnich, *Transforming Knowledge*, 167.

42. Elizabeth Young-Bruehl, "The Education of Women as Philosophers," *Signs* 12(2) (1987): 214–215.

43. Ibid., 217.

44. DuBois, *Torture and Truth*, 113.

45. See P. Freire, *Pedagogy of the Oppressed* (New York: Seabury Press, 1973) 56, for the notion of *co-intentional* education in which "teachers and students (leaders and people) co-intent on reality, are both Subjects. . . . As they attain this knowledge of reality through common reflection and action, they discover themselves as its permanent re-creators."

46. See H. A. Giroux, ed., *Postmodernism, Feminism, and Cultural Politics:*

Redrawing Educational Boundaries (Albany: State University of New York Press, 1991), for such a conceptualization.

47. See, e.g., Susan Stanford Friedman, "Authority in the Feminist Classroom: A Contradiction in Terms?" in *Gendered Subjects: The Dynamics of Feminist Teaching,* ed. Margo Culley and Catherine Portuges (Boston: Routledge & Kegan, 1985), 203–208; Margo Culley, "Anger and Authority in the Introductory Women's Studies Classroom," ibid., 209–217; Johnella Butler, "Toward a Pedagogy of Everywoman's Studies," ibid., 230–239.

48. Teresa de Lauretis, "The Essence of the Triangle or, Taking the Risk of Essentialism Seriously: Feminist Theory in Italy, the U.S., and Britain," *Differences* 1 (1989): 25.

49. Paula Gunn Allen, "Who Is Your Mother? Red Roots of White Feminism," in *Multi-Cultural Literacy,* ed. Rick Simonson and Scott Walker (Saint Paul: Greywolf Press, 1988), 18f.

50. This is a slightly revised and shortened version of a paper by Diana Scholl, "An Exercise in Biblical Imagination: The Gospel Story of Elizabeth," submitted in my course, "Gospel Stories of Women," Spring semester, 1990.

7. SHEBA – THE POWER OF WISDOM

This chapter is a revised and expanded version of my essay "Lk 13:10–17: Interpretation for Liberation," *Theology Digest* 12 (1990): 796–800.

1. Maya Angelou, "Still I Rise," in *And Still I Rise* (New York: Random House, 1978).

2. Audre Lorde, "An Open Letter to Mary Daly," in *This Bridge Called My Back: Writings by Radical Women of Color,* ed. Cherrie Moraga and Gloria Anzaldua (Watertown: Persephone Press, 1981), 95.

3. See Faye Levine, *Solomon & Sheba* (New York: St. Martins Press, 1980), 207–226. Archeologists still debate whether the territory of Sheba was located in the eastern region of present-day Yemen, or whether it belonged to Ethiopia, which has the most elaborate traditional claim on it. See the archeological report by Colin Campbell, "Was There A Queen of Sheba? Evidence Makes Her More Likely," *The New York Times,* February 4, 1986.

4. Mieke Bal, *Death and Dissymmetry: The Politics of Coherence in the Book of Judges* (Chicago: University of Chicago Press, 1987), 11.

5. Annette Kolodny, "Dancing Through the Minefield: Some Observations on the Theory, Practice, and Politics of Feminist Literary Criticism," in *Feminist Criticism: Essays on Women, Literature, Theory,* ed. Elaine Showalter (New York: Pantheon, 1985), 153.

6. For the expression "frame of meaning," see Anthony Giddens, *New Rules of Sociological Methods: A Positive Critique of Interpretative Sociologists* (New York: Basic Books, 1976), 64.

7. For the notion of "reading formation," see Tony Bennett, "Texts in History: The Determinations of Readings and Their Texts," in *Post-Structuralism and The*

Question of History, ed. D. Attridge, G. Bennington, and R. Young (Cambridge: Cambridge University Press, 1987), 68–78.

8. For a similar theoretical framework see bell hooks, *Feminist Theory: From Margin to Center* (Boston: South End Press, 1984).

9. Kolodny, "Dancing Through the Minefield," 162.

10. See the discussion of this text by J. A. Fitzmyer, *The Gospel According to Luke X–XXIV*, AB 28A (Garden City: Doubleday, 1985), 1009–1014, and M. Dennis Hamm, "The Freeing of the Bent Woman and the Restoration of Israel: Lk 13:10–17 as Narrative Theology," *Journal for the Study of the New Testament* 31 (1987): 23–44. Hamm shows that the evangelist has made this story "part and parcel of his narrative" to be a "vehicle of Lucan Theology."

11. Such a reconstruction of the text is different from that of R. Bultmann, *History of the Synoptic Tradition* (New York: Harper & Row, 1963), 12, who suggests that this variant of a Sabbath healing (cf. Mark 3:1–6 and Luke 14:1–6) was composed on the basis of the originally isolated saying in verse 15. However, he concedes that in the oral stage of development, the style of the miracle story could have influenced that of the controversy dialogue (13).

12. According to Fitzmyer, *The Gospel According to Luke*, 1012, the expression "spirit of infirmity" is "undoubtedly an Aramaism." R. Latourelle, *The Miracles of Jesus and the Theology of Miracles* (New York: Paulist Press, 1988), 194–196, concludes from this that the story is archaic and therefore situated in the ministry of the "historical" Jesus. However, he does not distinguish between the miracle story and the ensuing controversy dialogue as I have done.

13. According to J. Wilkinson, "The Case of the Bent Woman in Lk 13:10–17," *Evangelical Quarterly* 49 (1979): 195–205, the illness of the woman was probably *spondylitis ankylopoietica*, which results in a fusion of spinal joints. Although commentaries suggest that this spinal deformation marked the woman as a great sinner, or as unclean in the eyes of her contemporaries, the text does not allude to either.

14. In *In Memory of Her*, 152, I have argued that a feminist reconstruction needs to focus methodologically on story and characters, rather than eclipse them by concentrating on the "word" or "saying" of Jesus as the earliest component of a story, as form criticism and tradition history do. Moreover, this implies a shift in theological focus.

15. Although in *The Gospel According to Luke* Fitzmyer underlines this in his notes on this passage, he nevertheless asserts in his commentary: "the episode depicts Jesus once again making use of his power (recall 4:14.36; 5:17) to heal an unfortunate human being afflicted with physical ill" (101).

16. See Susan R. Garrett, *The Demise of the Devil: Magic and the Demonic in Luke's Writings* (Minneapolis: Augsburg Fortress Press, 1989), and my "Miracles, Mission and Apologetics," in *Aspects of Religious Propaganda in Judaism and Early Christianity*, ed. E. Schüssler Fiorenza (Notre Dame: Notre Dame University Press, 1976), 1–26.

17. I use this expression to distinguish analysis concentrating on the contemporary reader from reader-response criticism, which focuses on the reader as a formal-

istic feature inscribed in the text. For the "formalist" orientation of reader-response criticism in literary studies see Steven Mailloux, *Rhetorical Power* (Ithaca: Cornell University Press, 1989), 29–53, and in biblical studies see Stephen D. Moore, *Literary Criticism and the Gospels: The Theoretical Challenge* (New Haven: Yale University Press, 1989), 71–107.

18. For a general introduction see Jane P. Tompkins, ed., *Reader-Response Criticism: From Formalism to Post-Structuralism* (Baltimore: Johns Hopkins University Press, 1980), and E. V. McKnight, *The Bible and the Reader: An Introduction to Literary Criticism* (Philadelphia: Fortress Press, 1985).

19. See Susan Lanser, "(Feminist) Criticism in the Garden: Inferring Gen 2–3," *Semeia* 41 (1988): 67–84, for an inferential notion of reading as "contextualization" that foregrounds certain meanings and blends out others.

20. The ecclesiastical argument against the ordination of women has endowed the biological sex of Jesus with theological significance. However, such an understanding of the incarnation in terms of biological gender positivism does not square with the tradition according to which the *humanity* and not the *masculinity* of Jesus has saving significance. Patriarchal relationships of exclusion produce androcentric theology.

21. See Dennis Brandon, *Grammar and Gender* (New Haven: Yale University Press, 1986), on the history of sexual bias in grammar and diction.

22. Essays and books on feminist literary criticism abound. I have found *Making a Difference: Feminist Literary Criticism*, ed. G. Greene and C. Kahn (New York: Methuen, 1985) and R. Felski, *Beyond Feminist Aesthetics: Feminist Literature and Social Change* (Cambridge: Harvard University Press, 1989), especially helpful for articulating my own approach.

23. For this expression see J. Fetterley, *The Resisting Reader: A Feminist Approach to American Fiction* (Bloomington: Indiana University Press, 1978), xx: The United States' "cultural reality is not the *emasculation* of men by women but the *immasculation* of women by men. As readers and teachers and scholars women are taught to think as men" (emphasis added).

24. Patrocinio P. Schweickart, "Reading Ourselves: Toward a Feminist Theory of Reading," in *Gender and Reading: Essays on Readers: Texts and Contexts*, ed. E. A. Flynn and P. P. Schweickart (Baltimore: Johns Hopkins University Press, 1986), 42.

25. M. Crawford and R. Chaffin, "The Reader's Construction of Meaning: Cognitive Research on Gender and Comprehension," in Flynn and Schweickart, eds., *Gender and Reading*, 3–30.15f.

26. Virginia Fabella, "A Common Methodology for Diverse Christologies," in *With Passion and Compassion: Third World Women Doing Theology*, ed. Virginia Fabella and Mercy Amba Oduyoye (Maryknoll, N.Y.: Orbis Press, 1988), 116.

27. Catherine Belsey, "Constructing the Subject: Deconstructing the Text," in *Feminist Criticism and Social Change: Sex, Class, and Race in Literature and Culture*, ed. J. Newton and D. Rosenfelt (New York: Methuen, 1985), 50.

28. See my *The Book of Revelation: Judgment and Justice* (Philadelphia: Fortress Press, 1985).

29. J. Carlson Brown and R. Parker, "For God So Loved the World," in *Christianity, Patriarchy, and Abuse: A Feminist Critique,* ed. J. Carlson Brown and C. Bohn (New York: Pilgrim Press, 1989), 1–30. Brown and Parker rightly have criticized the atonement tradition as an abusive Christian tradition that justifies suffering. However, they are mistaken in assuming that it is the only New Testament theological interpretation of Jesus' execution.

30. See D. Soelle's *Political Theology* (Philadelphia: Fortress, 1974), a critique of R. Bultmann's demythologizing program in the interest of an existentialist theology.

31. For this understanding of patriarchy see my article "Breaking the Silence—Becoming Visible," in *Women—Invisible in Church and Theology,* ed. M. Collins and E. Schüssler Fiorenza (Edinburgh: T. & T. Clark, 1985), 3–16 and chapter 4.

32. See Susan Moller Okin, *Women in Western Political Thought* (Princeton: Princeton University Press, 1979), and Page duBois, *Centaurs & Amazons: Women and the Pre-History of the Great Chain of Being* (Ann Arbor: University of Michigan Press, 1982).

33. This is a condensed form of a reflection by Mary Lou Sleevi, *Women of the Word* (Notre Dame: Ave Maria Press, 1989), 51ff.

34. Teresa Ebert, "The Romance of Patriarchy," *Cultural Change* 10 (1988): 36.

35. See O. Lamar Cope, "On the History of Criticism of the Gospel of Luke," *Union Seminary Quarterly Review,* 42 (1988): 59–61.

36. For such a form-critical description see Martin Dibelius, *From Tradition to Gospel* (Cambridge: Clarke, 1971), 97f. See also Fitzmyer, *The Gospel According to Luke,* 1011. Although Joel B. Green, "Jesus and a Daughter of Abraham (Luke 13:10–17): Test Case For a Lucan Perspective on Jesus' Miracles," *The Catholic Biblical Quarterly* 51 (1989): 643–654, argues that the story must be interpreted as an integrated unity, by underlining the "internal connections" of this two-part story, he concedes that two "parts" or "forms" of the story can still be distinguished.

37. D. L. Tiede, *Luke* (Minneapolis: Augsburg Publishing House, 1988), 248.

38. See P. Achtemeier, "The Lucan Perspective on the Miracles of Jesus: A Preliminary Sketch," in *Perspective on Luke-Acts,* ed. C. H. Talbert (Edinburgh: T. & T. Clark, 1978), 153–167.

39. See Hamm, "The Freeing of the Bent Woman," 30f.

40. The appellation "daughter of Abraham" refers back to Luke 3:8 and forward to 19:9 where the toll-collector Zacchaeus is called "son of Abraham." The repentance sermon of John the Baptist in 3:7–9 insists that G-d does not depend on ethnic privilege to keep the promise to Abraham but can "raise up children of Abraham from these very stones." Luke 3:9 alludes to the parable of the fig tree (13:6–9) that precedes the story of the stooped woman.

41. For a discussion of the question of anti-Judaism in Luke-Acts see J. T. Sanders, *The Jews in Luke-Acts* (Philadelphia: Fortress Press, 1987) and J. B.

Tyson, ed., *Luke-Acts and the Jewish People: Eight Critical Perspectives* (Minneapolis: Augsburg Publishing House, 1988).

42. Jacob Jervell, "The Daughters of Abraham: Women in Acts," in *The Unknown Paul: Essays on Luke-Acts and Early Christian History* (Minneapolis: Augsburg Publishing House, 1984), 146–190.

43. For a survey of scholarly opinion on the travel narrative, see J. L. Ressegui, "Interpretation of Luke's Central Section (Lk 9:51–19:44) since 1856," *Studia Biblica et Theologica* 5 (1975): 3–36.

44. F. Danker, *Jesus and the New Age: A Commentary on St. Luke's Gospel*, rev. ed. (Philadelphia: Fortress Press, 1988), 370, argues to the contrary: "If the guilt of Jews in the crucifixion is in any way accented, Luke's intention is not to let Rome off lightly, but to prepare his public for the proclamation of forgiveness . . . No matter how great Israel's crime, God gives her [sic] a fresh chance." See, however, the balanced assessment of Jane A. Via, "According to Luke, Who Put Jesus to Death?" in R. Cassidy and P. J. Scharper, *Political Issues in Luke-Acts* (Maryknoll, N.Y.: Orbis Press, 1983), who concludes that by laying the responsibility for Jesus' death primarily on the religious Jewish authorities and by stressing that Pilate did not condemn Jesus to death because he found him guilty of any crime, Luke seeks to remove "theoretical obstacles to the legalization of Christianity as a religion in the Roman Empire. . . ." (140).

45. J. A. Sanders, "Hermeneutics," in *The Interpreter's Dictionary of the Bible*, suppl. vol. (Nashville: Abingdon, 1976), distinguishes between a *constitutive* reading, in which one identifies with Jesus, and a *prophetic* reading, in which one identifies with those who are challenged by Jesus. He suggests that established churches need to read in the prophetic mode, whereas minorities need to read in the constitutive one (407).

46. For this critique of Christian feminist apologetics, see especially Judith Plaskow, "Christian Feminism and Anti-Judaism," *Cross Currents* 28 (1978): 306–309, and Bernadette Brooten, "Jewish Women's History in the Roman Period: A Task for Christian Theology," *Harvard Theological Review* 79 (1986): 22–30, and the special section on "Feminist Antijudaism," in *Journal of Feminist Studies in Religion* 7(2) 1991: 95–134.

47. On the different articulations of feminist hermeneutics, see the diverse contributions in M. A. Tolbert, ed., *The Bible and Feminist Hermeneutics*, Semeia 28 (Chico, Calif.: Scholars Press, 1983) and L. M. Russell, ed., *Feminist Interpretation of the Bible* (Philadelphia: Westminster Press, 1985).

48. Compare, e.g., J. B. Green, "Jesus and a Daughter," who stresses that Jesus does not intend to provoke opposition or to express his attitude toward the Sabbath law *per se*, but rather acts in order to express G-d's mercy "in contradistinction to the Jewish institutions that threw up a dividing wall restricting access to God's mercy for this needy woman" (654). However, such an argument begs the question.

49. See my article, "The Politics of Otherness: Biblical Interpretation as a Critical Praxis for Liberation," in *The Future of Liberation Theology: Essays in Honor of Gustavo Gutiérrez*, ed. M. H. Ellis and O. Maduro (Maryknoll, N.Y.:

Orbis Press, 1989), 311–325 and the introduction to *Interpretation for Liberation*, ed. K. G. Cannon and E. Schüssler Fiorenza, Semeia 47 (Atlanta: Scholars Press, 1989).

50. Itumeleng J. Mosala, *Biblical Hermeneutics and Black Theology in South Africa* (Grand Rapids: Eerdmans, 1989), 167.

51. For an analysis of the Lukan infancy narrative from a somewhat different perspective, see J. Schaberg, *The Illegitimacy of Jesus: A Feminist Theological Interpretation of the Infancy Narratives* (San Francisco: Harper & Row, 1987), 78–144, and R. A. Horsley, *The Liberation of Christmas: The Infancy Narratives in Social Context* (New York: Crossroad, 1988).

52. For an analysis of the passage without attention to its anti-Jewish tendencies, see Marion L. Soards, "Tradition, Composition, and Theology in Jesus' Speech to the 'Daughters of Jerusalem' (Lk 23:26–32)," *Biblica* 68 (1987): 221–244; J. Neyrey, *The Passion According to Luke: A Redaction Critical Study of Luke's Soteriology* (New York: Paulist Press, 1985), 108–128.

53. R. C. Tannehill, *The Narrative Unity of Luke-Acts, Vol. I: The Gospel According to Luke* (Philadelphia: Fortress Press, 1986), 143–199. However, Tannehill's assertion that Luke portrays Jesus' rejection by his own people as "a situation of tragic irony" is rightly challenged by the Jewish scholar Michael J. Cook, "The Mission to the Jews in Acts: Unraveling Luke's Myth of the Myriads," in Tyson, ed., *Luke-Acts and the Jewish People*, 102–123.

54. See Ernst Lohmeyer, *Das Evangelium der Markus*, 16th ed. (Göttingen: Vandenhoeck, 1963) 253.

55. For a more extended discussion see my *In Memory of Her*, 262–315, and R. Joseph Hoffmann, *Celsus, On The True Doctrine: A Discourse Against the Christians* (Oxford: Oxford University Press, 1987).

56. James M. Dawsey, *The Lukan Voice: Confusion and Irony in the Gospel of Luke* (Macon: Mercer Press, 1986), 152.

57. See also Robert J. Karris, "Poor and Rich: The Lukan Sitz im Leben," in *Perspectives on Luke*, ed. C. H. Talbert (Edinburgh: T. & T. Clark, 1978): "Luke is primarily taken up with the rich members, their concerns and the problems which they pose for the community" (124).

58. Dawsey, *The Lukan Voice*, 154.

59. For the discussion of the *basileia* vision of the Jesus movement, see my *In Memory of Her*, 110–130, and B. Chilton and J. J. H. McDonald, *Jesus and the Ethics of the Kingdom* (Grand Rapids: Eerdmans, 1987), who offer a more ethical-individualistic view.

60. See Susan M. Praeder, *The Word in Women's Worlds: Four Parables* (Wilmington: Michael Glazier, 1988), 17–19.

61. The Greek word *endoxa* (LXX) alludes to the marvels of the exodus. For other verbal evocations of the meaning of the Sabbath with reference to the traditions of creation and exodus, see my *In Memory of Her*, 124f, and Hamm, "The Freeing of the Bent Woman," 28f.

62. Alice Walker, *Horses Make a Landscape Look More Beautiful* (New York: Harcourt Brace Jovanovich, Harvest Books, 1986), 1–2.

255

INDEX

African-American, biblical imagination of, 26–27; biblical interpretation, 38, 153–154, 162; feminist theory, 138, 152, 156–157, 159–160, 189; neglect of hermeneutic tradition of, 29, 32. *See also* Womanist

Alterity, 105–106, 115, 126, 131. *See also* Other

Androcentrism/Androcentric language, 5–8, 10, 13, 21–34, 40–43, 69–90, 113, 135, 145, 198, 200–201; in biblical texts, 21, 34–36, 69; as descriptive, 30–31; dualism, 40, 73, 125–126; feminist literary studies, as fostered by, 34–35; as ideological construction, 30, 34–35; marginality of women in, 25–26, 30–37, 86, 89, 113; relationship to historical reality of, 34; rhetorical silences of, 35, 93; values, 25–26, 30, 34–36, 83, 86, 113. *See also* Kyrocentric; Language; Patriarchy

Apologetics, 24, 59, 135–136, 139, 142, 144–146, 213

Apostolic succession, model of, 32–33

Aquila, 168–169

Arachne, 9, 52

Aristotle, 94, 119–120, 202

Asian feminist theology, 29, 32, 37–38, 155

Augustine, 136, 203

Authority, 35; biblical normativity and, 138–145; of Sophia-Spirit, 156–163; of women, 28–30, 163. *See also* Patriarchy

Basileia, 57, 132, 215–216

Biblical hermeneutics/interpretation, androcentric text, 23, 45; minimal history of women in, 29; and patriarchy, 4–5, 8–9, 26; women-church as hermeneutical center of, 5. *See also* Critical feminist theological hermeneutics; Women-church

Canon, 11, 139–140, 142, 146–150, 197; within canon, 140–144, 151, 156

Conscientization, 53, 185

Constructivism, 81, 105

Contextualization, 8, 10–11, 13, 25–26, 32, 36, 43, 62–64, 66, 70, 98, 161–62, 197, 201

Critical feminist biblical interpretation, 5–7, 24, 39–40, 47, 50, 152, 163; biblical criticism of, 135; contesting and transforming patriarchy by, 9, 68, 198; contrast to scientist interpretation, 46; critical evaluation in, 6, 26–28; deconstruction and reconstruction in, 5, 10, 30, 32–33, 36, 46, 53, 84, 87–90, 101; discursive problems encountered by, 12; historical interpretation for liberation, 5, 7, 10–11, 27–28, 30–50, 55, 62–63, 69, 75, 104, 113–114; historical questions in, 10, 29–31; imaginative reinterpretation in, 26–28, 48, 52–53, 92; methodology of, 35, 40, 52–76; politics of, 10, 46; reconceptualization in, 8, 10, 22;